INSOLVENCY ACCOUNTING

INSOLVENCY ACCOUNTING

Robert A. Wiener, CPA, New York

Vice President—General Auditor, Seeburg Industries, Inc.

Roger W. Christian

President, Creative Consulting Service

McGRAW-HILL BOOK COMPANY

*New York   St. Louis   San Francisco   Auckland   Bogotá   Düsseldorf
Johannesburg   London   Madrid   Mexico   Montreal   New Delhi   Panama
Paris   São Paulo   Singapore   Sydney   Tokyo   Toronto*

Library of Congress Cataloging in Publication Data

Wiener, Robert A., date.
Insolvency accounting.

1. Bankruptcy.   2. Accounting.   I. Christian,
Roger, joint author.   II. Title.
HF5686.B3W53   657'.7   76-21666
ISBN 0-07-070135-0

1 2 3 4 5 6 7 8 9 0   KPKP   7 8 5 4 3 2 1 0 9 8 7

The editors for this book were W. Hodson Mogan
and Carolyn Nagy, the designer was Elliot Epstein,
and the production supervisor was Teresa F. Leaden.
It was set in Palatino by Monotype Composition
Company, Inc.

Printed and bound by The Kingsport Press.

CONTENTS

PREFACE

This book has two mutually supportive functions and is intended to serve two groups of readers. For professional accountants, it is a pragmatic and detailed guide to the sometimes peculiar requirements and practices associated with serving companies involved in an insolvency proceeding, whether the matter is resolved informally—out of court—or under court protection under the provisions of the National Bankruptcy Act.

For business executives, controllers, and the officers of the various suppliers, banks, customers, and other organizations that occasionally find themselves caught up in some way with a company in financial crisis, this book is a guide to just what happens throughout an insolvency proceeding.

We describe exactly who does what, in which order, when, why, and how, in order to minimize the losses and irritation of everyone involved. This book does not address personal bankruptcies at all. Moreover, while we touch upon the more complex Chapter X proceedings typically associated with large public companies in distress, we concentrate on the more common—and much more promising—proceedings under Chapter XI.

Because the fundamental objective of Chapter XI is the rescue, recovery, and rehabilitation of insolvent companies, our emphasis is on the accounting and administrative aspects of bringing a company through a successful reorganization. However, the best-laid plans of companies, too, "gang aft agley," so we also deal with the accountant's role in litigation, in serving a trustee in bankruptcy, and in the ultimate liquidation of an enterprise whose affairs prove to be irretrievable.

During the course of all this, the various forms, financial statements, reports, schedules, court orders, and the like are fully described. In addition, a representative collection of such documents is reproduced as a series of exhibits in the main appendix. Throughout, we have tried to respond to the needs and interests of not only professional accountants but of the executives, owners, and other professionals who rely upon their services, advice, and expertise.

That said, however, we cannot stress too strongly that *this is not intended to be, and should not be used as, some sort of do-it-yourself kit* for the head (or accountants) of a company in financial distress. There is only one rational first step in dealing with an existing or imminent insolvency: immediate contact with an experienced attorney who specializes in such cases. The very survival of the organization is at stake, and an innocent misstep can doom any chance of salvaging the situation.

Further, missteps are easy to make. The rules and regulations are not only complex, but subject to change; and certain requirements laid down by bankruptcy judges vary from one jurisdiction to the next. Accordingly, attorneys and executives with no previous exposure to insolvency situations can quickly come to grief. For example, the payment of obligations incurred before and after filing for a Chapter XI proceeding is rigorously controlled, and the two are dealt with differently. As a result, a spontaneous "gesture of goodwill" on the part of a debtor is quite likely to run afoul of the bankruptcy court, the creditors, or both.

Similarly, some of the accounting procedures involved differ in important ways from those of generally accepted accounting practices, so despite heavy normal experience, a CPA unfamiliar with the peculiarities of insolvency accounting can easily bungle the assignment.

To avoid a bit of bungling ourselves, we want to gratefully acknowledge the contributions of two friends whose help was invaluable. Insolvency attorney Salvatore A. Adorno reviewed our efforts with a careful and experienced eye, and made many suggestions for improving the accuracy of our observations. Executive secretary Carolyn B. Shields stoically retyped the manuscript so often that she could probably recite it in her sleep, and it was letter-perfect every time. Our thanks to two fine craftspersons.

That strange expression brings us to a blanket disclaimer. Applauding as we do the growing number of female leaders in the world of business and the professions, we have tried to minimize so-called sexist language in this book. However, we have also tried to avoid such awkward constructions as "his/her" and "he/she," and the two objectives are not always compatible. Very rarely, we were forced to choose between an absurdly artificial expression and a more familiar masculine term, i.e., businessman. We opted for the latter, intending that the term be taken generically, to apply equally to both men and women.

Finally, we would like to point out that as this book goes to press, the Congress is very seriously considering some fundamental changes in the bankruptcy law. There is little doubt that certain changes are overdue and forthcoming, but a basic legislative restructuring is not likely to be completed in haste. Meanwhile several thousand companies every month find themselves in financial crisis, and their owners and advisors must respond in terms of the laws, rulings, practices, and procedures that currently apply. We are confident that this book will help them do so more effectively.

Robert A. Wiener
Roger W. Christian

Chapter One

A PERSPECTIVE:
Insolvency Is Serious,
but Survivable

Credit has been aptly called the lubricant of commerce, and without it, business on any significant scale would simply cease. Moreover, its importance has been recognized throughout the history of trade and commerce. References to the debtor-creditor relationship exist from the very beginning of record keeping. The business people of antiquity discovered, however, as have uncounted business people ever since, that credit—based as it is on intentions and expectations in an unpredictable world—can get out of hand. Enlightened acknowledgment of the resulting grief appeared at least as early as the Old Testament, which provided for the "release" of otherwise unresolvable debts every seven years.

More commonly, however, people in financial straits have been harshly, if not inhumanly, dealt with. Under early Roman law, creditors could literally exact their "pound of flesh," cutting off pieces of an insolvent debtor's body to satisfy their claims. Not until Julius Caesar's time was this modified—to provide, instead, for the distribution of a debtor's remaining personal assets. Capital punishment, imprisonment, and slavery were also abolished as legal punishments for the bankrupt. However, the initiation of action was still limited to creditors, so a merchant in distress could not minimize his losses by voluntarily throwing in the towel. Even worse, the distribution of his personal assets to creditors did not discharge the debts.

Throughout the Middle Ages, business failures were generally subjected to wide publicity, banishment from the business community, and public disgrace. The very term *bankrupt* (*banca rupta*, or broken bench) is derived from the Italian custom of breaking up the debtor's bench or stall which was used in the open markets of medieval times. When the custom emigrated to England, along with the merchants, the

English corruption of the French *banqueroute* became bankerout, which evolved finally into the term bankrupt. (And to this day, in slang parlance, a person without money is "broke.")

Progress in society's treatment of bankrupts has been painfully slow. The first English bankruptcy law—like its predecessors, a criminal statute—was enacted in 1542, during the reign of Henry VIII. It provided for the distribution of the bankrupt's assets by an agent, for the benefit of all creditors. Action could still be initiated only by the creditors, and the asset distribution still did not discharge the debts.

Full discharge of debts was not provided until about a century and a half later, by the English statutes enacted in 1705. Subsequent changes modified this right of discharge, and it is these statutes which served as the model for the United States bankruptcy laws.

Article I, Paragraph 8, of the Constitution provides that "the Congress shall have the power to establish uniform laws on the subject of bankruptcies throughout the United States." The first such statute was enacted in 1800, primarily for the benefit of creditors, and permitted discharge under very narrow restrictions. This law was repealed three years later. It was not until 1841 that a statute appeared providing for the rehabilitation of debtors and permitting a voluntary bankruptcy proceeding. This law, too, lasted only for three years.

In 1867, largely in response to the exigencies of the Civil War, Congress enacted a third bankruptcy act. This act, for the first time, permitted a debtor to propose terms of a composition which would be binding upon all creditors after its acceptance by a majority of them and its confirmation by the bankruptcy court. This act was repealed in 1878. (It is revealing to note that during our first eighty-nine years under the Constitution, we had a national bankruptcy act for only sixteen years.)

The present basic bankruptcy statutes were enacted in 1898, and the last broad revisions (the Chandler Act) were made in 1938. This statute, as amended, governs the administration of both companies and individuals who are subject to bankruptcy proceedings. It is administered under rules adopted by the Judicial Conference of the United States, which is directly under the jurisdiction of the United States Supreme Court.

These bankruptcy rules are further modified and elaborated upon by rules of practice formulated by district court judges. The district courts in each circuit provide the framework for administering bankruptcy and reorganization petitions. There are eleven circuits in the United States, and the rules of practice vary.

Actual administration of the bankruptcy courts is provided by bankruptcy judges who are appointed by the district judges in each circuit. In some localities, the district judges also empower the bankruptcy judges to fix some of their own rules. Some bankruptcy judges serve only part time, while maintaining independent law practices, but others have full-time careers as bankruptcy judges.

For instance, in the State of New York, which is divided into eight judicial districts, the Eastern District has five full-time judges, and the Southern District has six. Each judge is appointed to a six-year term, and can be reappointed at the discretion of the district judges.

A business* that finds itself either insolvent (i.e., its liabilities exceed its assets) or unable to pay its debts as they mature has only four fundamental options. The first is to level with its creditors promptly, once the financial difficulty is evident, and ask their cooperation in devising an out-of-court plan for salvaging the enterprise. The second is to petition for reorganization under Chapter X or Chapter XI of the National Bankruptcy Act. The third option is for the debtor company to voluntarily declare formal bankruptcy. The fourth is to do nothing until the situation disintegrates and creditors force the company into involuntary bankruptcy.

Only the first two courses of action hold real potential for rehabilitating the business—the latter under the protection of the courts. The other options entail liquidating the enterprise. In light of this, and the possibility that a plan to rehabilitate the business will fail in spite of everything if the circumstances prove to be irreversible, a company in distress should seek help early in the episode.

Unfortunately, most business people are too embarrassed or too proud to admit they are in trouble. The historic stigma that has clung to bankruptcy through the ages is still extremely powerful; many business people resort to desperate measures and irrational hopes in their fight to save the company—and to "save face" in the community. At last, when little or nothing can be retrieved, the truth is forced to the surface by lawsuits, property seizure by tax authorities, or the debtor's collapse for want of operating funds with which to meet the payroll or pay for utilities.

A business in financial distress can be compared to a person who is seriously ill. Medication and intensive care are required if the patient is to recover and thrive again. In the case of a financially embarrassed company the healing services are provided by technical experts: attorneys, accountants, perhaps consultants, and the advice and cooperation of creditors—especially the creditors' committee. Money—the cash or credit a business needs—is its lifeblood, and must be carefully marshaled and monitored, or all is lost. Taking the analogy one step further, if one of the patient's limbs or organs is not responding to treatment or is threatening the survival of the entire entity, surgery may be required.

*Individual (personal) bankruptcies do not fall within the scope of this book.

When a debtor company finds itself in financial difficulties, it should move promptly to identify the exact nature and magnitude of the problem, so that more serious trouble can be headed off. A logical first step is a stern appraisal of the company's financial condition, including a skeptical reexamination of all the traditional financial statements.

Next, a realistic budget of future operations should be prepared, including some provision for the necessary funds or credit with which to continue operating the business. Company officials should then consult with the company's larger trade creditors and its lending institutions and ask for their assistance. Preferably, this should be done well before the commencement of any proceeding in the bankruptcy court.

In almost all instances, if the debtor is honest and forthright in dealing with creditors, they will be cooperative and willing to help. The debtor should ask them to form a committee, select counsel, and consider the circumstances that brought the company to consult with its creditors.

If this procedure is followed, and there is goodwill on both sides, the debtor commonly will find that some informal and confidential arrangement can be worked out to continue an essentially normal business relationship while the company systematically puts itself back on a sound footing and gradually settles its creditors' claims. Moreover, even if a court proceeding is later forced upon the company to protect it from judgment or lien creditors, these earlier discussions and the climate of sincerity they create will make dealing with these unsecured creditors much easier.

With these important preliminaries behind it, the troubled business will know in some detail (1) where it is, financially, and (2) where it must go, over a reasonable period of time. The next big issue to be addressed is: specifically how will it get there? That is, the debtor now must seek a specific and workable plan for its financial rehabilitation. It is, of course, in the mutual best interest of all parties concerned to evolve such a plan.

The responsibility for developing and implementing a realistic recovery plan is shared by the two groups. Within the larger objective of avoiding a liquidation of company assets, each party has competitive objectives of its own. The debtor naturally wants to strike the best bargain possible in its straitened circumstances. On the other hand, creditors want to exact the largest practical portion of the amount owed them by the debtor.

Generally, both groups know that the pragmatic settlement price lies somewhere between liquidation value and going-concern value. There also may be intangibles to be considered, the value of which is not included on the debtor's books. These might include goodwill, patent rights, trade names, tax loss carry-forwards, and so forth.

Normally, once the creditors have formed their committee—usually consisting of representatives of the largest creditors, who not only have the largest stake in the settlement, but who can exert the greatest leverage—the committee suggests that a firm of experienced insolvency accountants take a look at the debtor's affairs. Hopefully, this can be accomplished without resort to a court proceeding. Hopefully, too, this accountant's examination will reveal nothing untoward; the debtor and the creditors' committee will proceed to negotiate a mutually acceptable settlement and recovery plan, and the whole affair will be resolved with a minimum of embarrassment and rancor.

Sometimes, however, this desideratum cannot be achieved for one reason or another, and the debtor feels obliged to seek shelter until an equitable arrangement can be hammered out. Accordingly, the be-leaguered business initiates a bankruptcy proceeding in the U.S. District Court, a step explored in more detail in the next chapter.

Chapter Two

HOW AND WHY TO INITIATE
A BANKRUPTCY PROCEEDING

When a financially strapped company becomes subject to the bankruptcy courts either voluntarily or involuntarily, the immediate effect is to place the company under the protection of the courts, and to freeze in place, as it were, all the company's unsecured creditors. That is, the court figuratively steps between the debtor and the creditors, and prevents creditors from taking legal steps to collect the amount owed to them. This injunction against pressing claims applies to all creditors, secured and unsecured alike, including public utilities and the tax collectors.

It is important to recognize that a company may feel obliged to seek relief under the bankruptcy statutes for reasons other than an inability to meet its debts as they mature. The company may realize, for example, that its survival depends on reducing the amount of its unsecured obligations. It may be encumbered by uneconomical leases, it may want to disaffirm onerous executory contracts, or it may seek to restructure the repayment terms of burdensome short-term debt. Finally, it may have to head off action by judgment creditors, lien creditors, taxing authorities, or others.

Whatever its reasons, a company can place itself under the protection of the courts in any one of three ways, depending on the circumstances involved. It can also be petitioned into bankruptcy against its will, if creditors perceive the need for drastic action before the debtor does. However, creditors filing such an Involuntary Petition in Bankruptcy, as it is called, must go further than merely proving that the debtor is in trouble and owes money to the creditors. The petitioning creditors must allege that the debtor committed certain "acts of bankruptcy."

The law is very specific about what constitutes an act of bankruptcy, and the matter is explained in some detail in Chapter Six of this book.

For now, suffice it to say that such acts include falsifying or destroying records, concealing assets, using false financial statements to obtain credit, and the like.

If a debtor has twelve or more creditors, at least three of them, with claims aggregating $500 or more, must join in filing an Involuntary Petition in Bankruptcy, naming the debtor. A single creditor with a claim of $500 or more may file such a petition if the debtor has fewer than twelve creditors.

The affected debtor may challenge such a petition, of course. The bankruptcy statute includes guidelines for contesting a petition, but an attorney should be consulted for advice on the proper procedures. Alternatively, the debtor has the option, under Sections 127 and 321, respectively, of the Bankruptcy Act, to file a voluntary petition under Chapter X or Chapter XI of the act, and get the court to stay the involuntary proceeding. No such legal maneuvers should be attempted, of course, without an attorney's guidance. Accordingly, we shall dismiss the subject as beyond the scope of this book, adding only that if such an involuntary petition is not contested, it is treated by the bankruptcy court the same as a voluntary petition.

Returning, then, to the broader subject of voluntary bankruptcy proceedings, there are, as already mentioned, three basic categories of bankruptcy proceedings. They are straight bankruptcy—which is simply recognition of outright business failure on an irretrievable scale—and petitions for reorganization under either Chapter X or Chapter XI of the Bankruptcy Act. The latter two constitute attempts to salvage the situation by working out an accommodation with creditors that will permit the business to survive the crisis and, it is hoped, recover from it.

STRAIGHT BANKRUPTCY

When a petition in bankruptcy, whether voluntary or involuntary, is filed with the U.S. District Court, the petitioner can apply to the court for the temporary appointment of a receiver to take possession of the bankrupt company until he or she is succeeded by a trustee in bankruptcy. The trustee is usually elected by the creditors at their first formal meeting, but may be appointed by the bankruptcy judge if the creditors cannot agree on a trustee.

The receiver may continue to operate the business temporarily, under certain circumstances. For example, when a food processor goes bankrupt, there may be large quantities of perishable produce on hand or en route to the company. If the facility were simply padlocked pending the auction, as normally occurs, spoilage losses would needlessly make the company's situation worse. When the elected or appointed trustee in bankruptcy takes over from the receiver, he or she marshals the bankrupt's assets—now referred to as the estate—for the benefit of creditors, working under the supervision of the bankruptcy court.*

Eventually, the bankrupt company's assets are liquidated, and the proceeds, after the expenses of administration are paid, are distributed to creditors. Creditors are paid in the order of priority provided in the Bankruptcy Act. These priorities, and the mechanics and procedures involved in converting the company's assets into cash and otherwise winding up its affairs, are dealt with at length in Chapter Eleven of this book. The point to be made here is that a petition in straight bankruptcy leads inevitably to the dissolution of the debtor company.

CHAPTER X REORGANIZATION

As we have seen, a proceeding under either Chapter X or Chapter XI of the Bankruptcy Act prevents creditors from pressing their claims or taking any legal action to collect the amounts owed them by the debtor company. There the similarity ends, for most practical purposes, for the rules and practices attending the two kinds of bankruptcy proceedings differ in a number of important respects. For instance, the rights of secured creditors are theoretically not affected by a filing in Chapter XI, nor are equity interests changed. In Chapter X proceedings, however, the rights of all creditors, secured and unsecured, are considered. Stockholders whose equity interests predate a Chapter X proceeding may also find their interests modified, or even eliminated.

Chapter X proceedings are normally chosen by (or imposed upon) large, geographically dispersed and publically held corporations with complex financial structures. The precedents and procedures, rules, and regulations involved are not only extensive enough to warrant a book in their own right, but as noted, are quite distinct from those involved in a Chapter XI proceeding. In consequence, and in light of the almost exclusive choice of Chapter XI proceedings by small- and moderate-sized businesses, the balance of this book will deal primarily with

---

*Alternatively, the debtor may, under the state statutes, make an assignment of assets for the benefit of creditors. In this case, the assignee, rather than a trustee, administers the estate for the benefit of all creditors. Such an assignment constitutes an act of bankruptcy, however, so if three or more creditors object to the assignment, they can petition the debtor into involuntary bankruptcy, placing the matter under federal jurisdiction. The procedures relating to assignments are regulated by the debtor-creditor statutes of the particular state or states involved. In either an assignment or a formal bankruptcy proceeding, the accounting work and the basic rules and steps to be taken are very similar, but legal counsel should be consulted about the procedures to be followed in each set of circumstances.

Chapter XI insolvencies. (Bear in mind, however, that Chapter XI proceedings can, and occasionally do, fail to achieve their objective, and they then end up as straight bankruptcies.)

CHAPTER XI REOGRANIZATION

Filing a voluntary petition under Chapter XI initiates a process directed at eventually providing some accommodation with general unsecured creditors, either by way of composition of debt or extension of the time for payment, or both. (To repeat: The rights of valid *secured* creditors are not affected in a Chapter XI proceeding, although their rights to the secured property may be delayed.)

The first step to be considered is selection of counsel, and because of the complexities that can arise in such a proceeding, retention of a law firm that specializes in insolvency work is strongly recommended. General and corporate lawyers know, or can easily find out, who these specialists are, and in fact a number of them have built national reputations.

These insolvency attorneys are experienced and familiar not only with bankruptcy law and procedures, but with local practices and preferences. They know all the shortcuts and can "boiler-plate" many of the legal requirements. Above all, they are familiar with the judges, credit and collection agencies, attorneys for banks, large creditors, and trade associations, and with the accountants who are experienced in the insolvency field. Accordingly, they can and do make the process much more efficient, faster, and easier for all parties concerned. It is also worth noting that the acts and decisions of bankruptcy judges are subject to higher review within the judicial system, and this provides another argument for retaining an experienced attorney who specializes in handling insolvency cases.

Furthermore, every action of a company in bankruptcy or in reorganization is subject to the supervision of the bankruptcy judge. Accordingly, attorneys, like accountants, appraisers, and any others who expect to be paid for their services, must serve only upon order of the bankruptcy court. Attorneys, accountants, appraisers, and any others who render services to a creditors' committee in the course of a *successful* reorganization may also apply to the bankruptcy court for compensation.* This can also be done by those serving or employed by an assignee for the benefit of creditors, under state statutes, if, after the assign-

---

*If an acceptable reorganization plan cannot be worked out, and the company is liquidated, those who served the creditors' committee may have to look to the disbanded committee for their fees, which might well prove to be uncollectible. The temptation this creates to gloss over matters that could threaten the debtor-creditor negotiations is expanded upon in Chapter Four.

ment is made, the debtor estate is adjudicated a bankrupt and liquidated.

The debtor's counsel files the Chapter XI petition with the clerk of the appropriate United States District Court, and it must be accompanied by a filing fee of $50 and certain information as set forth in the statutes. Four copies of the petition are required, subject to local rules.

Among other requirements, the petition must state that the debtor intends to propose an arrangement, although the details need not be included with the initial filing. (Prior to 1958, each petition had to include a proposed arrangement. In practice, however, it proved that a debtor's initial proposal was very rarely the final one, which was negotiated subsequently with creditors, so this proviso was dropped from the statute.)

If the debtor has been successfully negotiating with creditors, out of court, prior to the inception of a formal proceeding, and has developed a proposal that has been accepted by a majority of the creditors, the debtor can accelerate matters by filing the Plan of Arrangement, already adopted, along with the Original Petition. If the previously solicited consents are in proper form, they may be filed as acceptances to the plan.

The Original Petition under Chapter XI requires a detailed statement of all the company's debts, indicating the full name and address of each creditor, a complete list of the company's assets, and a statement of all executory contracts, as well as other general information regarding the company's affairs. This information is set forth in a series of statements and schedules (see Appendix, Exhibit B).

Usually a Chapter XI filing is decided upon suddenly, before the debtor's books and records have been closed. Under these circumstances, a summary statement of assets and liabilities is filed, together with a detailed list of the names and addresses of all creditors. Current rules provide an automatic extension of ten days for preparing and filing a complete set of schedules. Moreover, the court may, at its discretion, grant additional extensions of up to thirty days, if the debtor can demonstrate good cause for such an extension. Meanwhile, the bankruptcy court can at least notify creditors that a Chapter XI proceeding has begun.

A local rule in effect in the Southern District of New York State and in some other jurisdictions requires that the debtor also file an affidavit describing the history of the company, anticipated operating expenses over the thirty days following the filing, executory contracts in existence, the past and proposed salaries of company executives, and similar information. Counsel often elicits these details from the debtor's officers by asking them to complete a questionnaire similar to that shown as Exhibit A in the Appendix.

The required schedules include a Statement of Affairs, which addresses itself to specific matters regarding the debtor's affairs that will be of interest to creditors and the court in considering the proposed arrangement. An example of such a Statement of Affairs, as well as the various supporting schedules required, is shown in the Appendix of this book as Exhibit B, "Original Petition under Chapter XI."

The following information is also required and should be furnished to counsel as promptly as possible:

1. The latest available balance sheet and profit and loss statement.

2. Name, address, phone number, and specific contact at the debtor's accounting firm.

3. All financial statements issued within the last two years, including their dates and the identity of all persons to whom they were issued.

4. Copies of office and plant facility leases and of major contracts.

5. The exact name of the corporation and its state of incorporation.

6. All assumed, trade, and any other names or designations by which the debtor has been known, or under which it conducted any business, within the six years preceding the petition filing.

7. The company's Federal Tax Identification Number.

8. The full address of the principal place of business for the longer portion of the six months immediately preceding the filing.

9. A description of the general nature of the business in which the debtor is engaged.

10. The location of the debtor's bank accounts. (Alert counsel will immediately ascertain if the debtor is indebted to any of the banks named and will take steps to prevent a "setoff" of the account.)

11. Details of any proceedings under the Bankruptcy Act that may have been instituted by or against the debtor within the preceding six years.

12. The names, addresses, and titles of top executives, especially the managing executive. If the debtor is a privately

held corporation, the names and addresses of each stock-holder also should be submitted.

13. Evidence that the requisite majority of the debtor's board of directors has authorized the Chapter XI petition filing. If it has not yet done so, substitute an assessment of any fore-seeable difficulty in obtaining such authorization.

14. The location of the debtor's corporate seal, minute books, stock books, and stock transfer records.

15. The names, addresses, and amounts due and owing to the ten largest *unsecured* creditors. The following creditors should *not* be included in such listing:
    a. Priority creditors (e.g., taxing authorities and wage and salary claimants).
    b. Creditors employed by the debtor at the time of the petition filing.
    c. Officers, directors, and stockholders of the debtor.

16. A comprehensive listing of the nature and status of each action or proceeding, pending or threatened, against the debtor or its property, in connection with which a judgment against the debtor, or the seizure of its property, may be imminent. This list should set forth, with respect to *each* pending action:
    a. The exact title of the action.
    b. The court in which the action has been instituted.
    c. The name and address of the plaintiff's attorney.
    d. The cause and nature of the action alleged against the debtor (e.g., goods sold and delivered, work, labor and services, money loaned, rent due, etc.) and the amount demanded in each complaint.
    e. The status of each action (e.g., answer not yet due, issue joined by the service of an answer, counterclaim asserted, notice of trial received, motion for summary judgment pending, etc.).

17. A list of any property of the debtor that is in the possession or custody of any public officer, receiver, trustee, mortgagee, pledgee, or assignee of rents. This list should include names and addresses of such persons and the court in which such proceedings are pending.

18. If stock, debentures, or other securities of the debtor or any of its subsidiaries are publicly held, a list of the number and class of such securities, along with the number of hold-

ers of each, plus a separate listing of the amount of each such security held by the debtor's officers and directors.

19. Information as to which premises the debtor is occupying under the lease, the term of the lease, the rent reserved, the amount, if any, owing for rent, and what negotiations, if any, have been held for a modification of the lease.

20. If the debtor company is to continue operating, as is normally the case, the following additional information is required:

    a. The estimated amount of the weekly payroll to employees (*exclusive* of the officers, stockholders, and directors of the corporation) for a thirty-day period following filing of the Chapter XI petition.

    b. The amount now being paid, and proposed to be paid, to officers, stockholders, and directors for a period of thirty days following the filing. (As justification for this pay, include a statement of the background, qualifications, other income, etc., of each such person.)

    c. The estimated additional thirty days' operating expenses.

    d. The estimated gain or loss from the next thirty days' operation of the debtor's business.

    e. Such additional information as may fully inform the court as to the desirability of the debtor's continuing in business. The principals of the debtor should prepare a written statement as to the nature of the debtor's business and a brief history, the nature and causes of its financial difficulties, and what steps have been or will be taken to overcome such difficulties (e.g., reducing the number of employees, relocating the plant to reduce overhead, etc.).

21. If an involuntary bankruptcy proceeding has been launched against the debtor, the following additional information should be provided:

    a. The name and address of any receiver or trustee that was appointed, along with the name of his or her attorney.

    b. The names and addresses of the members of the creditors' committee, if one has been established.

All this done, the company has taken its first step on the way back to financial health, and creditors are immobilized while they await the examining accountant's report on the affairs of the debtor. If the proceeding is in the bankruptcy court (as opposed to being an informal, out-of-court effort), the bankruptcy judge may wish to meet with the debtor to receive a firsthand report of the debtor's future plans. Such a meeting is both desirable and recommended. Business people will find the judges realistically interested in seeing the debtor company rehabilitated.

The formal procedure requires that a hearing date be set for the near future (within ten days if the proceeding is in the Southern or Eastern District of New York). At the hearing, an officer of the debtor appears before the judge to answer questions about the future conduct of the business, and about the facts set forth in the debtor's petition or in the accompanying schedules and Statement of Affairs.

This hearing is called the "first meeting of creditors," and it may be adjourned from time to time as the proceeding progresses. At the initial meeting, the judge may ask an officer of the debtor to state under oath that he or she is familiar with the contents of the schedules and has signed them with full knowledge of their contents.

At the same time, any creditor may examine the debtor's officers regarding "the acts, conduct, and property of the debtor." Usually this first hearing is more or less routine. If an informal creditors' committee has been formed previously, as the result of a meeting called by the debtor or the creditors, it may be nominated and designated as the official creditors' committee. An informal meeting of this kind is normally arranged just before or immediately after the debtor files, to give the creditors time to select a lawyer, accountant, and recording secretary, and to form an ad hoc creditors' committee to function until the official first meeting of creditors. If no such committee was formed, or if another group of creditors nominates a rival committee, the judge may adjourn the hearing for a time, while the creditors elect an official creditors' committee. (If the creditors cannot agree on a committee, the judge may appoint one.)

Recent rules specify how a creditors' committee must be formed, and require that it have between three and eleven members. The rules further require that a secretary take minutes of the first informal meeting of creditors, and that invitations to the informal meeting be sent to every creditor with a known claim of $500 or more. (If inviting all such creditors proves too cumbersome, the creditors with the 100 largest claims must be invited.)

After the Chapter XI petition has been referred to a judge, the debtor must file a number of legal papers, each of which is necessary to permit the continued conduct of the debtor's affairs. The most important of these is the order continuing the debtor in possession of the business (see Exhibit C in the Appendix) or appointing a receiver instead. The filing of the bankruptcy proceeding automatically restrains creditors from satisfying judgments or seizing the debtor's property as the result of tax liens.

Exhibit D in the Appendix is a typical letter of instructions to the debtor, of the kind with which seasoned insolvency attorneys reinforce and clarify the official orders and rulings of the bankruptcy judge. By strongly calling the debtor's attention to specific requirements and responsibilities, such letters can minimize careless and ignorant actions or oversights that might easily threaten or compromise the outcome of the reorganization effort.

Counsel may also submit at this time, for the bankruptcy judge's signature, an order providing for the retention of the company's accountant to perform routine, regular accounting services. Typically, these include aid in closing the company's books, help in preparing the required schedules, assistance in opening up new books, preparing the financial reports required for the operations of the debtor-in-possession, and the preparation of tax reports.

This last point deserves emphasis. Among the refinements developed since World War II are those requiring strict tax reporting. Previously, the debtor-in-possession would frequently incur new tax obligations, which, when superimposed on the amounts previously due, would completely wipe out the estate if the proceeding terminated in a bankruptcy instead of a reorganization.

As the result of this, a debtor-in-possession is now required to maintain a special tax account* in which all taxes due are deposited, as the tax liabilities are incurred. The Internal Revenue Service requires that reports be filed as these tax monies are deposited. (This form, NAR 2-13, is shown on page 128.) The initial procedures in this connection related solely to federal taxes, but today all taxes, whether withheld or accrued, are included. The bankruptcy judges have shown no sympathy for violations of the tax reporting provisions of the bankruptcy rules.

Many of the acts of the bankruptcy court, dealing with companies subject to its jurisdiction, require that adequate notice be given to creditors. Every company engaged in a bankruptcy proceeding is required to note the fact on all checks, letterheads, and the like, so that all parties dealing with the company are aware of its situation. Particular effort is made to notify the company's creditors that a bankruptcy or reorganization petition has been filed, and to keep them informed of key developments throughout the proceeding.

Typically, notice is mailed to all creditors whose names and addresses were filed by the debtor. To hedge the possibility of a debtor's oversight, notice by publication is also provided for. Each district court selects at least one official newspaper of record, which is the official medium for all advertisements in bankruptcy cases in that district.

---

*It is prudent, when opening such a "tax and trust account," as it is called, to insist upon a letter from the bank, acknowledging that the bank is accepting the deposits as a trust account, and is waiving any rights to "set off" the contents.

Other newspapers are also free to publish these notices as items of public interest, and many do. A typical notice, in this case regarding the first meeting of creditors, is reproduced below.

ARRANGEMENT

UNITED STATES DISTRICT COURT, Southern District of New York. In the Matter of YOUNG ROYALTY, INC. of 115 West 30th Street, New York, N.Y. 10001. Debtor No. 75-B-1282—Tax I.D. # 13-275-7556.

NOTICE IS HEREBY GIVEN that on July 18th, 1975 the above named debtor filed a petition under Chapter XI of the Bankruptcy Act and states that it intends to propose an arrangement with its unsecured creditors. A first meeting of creditors will be held before the undersigned Bankruptcy Judge, in the courtroom, Room 237, United States Court House, Foley Square, New York, N.Y. 10007, on September 2nd, 1975, at 10:00 A.M., at which place and time the creditors may attend, prove their claims, nominate a trustee, appoint a committee of creditors, examine the debtor and transact such other business as may properly come before said meeting, including hearing and determining whether the debtor should be adjudged a bankrupt, and bankruptcy proceeded with, or the proceedings dismissed on any of the grounds specified in Section 376 of the Act.

NOTICE IS HEREBY GIVEN that at such meeting the court will fix a time within which the proposed arrangement shall be filed and will fix a time for the filing of the applications to confirm the arrangement and for hearing on the confirmation thereof, and of such objections as may be made to confirmation.

NOTICE IS ALSO GIVEN that the 2nd day of October, 1975 is hereby fixed as the last day for the filing of applications, as provided in Section 17C(2) of the Bankruptcy Act, to determine the dischargeability of debts claimed to be nondischargeable pursuant to Clauses (2), (4) or (8) of Section 17A of the Bankruptcy Act.
DATED: New York, New York
July 28th, 1975

JOHN J. GALGAY
Bankruptcy Judge

NOTICE

YOU MUST FILE A CLAIM BEFORE CONFIRMATION IN ORDER TO PARTICIPATE IN THE DISTRIBUTION OF THE CONSIDERATION, IF ANY, TO BE DEPOSITED.

By the time a notice such as this appears in the press, the Chapter XI proceeding is a legitimate fait accompli, and the distressed debtor is in a position to pursue its goals, free of the threat of creditor court actions that might prevent, or at least prolong, its recovery. Nevertheless, creditors unwilling to cooperate are still in a position to force the debtor out of business entirely and into liquidation, as we shall see in the next chapter.

Chapter Three

THE SEQUENCE OF EVENTS IN A CHAPTER XI PROCEEDING

The debtor company has filed its petition, company officers have appeared in court, and the creditors have selected a creditors' committee. The next pivotal step in the proceedings is to hammer out a settlement proposal on which the committee and the debtor can agree. The speed with which this can be done is determined by the intensity of interest the debtor and its creditors exhibit in coming to grips with a reality that is distasteful to all concerned.

While the creditors' committee awaits its accountants' report, the debtor continues to do business as best it can, dealing with the same customers and the same suppliers. If it is fortunate and has planned properly, the debtor company will have sufficient working capital with which to purchase necessary raw materials and to pay operating expenses.

Normal trade credit will have disappeared, of course, and dealings with most creditors will be on a COD, or even cash-in-advance, basis. Needless to say, such constraints on a company already short of cash make operations very difficult, so it is clearly in the best interest of the debtor and creditors alike to expedite completion of the accountants' report. Only then can it be studied and used as the basis for negotiating an acceptable proposal for settlement or extension of the debt.

As soon as the creditors' committee has been formed, it will generally communicate with all creditors, asking that each file a proof of debt, and asking that the committee be authorized to act on behalf of all creditors. In addition, it will report its formation and recap its activities to date.

Here is a typical committee's letter to unsecured creditors:

To the Creditors of Acme Corp.
New York, New York

Gentlemen:

This letter is addressed to you as an unsecured creditor in the
Acme Corporation.

Please be advised that on July 25, 1975, Acme—the debtor corporation—filed a Petition for an Arrangement under Chapter XI of
the Bankruptcy Act. The matter is pending in the United States
District Court, Southern District of New York, and has been
referred to the Honorable Jay Schramm, Bankruptcy Judge, and
assigned case #54882.

On August 2, 1975, a meeting of the larger creditors was convened
by debtor's counsel. Part of Acme's financial plight is apparently
attributable to a large volume of sales made at less than cost.
The figures presented then, as of June 11, 1975, are enclosed. While
the debtor was prepared to discuss a plan at this meeting, the
creditors present refused to consider any offer until after an independent accountant had reviewed the debtor's books and records
and submitted a report of his findings.

As is normal in this type proceeding, a committee of creditors
was organized, whose duty it will be to negotiate with the debtor
corporation toward an equitable Plan of Arrangement which
can be recommended to all concerned.

It is now in order for you to file your Proof of Debt. The appropriate
form is enclosed. We ask that you execute this document
promptly, before a notary public, that you *attach a statement of
your account,* and return the whole to this office.

Notice that the Proof of Debt contains a Power of Attorney, which
runs to the Creditors' Committee. Be assured that this Power
will only be used to make the committee official before the court,
and to vote for a tentative Trustee to serve in the event of a liquidation.
There will be no charge by the committee or any of its employees
for filing your claim.

You are reminded that an amendment to the Bankruptcy Act disposed of the former six-month filing period in an Arrangement proceeding. You now must file your Proof of Debt prior to confirmation of a Plan of Arrangement, or within the 30-day grace period thereafter. If your Proof of Debt is filed during the latter period, you will be bound by the debtor's books and records. If you do not file your claim in the required period, you will not participate in any dividend* that may eventually be paid. Therefore, to protect your interests, we urge that you file your Proof of Debt at once.

If you have any questions relative to this matter please contact the writer, any other member of the committee, or its counsel. Your committee will report back to you when the accountants have completed their report.

Very truly yours,

Secretary, Creditors' Committee

abc:de
enc.

CREDITORS' COMMITTEE

(list names)   (company name)

COMMITTEE COUNSEL

(list names)   (address)

COMMITTEE ACCOUNTANT

(list name)

*i.e., any payment to creditors.

ACME CORP.
BALANCE SHEET*
June 11, 1975

ASSETS

Current Assets

Cash on hand				$ 16
Receivables:				
Trade accounts	$20,694			
Less: allowance for doubtful accounts	1,144	$ 19,550		
Officers' advances		42,775		
Sundry		1,100	63,425	
Inventory			339,009	
Unexpired insurance			3,591	
Prepaid interest			68	
Total current assets				$ 406,109

Fixes Assets	Cost	Accumulated depreciation	Net	
Furniture and fixtures	$ 1,748	$ 1,210	$ 538	
Auto	6,055	505	5,550	
Leasehold improvements	825	83	742	
Total fixed assets	$ 8,628	$ 1,798		6,830

Other Assets

Deposits	$ 115	
Organization costs	102	
Total other assets		217
TOTAL ASSETS		$ 413,156

*For management purposes only.   Certification is not to be implied.

LIABILITIES AND CAPITAL

Current Liabilities

Cash in bank—overdraft		$ 2,391	
Payables:			
Trade accounts	$ 603,221		
Financed insurance premiums	2,355		
Payroll taxes	1,466		
Accrued expenses	1,856	608,898	
Total current liabilities			$ 611,289

Capital

Common stock		$ 10,000	
Capital contributed in excess of par value of stock		81,065	
Deficit, September 1, 1974	$ (12,170)		
Net (loss)—Exhibit B	(277,028)		
Deficit, June 11, 1975		(289,198)	
Total capital (deficit)			(198,133)
TOTAL LIABILITIES AND CAPITAL			413,156

SOUTHERN DISTRICT OF NEW YORK

IN THE MATTER OF _____ *Debtor*	*In Proceedings for an Arrangement Under Chapter XI of the Bankruptcy Act.* *File No.* _____

STATE OF
COUNTY OF

Mr.   *of No.*
in   *County of*   *State of*
being duly sworn, deposes and says:

1. (a) INDIVIDUAL

     That he hereinafter designates himself as claimant. (or as appears below)

     (b) CO-PARTNERSHIP

     That he is a member of
a co-partnership, hereinafter designated as claimant, composed of deponent and
                                    of
and carrying on business at No.
County of   *State of*   *(or as appears below)*

     (c) CORPORATION

     That he is the   *of*
a corporation organized and existing under the laws of the State of
and is duly authorized to make this proof of claim on its behalf. Said corporation
is hereinafter designated as the claimant.
     CORPORATION ADDRESS

2. *That the above named debtor was at and before the filing by said debtor of the petition for an arrangement and still is justly and truly indebted (or liable) to claimant in the sum of $*

3. *That the consideration of said debt (or liability) is as follows: Goods, wares and merchandise sold and delivered to the said debtor at the special instance and request of said debtor at the agreed price and reasonable value set forth in the annexed statement which is made a part hereof.*

4. *That no part of said debt (or liability) has been paid. That there are no set-offs or counterclaims to said debt (or liability). That claimant does not hold, and has not, nor has any person by his order, or to deponent's knowledge or belief for his use had or received any security or securities for said debt (or liability). That the instrument upon which said debt is founded is attached hereto. That no note or other negotiable instrument has been received for such account or any part thereof (or that the said debt is evidenced by a note (or other negotiable instrument), which is attached hereto); that no judgment has been rendered thereon, except*

POWER OF ATTORNEY

TO THE CREDITORS' COMMITTEE, OF WHICH (name)
IS COMMITTEE SECRETARY AND (name)   ESQ.
IS COMMITTEE COUNSEL.

   The undersigned, of
City of   State of
does hereby authorize you, or any one of you, or your representative with full power
of substitution, to attend all meetings of creditors of the debtor aforesaid, and all
adjournments thereof, at the places and times appointed by the court, and for the
undersigned and in the name of the undersigned, to vote for or against any proposal
or resolution that may be then submitted under the Act of Congress relating to bank-
ruptcy, to vote for a trustee or trustees of the estate of the said debtor and for a
committee of creditors, to accept any arrangement or wage earner's plan proposed
by said debtor in satisfaction of his debts, and to receive payment of dividends, and
payment or delivery of money or of other consideration due the undersigned under
such arrangement or wage earner's plan, and for any other purpose in the under-
signed's interest whatsoever: and with like powers to attend and vote at any other
meeting or meetings of creditors, or sitting or sittings of the court, which may be held
therein for any of the purposes aforesaid. All prior powers of attorney are hereby
revoked.

   IN WITNESS WHEREOF the undersigned has hereunto signed his name and af-
fixed his seal the   day of   19

Sworn to before me this   day
of   19 , said subscriber   _____(L.S.)
being known to me to be the person de-   *Sign name of individual, partner*
scribed in and who signed and swore to the   *or officer here*
above instruments and duly acknowledged
that he executed them and was authorized
to execute them.

_____   _____(L.S.)
Notary Public or Commissioner of Deeds   *Sign name of firm here*

                                                  Annex duplicate of your invoice
                                                  Corporation affix seal here

During the interim period, while the court awaits the result of negotiations between the debtor and the creditors' committee, the judge will postpone hearings. The judge may, however, ask the debtor to post an indemnity bond to protect the insolvent estate against losses resulting from the continued operation of the business.* (The judge may also require indemnity for any other reason.) Usually, such indemnity is required from *outside* of the assets of the troubled business.

At the first meeting of creditors, the judge will generally ask the creditors' representatives if they recommend waiving this requirement, and in the initial stages of a proceeding, indemnity is generally waived. As the proceeding progresses, however, and particularly if the debtor reports continuing operating losses, the judge may require, or creditors may urge, that indemnity be posted. Usually, such a requirement is taken as a signal that the situation is irretrievable. It is therefore the equivalent of aborting the reorganization proceeding, and the debtor may be adjudicated a bankrupt. In this event, the business will be liquidated.

On the other hand, if all goes reasonably well, the company manages to prove itself still viable, and if the debtor and the committee are satisfied with the accountants' report, they will negotiate. The mutual objective is to develop a proposal which the committee is willing to recommend to the general body of the unsecured creditors. The committee itself, acting on behalf of the debtor, solicits consents to the proposal. A characteristic solicitation of this sort is shown on the opposite page.

---

*In jurisdictions that appoint a receiver to operate the company, instead of letting the debtor's executives remain in possession, the receiver must post a fiduciary bond.

TO THE CREDITORS OF Acme Corp.

Gentlemen:

Please let this letter serve to supplement your committee's original letter of July 30, 1975, informing you of the pending proceedings.

The committee has met on several occasions in an effort to negotiate a Modified Plan of Arrangement. The basis for these negotiations was the report of the independent accountants, indicating that certain of the debtor's assets were probably undervalued. We enclose the balance sheet as of September 1, 1975, taken from this report. The committee had the benefit of an estimated value for the liquidation of the inventory under forced sale, which estimate was $280,000. These figures were submitted by an auctioneer who has conducted many such sales in the United States District Court.

To describe the various offers and counteroffers that were made would serve no useful purpose. It is sufficient to state that the committee has negotiated what it considers to be an equitable plan, which it now recommends to you for your acceptance.

THE PLAN

All unsecured creditors will receive 35% in full settlement, payable as follows:

> 30% upon confirmation
> 5% six months after confirmation

The deferred payments will be evidenced by a certificate of indebtedness, which certificate will be endorsed by Acme's executive committee.

The creditors' committee submits that this plan will offer creditors a sum far in excess of what they might receive as a dividend in liquidation.

Accordingly, we enclose a Form of Acceptance and recommend that you execute and return the same to our office.

If you have any questions relative to this matter, please contact the writer, any other member of the committee, or its counsel.

Very truly yours,

Secretary, Creditors' Committee

WNO:as
Enc.

CREDITORS' COMMITTEE
(list Names)

(Company)

COMMITTEE COUNSEL

(List Names)

ACME CORP.

STATEMENT OF FINANCIAL CONDITION

(Unaudited)

ASSETS

Current Assets

Cash in banks		$ 12,744
Accounts receivable (Schedule A-I)	$19,804	
Less: Allowance for doubtful accounts	1,143	
Net accounts receivable		18,661
Inventory (Note 1)		290,000
Total current assets		321,405

Fixed Assets

Store fixtures and leasehold improvements	2,573	
Less: Depreciation accumulated	1,359	
Net depreciated value of fixed assets		1,214

Other Assets

Loans receivable (Schedule A-II)	47,600	
Employee loans receivable:	1,000	
Unexpired insurance	3,000	
Organization expenses	101	
Deposit	115	
Total other assets		51,816
TOTAL ASSETS		$374,435

The accompanying notes are an integral part of this unaudited report.

LIABILITIES AND STOCKHOLDERS' DEFICIENCY

Liabilities Having Priority

Taxes payable (Schedule A-IV)	$ 2,957	
Wages unpaid	483	
Total liabilities having priority		$ 3,440

Unsecured Liabilities

Accounts payable (Schedule A-III)	638,115	
Union pension and welfare (local 815)	1,254	
Expenses accrued	700	
Total unsecured liabilities		640,069
Total liabilities		643,509

Stockholders' Deficiency

Capital stock—issued and outstanding		10,000	
Paid-in surplus		81,065	
Deficit—September 1, 1974	($ 12,170)		
Add: Loss—Exhibit B	(347,969)		
Deficit		(360,139)	
Stockholders' deficiency			(269,074)
TOTAL LIABILITIES LESS			
STOCKHOLDERS' DEFICIENCY			$374,435

UNITED STATES DISTRICT COURT
SOUTHERN DISTRICT OF NEW YORK

_____

IN THE MATTER
OF

_____ Debtor.   FORM OF ACCEPTANCE

                The undersigned, an unsecured
creditor of the above debtor, hereby consents to the debtor's
Modified Plan of Arrangement dated   which
Modified Plan calls for 35%, payable as follows:

        30% upon confirmation
        5% six months after confirmation

_____

CREDITOR

BY: _____

_____

TITLE OF OFFICER

_____

ADDRESS

DATED: _____

Concurrent with the committee's solicitation of consents to the Plan of Arrangement, public notice is given, so that other parties to the settlement, who may not have been known to, or reached by, the creditors' committee, can learn of the proposed arrangement. A typical notice, like the actual one reproduced below, would appear in appropriate newspapers, well in advance of the confirmation meeting.

ARRANGEMENT

UNITED STATES DISTRICT COURT, Southern District of New York. In the Matter of: THE PAN-AMERICAN BARTER CO., INC. of 417 Fifth Avenue, New York, N.Y. Debtor No. 72-B-606—Tax I.D. #13-1573074.

NOTICE IS HEREBY GIVEN, that the above-named debtor has filed its proposed amended arrangement and that the adjourned first meeting of creditors will be held before the undersigned Judge, in the courtroom, Room 236, United States Court House, Foley Square, New York, N.Y., on November 10th, 1972 at 10:00 A.M., at which place and time the creditors may attend, present written acceptances of the proposed amended arrangement and transact such other business as may properly come before said meeting.

NOTICE IS ALSO HEREBY GIVEN that the application to confirm said amended arrangement shall be filed with this court on or before November 29th, 1972, and that the hearing on the confirmation and objections thereto, if any, will be held before the undersigned Judge, in Room 236, United States Court House, Foley Square, New York, N.Y., on November 29th, 1972, at 10:00 A.M. All applications for allowances should be filed on or before November 29th, 1972.

Accompanying this notice is a copy of the amended arrangement with its unsecured creditors proposed by said debtor under the provisions of Chapter XI of the Bankruptcy Act.

DATED: New York, New York
    October 25th, 1972.

          EDWARD J. RYAN
          Bankruptcy Judge

(Notice that two distinct meetings are referred to in this announcement: a hearing with regard to acceptance of the recovery plan by creditors, and a hearing with regard to the court's confirmation of the plan. Normally, there is much to be done in the interval between the two. Other meetings and hearings may also be required, in which case the hearing on confirmation is postponed until everything else is in order.)

In a reorganization proceeding, as in many other situations that find humans with conflicting interests in confrontation, however, the ideal atmosphere of accommodation and enlightened self-interest does not always prevail. Each side is understandably trying to salvage as much as possible, so the debtor and the committee sometimes cannot agree on an acceptable proposal.

Under these circumstances, the debtor may attempt to communicate its proposal directly to the creditor body and solicit its own consents.

This ploy is rarely successful, however, because the consent of a majority, both in number and amount, of the creditors who have filed claims must be obtained; and generally the committee itself represents a majority, at least in amount. In addition, since any party at interest may be heard in the bankruptcy court, any disgruntled creditor can file Specifications of Objection to the debtors' proposal.

A court hearing on confirmation of the plan is required by the bankruptcy statute. It is held after the bankruptcy court has tallied the consents and found that a majority in number and amount of creditors has agreed to the plan. Testimony by an officer or other representative of the debtor, such as its accountant, must indicate that confirmation of the plan would serve the "best interests" of creditors, since bankruptcy and subsequent liquidation would yield less for creditors than would the proposed reorganization. The second hurdle is the "feasibility" test. This requires testimony indicating that after confirmation of the plan, the debtor can in fact comply with its provisions.

Clearly, the debtor's testimony on both of these points is self-serving, and readily subject to attack by hostile creditors. The cooperation of creditors is therefore imperative.

After the creditors' committee has negotiated and approved of the debtor's proposal, the taxing agencies must be consulted. The statutes provide for full payment, upon confirmation, of priority obligations. If an extension of the terms of payment of tax obligations is desired, some accommodation must be secured from the interested taxing agencies. (See Chapter Ten for a fuller discussion of the tax problems and the taxing agencies involved in reorganization or bankruptcy proceedings.)

All the preliminaries having been disposed of, the plan may now be confirmed. Generally, under the best of circumstances, it will take a minimum of at least six months between the debtor's initial petition and the court's final confirmation of the plan of reorganization. It commonly takes a year or more. It can take additional years to carry out the plan after it is confirmed. The chapters that follow deal in greater detail with the specifics and the mechanics that must be mastered.

Chapter Four

CONFLICTS AND QUANDARIES: THE ACCOUNTANT IN AN INSOLVENCY PROCEEDING

An accountant who renders services in connection with an insolvency serves various functions and roles, depending on the circumstances, the terms of the engagement, and the accountant's own posture vis-à-vis the parties to the proceedings. Shown below and on page 34 is one form of docket card that has proved useful, whether the accountant is serving the creditor or the debtor side of an insolvency case.

Generally, the creditors' accountant will not perform an audit, as part of the debtor-creditor confrontation. The debtor company's regularly employed accountant, who was rendering routine professional services prior to the inception of the insolvency, may continue to do so.

More often, however, the creditors insist that an accountant of their own selection replace the debtor's accountant. This practice can create

DOCKET CARD	
Name:	Date Called In:
Address:	Type of Case:
Telephone:	Case No:
Officers of Debtor:	Date Filed:
Accountant for Debtor:	District or County:
Attorney for Debtor:	Judge:
Attorney for Committee, Assignee or Trustee:	
Secretary to Committee:	Trustee or Assignee:
Case Called in By:	

```
Dun and Bradstreet Requested: _____

Form Letter Mailed: _____        ORDER OF
                                                        RETENTION_____
Premises Visited: _____

Books Picked Up: _____

Report Mailed or Committee Meeting Held: _____

Books in Storage At: _____

Auctioneer: _____

Miscellaneous Comments: _____

_____

_____

_____

_____
```

conflicting objectives which are often difficult to resolve. Alternatively, the debtor may insist that both accountants be employed. This, too, presents risks and conflicts. The main risk for the debtor's regular accountants is that their fees cannot be paid without either creditor review and consent or court approval; and the courts, in turn, often require creditor approval.

The courts get involved, of course, only after formal court proceedings have commenced, but if the debtor's accountants render their services prior to the inception of the court proceeding, they are still at risk, because as soon as the petition in bankruptcy is filed, they become additional unsecured creditors.

This is doubly unfortunate, because, in addition to their audit function, independent accountants normally furnish financial guidance to small businesses which cannot afford to have sophisticated accounting personnel on staff. As a result of the compensation dilemma, a business in financial difficulty may be unable to turn to its accounting firm in its hour of greatest need.

Yet, if the financially embarrassed company seeks professional advice from accountants suggested by the creditors' committee, those accountants may find that they are being asked to serve two masters, with commonly divergent interests. Professional objectivity under these circumstances would be a challenge even to a person of antiseptic judgment.

When accountants suggested by creditors meet the debtor for the first time, they try to set the debtor's mind at ease by describing the accounting function as a helpful one. Basically, they have three objectives. First, they have to determine the debtor's financial condition, with reasonable accuracy, but without conducting an audit. Second, they seek the underlying cause, or causes, of the debtor's financial difficulty, and are expected to monitor the debtor's business activities. In this connection, they are free to suggest economies and improvements that might help the debtor survive the crisis.

Third, creditors' accountants intend to probe the debtor's actions prior to the inception of the insolvency to ascertain if any acts were committed which would bar the debtor's discharge in bankruptcy. Such acts include fraud, concealment of assets, the solicitation of credit based on false financial statements, and other deceptive conduct, as set forth in Section 14C of the Bankruptcy Act.

It is important, however, that accountants confine themselves to determining the facts, without presuming to draw legal conclusions. They should simply report the debtor's acts as they find them, without editorial comment.

Among other things, creditors' accountants are expected to report possibly recoverable "preferential transfers." These involve a transfer of assets to a creditor in payment of an antecedent debt, the effect of which is to prefer, or favor, that creditor over other creditors of the same class. To be recoverable, such a transfer must have been made within four months of the commencement of a proceeding under the Bankruptcy Act, and at a time when the debtor was insolvent. Moreover, the preferred creditor must have had knowledge or "reasonable cause to believe" that the debtor was insolvent. (Similar provisions are found in most state debtor-creditor statutes.)

In a more general way, creditors' accountants are expected to review the acts of the debtor for evidence of good faith in the conduct of the troubled business. For example, substantial purchases beyond the normal needs of the business at a time when the debtor is contemplating, or on the verge of, bankruptcy would represent a breach of good faith. Excessive withdrawals of expense money, beyond the normal needs of the business, or large personal loans to, and withdrawals by, stockholders, officers, or their families or friends would also represent a breach of good faith. Creditors expect their accountants to detect and report all such actions.

For a number of years, creditors' committees also insisted that their accountants countersign debtors' checks, at least during the period of debtor-creditor deliberations, and often thereafter. The imposition of broadened legal liabilities has since discouraged this practice, and most public accountants now refuse to countersign checks. However, in the course of generally monitoring the operations of debtors, they may be asked to report any violations of debtor-creditor understandings or court-directed procedures.

Again, this situation raises ethical problems regarding the privileged client-accountant relationship. Generally, creditors' accountants would be well advised to secure the debtor's consent in writing to this reporting requirement. If the accounting services are being rendered under the provisions of a court order, the accountants' affidavit and the debtor's petition should explicitly define the services and terms of the engagement, including the obligation of disclosure and reporting to all interested third parties.

The initial visit by the creditors' accountant is normally in the nature of a survey. The accountant is interested in determining the condition of the debtor's books and records, their adequacy, and their completeness. The accountant should also estimate the amount of time the debtor will require to close the books of account as of the most recent, regular fiscal date. (In a court proceeding, the date of the court order continuing the operation of the business [normally the same date the petition was filed] is taken as the closing date.)

The accountant will estimate the cost of the accounting services, and seek agreement on the amount and the method of payment. If the services are rendered in connection with an out-of-court proceeding, the accountant will strive for payment of a retainer fee, along with a clear understanding regarding payment of the balance. A common arrangement is for payment of the balance of the fee upon delivery of the accountant's report, and before the meeting with creditors.

The accountant should prepare a letter of engagement, detailing the scope of work and the fee anticipated, and have this letter approved, at least by the debtor, and preferably by the creditors' committee as well.

The bankruptcy rules provide that the employment of an accountant in any insolvency proceeding must be approved in advance by the bankruptcy judge. In an affidavit, submitted with the petition and order for retention, accountants often quote the rates to be charged for all types of personnel, the total number of hours of work anticipated, by type of personnel, and the maximum total fee contemplated.

Bankruptcy judges can issue orders for the retention of accountants *nunc pro tunc* (retroactively), and can broaden or extend retention orders to modify the scope of work, adjusting the accountant's fees accordingly. Notice, too, that when an accountant applies for his or her allowance, the debtor or any creditor may object to it, in which case the bankruptcy judge may reconsider the amount to be approved for payment.

Rule 219, effective August 1, 1975, extends to accountants the same rules of practice with regard to compensation that apply to attorneys. That is, the fees are fixed, ex post facto, by the bankruptcy judge after review of the fee application, and the judge's evaluation of the services rendered. Despite this rule, it is important that the bankruptcy judge, the creditors, and the debtor understand in advance the scope of the accounting examination and its approximate cost.

In some instances, the judges have taken the position that routine, day-to-day accounting services need not be subject to court orders which sanction the performance of, and payment for, these services. Nevertheless, there is nothing lost, and at least a predictable outcome to be gained, by having proper orders entered to protect accountants.

The services performed by the debtor's regular accountant and by the accountants for the creditors cover different aspects of the debtor company's affairs and are necessarily oriented differently. Normally, though, when orders for regular accounting services are authorized, the practice has been that payment is made monthly.

In the course of a bankruptcy proceeding, it often develops that third parties—banks, finance companies, or private investors—agree to finance a Plan of Arrangement. In connection with this, such third parties frequently negotiate privately, outside the jurisdiction of the courts, the fees to be paid for lawyers and accountants for their services in connection with the proceeding. This practice is frowned upon by bankruptcy judges, who sometimes insist that these fees be subject to judicial review.

For all that, it is not at all unusual for the creditors' accountants to serve a dual function. First, they are retained to perform the monthly or regular accounting services, for which they are paid currently. At the same time, the order of retention provides them with a separate insolvency engagement, for which they are paid only after application and review by the bankruptcy judge.

In some jurisdictions, bankruptcy judges have refused to sign orders for the retention of insolvency accountants representing creditors. This refusal can hardly foster achievement of the ostensible objectives of the Chapter XI proceeding—namely, rehabilitation of the debtor.

If accountants who are investigating and evaluating the affairs of a debtor on behalf of creditors must rely for their compensation upon the successful completion of a composition, they indeed must be purer than Caesar's wife. If a proceeding ends in straight bankruptcy, for whatever reason, the accountants might well be left empty-handed.* Considering the attractive options open to an able accountant for investing talents and energies in alternative pursuits, this policy of some bankruptcy judges is simply unrealistic.

As soon as the accountants have finished their report, and before they present it to the creditors, they should discuss the report with the debtor. This affords the debtor an opportunity to explain any actions which the accountants question in their report. If this seems imprudent

---

*Recent court decisions have established the right of the creditors' committee to make its own application for allowances, even if a Chapter XI proceeding ends in straight bankruptcy. Compensation for the accountants and others who have served the committee naturally represent the lion's share of the committee's expenses; but the bankruptcy judge decides what value, if any, to place on the services provided to the committee by each person.

or futile in a particular situation, the accountants may wish to prepare a separate, confidential report to the creditors' committee. Especially where the details of the report are withheld from the debtor, the accountants should assure themselves that their findings are accurate, not susceptible to challenge, and not likely to be misinterpreted by other parties.

Creditors' accountants are often asked to participate in the negotiations between the debtor and the creditors' committee. This should be avoided wherever possible. Accountants should restrict themselves to determining the facts, leaving evaluation and interpretation to others.

Of course, this may be an unrealistic posture in certain circumstances. Creditors, being business people, are accustomed to having their accountants be part of the decision-making process. Moreover, no party to an insolvency proceeding is better able to calculate, with any degree of sophistication, the ability of the debtor business to meet the long-term payments to which a Plan of Arrangement commits it. Nevertheless, the accountant's proper role is advisory, and actual negotiations are best left to the creditors themselves.

This is not to say that accountants should restrict themselves to routine, regular reviews of the debtor's operations and to preparing the report used as a working tool by both parties in negotiating toward agreement on a proposal. In the course of their work, the accountants may be able to suggest important reductions in inventory or overhead, for example. In addition, accountants may be, and commonly are, engaged to make the audits required for filings under the Securities acts.

They also represent the debtor in tax examinations or other matters involving the Internal Revenue Service. In addition, they participate in other sensitive areas, such as the renegotiation of government contracts, price redetermination, systems analysis, and the many other functions that modern accounting firms routinely perform for their clients. In cases of this sort, the bankruptcy judges may sign orders permitting payment for these services without a formal application.

In practice, once the creditors' committee has approved a proposal made by the debtor, the independent public accountants proceed to render all the accounting services normally provided to any other client. When retained to serve the debtor, of course, the accountants perform subject to any obligation imposed by the terms of the court order authorizing the service. Such obligations characteristically include reviewing the business conduct of the debtor, so that the court remains in position to protect the interests of creditors.

The procedures and practices involved in rendering accounting services to a debtor-in-possession, trustee in bankruptcy, or receiver are explored more fully in the next chapter.

Chapter Five

ACCOUNTING FOR A DEBTOR-IN-POSSESSION, RECEIVER, OR TRUSTEE

As mentioned earlier, certain administrative practices of the bankruptcy courts vary from one jurisdiction to the next. A company involved in a Chapter XI proceeding in the Eastern or Southern Judicial District of New York is normally operated by a debtor-in-possession. In many other jurisdictions, notably California, this is not permitted; the court insists upon appointing a receiver to operate the company instead. Throughout the country, if the insolvent company is to be liquidated, the courts turn it over to a trustee in bankruptcy.

Like a trustee or a receiver, the officers of a corporate debtor-in-possession are in a fiduciary capacity to the bankruptcy court, and they operate the company under the provisions of court orders. Moreover, the same accounting procedures are used, whether the company is operated by a debtor-in-possession, a receiver, or a trustee. Accordingly, we shall use the term debtor-in-possession generically in this volume. What is said of the debtor-in-possession would apply equally to a receiver or a trustee, unless otherwise specified.

Court orders normally place various restrictions upon the debtor-in-possession, such as directing the establishment and location of new bank accounts,* requiring the maintenance of tax accounts, fixing officers' salaries, limiting new purchase commitments, and establishing such other controls as may be deemed necessary to the success of the particular Chapter XI proceeding. The debtor-in-possession may not

---

*Certain banks throughout the country have been specified by the federal government as "designated depositories," and bankruptcy judges choose from among them when specifying which bank a particular debtor company must use. Usually, the bank the debtor was using previously is one of the designated depositories, and the judge will allow the debtor-in-possession to continue using that bank.

borrow money except as specified by court order, which constrains both the amount and the terms of each loan.

The order continuing the debtor in the possession of the business also generally directs that new books of account be opened. As a practical matter, not *all* books need be opened anew. The underlying concept is that the assets of the debtor are made available for the new debtor-in-possession to use, subject to the various creditor security interests which must be recognized.

Liabilities existing when the petition is filed are frozen, and cannot be paid except with the explicit permission of the bankruptcy court as spelled out by court order. Customarily, permission is granted for the payment of wages accrued prior to the filing and for such other unpaid expenses as utilities, rents, employee expense accounts, vacation pay, hospitalization, etc. Payment of these and similar obligations are routinely approved as being conducive to the orderly continuance of the business.

Similarly, holders of liens on the debtor company's property are automatically stayed from exercising them. The rationale is that if lienholders were free to move in and seize assets the company needs in the normal course of business, all hope of salvaging the situation would collapse. Only rarely can a lienholder convince the court that exercise of a particular lien will not jeopardize the success of the proceeding. (Notice, though, that the *rights* of lienholders remain intact, which protects them in the event the reorganization fails.)

A creditor may have rights of reclamation for last-minute shipments to a debtor (those the debtor received within ten days prior to the filing of a Chapter XI petition) or for shipments made within three months of the filing if the creditor was misled by the debtor's representations of solvency. All such creditors are obligated, immediately after the filing, to take prompt action to protect their interests. The bankruptcy courts will determine their rights of reclamation, or, in some districts, their rights to liens on merchandise. Alternatively, if the merchandise is required for the continued operation of the debtor company, the bankruptcy court will require the receiver or debtor-in-possession to pay for it.

Generally, the task of opening the necessary new books of account for a debtor company is not particularly complex, but several quite understandable rules apply and should be carefully followed.

Books of original entry, such as cashbooks, sales journals, purchase journals, general journals, and the like, must be opened anew. New binders are not required, but new pages must be headed up, commencing with transactions that occur the day after the petition is filed.

New accounts payable ledgers also must be opened, because liabilities accrued after the filing have a prior right to payment over those that accrued before the petition was filed. The same holds true for any other subsidiary ledgers that record liabilities, such as notes.

Subsidiary accounts receivable and note receivable ledgers need not be opened anew. Business transactions generally continue with the same customers, so normally no distinction is necessary in the accounts receivable ledger between shipments made before and those made after the petition is filed. However, an exception arises if the debtor's new financing arrangements include a loan secured by accounts receivable. Since any deficiency in loans secured by previously pledged accounts would result in a general claim by the moneylender, new ledger accounts must be opened to isolate customers' accounts pledged under the new financing agreement.

The book of final entry, the general ledger, may be kept in either of two ways. A new general ledger may be opened by debiting all the assets—subject to secured liabilities—and crediting the difference to an account called "(Jones) Company—Debtor." Thereafter, transactions of the debtor-in-possession are posted to this new general ledger. In the event that corrections to the original opening entries prove necessary, they are recorded in this new general ledger and the debtor account is adjusted accordingly.

The other, and often preferable, method is to continue using the old general ledger, but to segregate all unsecured liabilities and all income and expense accounts of the debtor. Additional general ledger accounts are then opened for the new unsecured liabilities and the new income and expense accounts. Thereafter, as adjustments are required to the old accounts, they may be made directly in the old ledger. This approach greatly simplifies general ledger bookkeeping when, for example, accrued wages or other liabilities accrued prior to the inception of the proceeding are paid by court order.

Taxing authorities may not charge interest or penalties on any obligations accrued prior to the filing of the petition. Nevertheless, all tax reports should be submitted promptly, because penalties have on occasion been assessed for late *filing*, although they cannot be levied for late *payment*.

From time to time, questions may arise regarding tax claims which are protected by liens that predate the petition or which have lien rights as a matter of law; i.e., real estate taxes. Advice of counsel should be requested as to whether such tax claims are best treated as liabilities of the old debtor or of the new debtor-in-possession. Payment of some taxes may be avoidable even though liens have been filed, but real estate taxes may have to be paid to maintain property interests.

Certainly, public accountants serving the operators of an insolvent company can make a number of important contributions beyond merely opening new books of account. These services might range from evaluating the capability of the company's accounting personnel or suggesting potential new investors, to preparing special schedules and presentations for meetings with creditors.

Since the trustee, receiver, or debtor-in-possession must report periodically (usually monthly) to the bankruptcy court, separate records, clearly distinguishing activities of the debtor-in-possession from those of the old debtor, are essential. Accrued expenses of the old debtor, paid pursuant to court order, are not operating expenses of the debtor-in-possession.

After the petition is filed, the debtor's unsecured obligations no longer accrue interest. Interest-bearing secured obligations of the debtor may be treated differently from those of the debtor-in-possession. For example, interest on an accounts receivable loan of the old debtor is not chargeable to operations of the new debtor-in-possession, even though the lender accrues the interest and deducts it from the proceeds of the disposition of the collateral. On the other hand, interest on mortgages is chargeable to the operations of the debtor-in-possession.

While depreciation, amortization of leaseholds, and similar deferred charges are not chargeable to the debtor-in-possession's operations for purposes of reporting to the bankruptcy court, they are chargeable to operations for general reporting purposes (i.e., to the SEC or public stockholders). The following pages contain a typical set of financial statements of a debtor-in-possession (company name fictitious):

FINANCIAL STATEMENTS

THE PRUDENTIAL DRYCLEANERS, INC.

Debtor-in-Possession

September 30, 1975

THE PRUDENTIAL DRYCLEANERS, INC.
Debtor-in-Possession
STATEMENT OF ASSETS AND LIABILITIES
September 30, 1975
(unaudited)

ASSETS

Current Assets

Cash			$ 1,150
Accounts receivable			
Unbilled		$ 13,146	
Billed, less allowance for doubtful accounts of $2,741		80,669	93,815
Inventories			
Production supplies		42,102	
Linens		131,168	
Linens in circulation		13,247	186,517
Miscellaneous receivables			10,100
Prepaid expense			2,517
Total current assets			294,099

Fixed Assets (pledged)

Land and buildings		1,126,321	
Building equipment		275,551	
Machinery and equipment		303,515	
Furniture and fixtures		6,482	
Building improvements		18,142	
Delivery equipment		22,585	
		1,752,596	
Less accumulated depreciation		719,294	1,033,302

Other Assets

Investment at amortized value—$22,000 New York City, 3% due 6/1/80 (held as deposit by New York State Industrial Commission)		22,550	
Due from Irving Mallon		73,000	
Utility deposits		5,750	
Deferred mortgage costs, net of amortization		62,837	
Cash—security deposit	$ 4,000		
Less security deposit payable	(4,000)	—	164,137
			$1,491,538

This statement has not been audited by us, and accordingly we do not express an opinion on it. This statement is solely for the information of the Federal Bankruptcy Courts and is not accompanied by a statement of changes in financial position and does not necessarily include all disclosures which might be required for fair presentation. No depreciation has been reflected on an

LIABILITIES

Collateralized Liabilities

11% mortgage payable, Brinkman-Perchiet Assoc.		$ 574,282
Capitalized leased obligation		29,892
Other		18,123
		622,297

Debtor-in-Possession Liabilities

Bank overdraft	$ 14,313	
Accounts payable	29,794	
Taxes payable	17,552	
Wages payable	13,810	
Accrued expenses	8,100	
Real estate taxes payable	20,116	103,685

Priority Liabilities

Taxes payable (subject to audit by taxing authorities)	25,448	
Wages and vacation payable (subject to claims for vacation and termination pay)	1,164	
Due to union—dues withheld from employees	3,618	
Other	13,164	43,394

General Liabilities

Accounts payable	415,353	
Employment contracts payable	12,029	
Due to the Greater New York State Bank for The Prudential DryCleaners, Inc. Employees Retirement Fund	80,000	
5% twenty-five year debentures	257,842	
Debenture bond subscription paid	1,919	
Due to Phillip A. Sherman	100,000	
Due to Julius L. Linden	25,108	892,251

Deficit in Stockholders' Equity

Common stock—authorized, 80,000 shares no par value; issued, 80,000 shares	200,600	
Appraisal surplus	590,304	
Accumulated deficit	(959,693)	
	(168,789)	
Less 50 shares of common stock in treasury—at cost	(1,300)	(170,089)
		$1,491,538

Subject to claims filed in the proceedings.

appraisal revaluation of $590,304 which was recorded prior to 1972, a practice which is at variance with generally accepted accounting principles.

THE PRUDENTIAL DRYCLEANERS, INC.

Debtor-in-Possession

STATEMENT OF OPERATIONS AND ACCUMULATED DEFICIT

For the period January 1, 1975 to September 30, 1975
(unaudited)

Sales		$1,209,572
Prime cost of sales		
Production labor	$ 267,504	
Production supplies	62,359	329,863
Prime gross profit		879,709
Operating overhead		734,171
Gross profit		145,538
General and administrative expenses	137,737	
Interest expense	49,962	187,699
Net loss from operations		(42,161)
Other income		
Rental	19,395	
Gain on sale of trucks	2,200	
Sundry	5,865	27,460
		(14,701)
Other expenses		
Depreciation	32,400	
Amortization of deferred mortgage costs	3,491	
Amortization of linens	14,895	50,786
NET LOSS		(65,487)
Accumulated deficit—January 1, 1975 as originally stated	(797,100)	
Adjustment to linens on hand at January 1, 1975	47,813	
Accumulated deficit—January 1, 1975 restated	(749,287)	
Loss arising from sale of treasury stock in excess of		
amounts charged to capital contributed	144,919	894,206
Accumulated deficit—September 30, 1975		$ (959,693)

This statement has not been audited by us, and accordingly we do not express an opinion on it. This statement is solely for the information of the Federal Bankruptcy Courts and is not accompanied by a statement of changes in financial position and does not necessarily include all disclosures which might be required for fair presentation. No depreciation has been reflected on an appraisal revaluation of $590,304 which was recorded prior to 1972, a practice which is at variance with generally accepted accounting principles.

THE PRUDENTIAL DRYCLEANERS, INC.
Debtor-in-Possession
SUPPORTING SCHEDULES
For the period January 1, 1975 to September 30, 1975
(unaudited)

Operating Overhead

Superintendent labor	$ 47,918
Indirect labor	36,623
Power plant labor	18,614
Power expense	49,637
Building overhead	41,770
Machinery overhead	1,854
Factory expenses	16,802
Factory labor	25,843
Welfare and pension costs	58,687
Payroll taxes	50,948
Workmen's compensation	11,221
Labor—routeman	208,996
Collection and delivery expenses	132,524
Vacation payroll	22,942
Commissions	9,792
	$734,171

General and Administrative Expenses

Officer's salary	$ 15,900
Sales promotion	3,858
Claims	11,441
Claim department expenses	6,184
Office salaries	52,504
Office expenses	12,035
Professional fees	8,235
Executive office payroll and expenses	15,074
General expenses	12,506
	$137,737

These schedules have not been audited by us, and accordingly we do not express an opinion on them. These schedules are solely for the information of the Federal Bankruptcy Courts and are not accompanied by a statement of changes in financial position and do not necessarily include all disclosures which might be required for fair presentation. No depreciation has been reflected on an appraisal revaluation of $590,304 which was recorded prior to 1972, a practice which is at variance with generally accepted accounting principles.

The proper treatment on financial statements of the costs associated with a Chapter XI proceeding appears to be an unsettled area of accounting practice. No clear weight of authority is evident, and there are no official pronouncements furnishing absolute guidelines. There is considerable flexibility, for example, in the treatment of a reduction in debt occasioned by confirmation of a Plan of Arrangement. Accordingly, a decision on just how to treat certain transactions should probably be deferred until the implications and final outcome of the particular proceeding are clearly in view. For the most part, however, such costs can be thought of as falling into one of four general categories, which are usually dealt with as follows:

1. Costs directly and specifically attributable to Chapter XI proceedings—such as debtor's counsel fees, costs of meeting halls, and the like—are so identified, and recorded as period extraordinary charges.

2. Expenses that would in any event be treated as extraordinary items, including losses resulting from the termination of leases, moving expenses forced by the relocation of facilities, and so forth, should be so classified, and charged currently.

3. Imputed, indirect, and less identifiable costs should not be separately stated. The imputed profit on sales that are lost because a supplier refused to deliver, and the underabsorbed labor and overhead costs resulting from the cancellation of contracts or a brief plant shutdown, are examples. These and similar economic losses may indeed reflect the company's financial difficulties, but they are more properly treated as normal elements of the new debtor-in-possession's operating income or loss. However, a footnote to the financial statement should disclose that the company is in a Chapter XI proceeding and that numerous abnormal and nonrecurring economic losses were sustained.

4. Some costs cannot be accurately known until confirmation of the plan. These costs, such as creditors' counsel and accountants' fees and court costs, should not be accrued. Here again, though, a footnote disclosure is in order, indicating the approximate total of such costs that can be anticipated, and emphasizing the fact that they are not provided for in the accounts. When these costs are finally determined, they are generally treated similarly to the credit, if any, arising on confirmation of the plan. That is, if the reduction in liabilities is treated as income, these costs are netted against

the income. If the reduction in liabilities is treated as additional capital, these costs would reduce the capital.

So long as the philosophical and legal distinction between the debtor and the debtor-in-possession (or receiver or trustee) who succeeds the debtor in the management of the company's affairs is kept clearly in mind, the accounting services to be performed are clear, straightforward, and relatively routine. By contrast, the accountant serving the creditors faces a challenging and sometimes exciting task, which might well take on elements of detective work, as we shall see in the next chapter.

Chapter Six

ACCOUNTING FOR CREDITORS:
The Insolvency Examination

A meticulous examination and report of the financial status and activities of the insolvent company plays a pivotal role in the resolution of the company's difficulties. Accordingly, it constitutes the examining accountant's most important single contribution to the entire proceeding. Basically, the examining accountants have six key objectives:

1. To provide enough objective information about the distressed company's assets and liabilities to establish its "going concern" and liquidation values.

2. To analyze the operations of the debtor for several accounting periods prior to the filing of the proceeding—both to ascertain if all transactions were in the ordinary course of business, and to seek an explanation for the debtor's inability to operate profitably.

3. To uncover any transactions that might represent preferential transfers of company assets, which are recoverable under the Bankruptcy Act.

4. To detect any evidence of bad faith on the part of the debtor immediately prior to the filing of the petition, i.e., substantial extraordinary purchases of material or payment for services by a debtor with knowledge of the imminent possible filing of a reorganization petition.

5. To determine if there have been any transactions that might bar the debtor's discharge under the Bankruptcy Act.

6. To guide the debtor and creditors in the formulation and consideration of a plan of reorganization.

Generally, the information of most value and interest is that regarding the debtor's activities during the twelve months preceding the filing of the petition or the initiation of the out-of-court negotiations. The inquiry, therefore, is initially confined to this period, although extraordinary developments occasionally warrant a wider probe. In addition, summary data from prior periods should be included in the examining accountant's report, as they often prove helpful, particularly for comparative analysis.

Generally, the financial information is unaudited. The term *audit* is a word of art as defined by the American Institute of Certified Public Accountants.* Rarely does the examining accountant have time to comply with all the standards required for an audit, nor can the debtor's financial condition support the cost that would be involved. In very unusual circumstances, creditors may pool their resources and pay the cost of an audit and be willing to wait for its completion. Normally, however, the situation is urgent, so a timely report is much more important than the incremental accuracy that might result from working to audit standards.

The independent accountant's report to the debtor and the creditors may be as comprehensive and as detailed as the examiner considers warranted under the circumstances.** The report routinely includes comparative financial statements, setting forth operating results of the period immediately prior to the petition, along with those of several previous years. The report also includes a statement of assets and liabilities as shown on the company's books and records as of the date on which the bankruptcy proceeding was initiated.

Although the assets are classified in the traditional manner, liabilities are classified according to the priority of payment provided for in the Bankruptcy Act (see Appendix, Exhibit B). Bear in mind that the expenses of administering the Chapter XI proceeding itself constitute a

---

*It is interesting to note that the Statement of Affairs in the Original Petition under Chapter XI, includes question 2, item (*b*): "By whom have your books of account and records been audited during the two years immediately preceding the filing of the original petition herein? (Give names, addresses, and dates of audits.)" Your authors submit that the use of the word "audit" in this question is misleading. It was not the intention of the Judicial Conference to inquire as to *audits*, but rather to inquire regarding the name of the accountant who might have been retained by the company for accounting services prior to the filing of the petition. These services would include the preparation of unaudited, as well as audited, financial statements. Most small companies do not have regular audits, although almost all have accountants who regularly prepare unaudited financials.

This interpretation has been confirmed by correspondence and discussions with leading representatives of the accounting profession as well as with members of the panel who assisted in the preparation of the new bankruptcy rules and forms.

**See Appendix, Exhibit I, for an example of such a report, in this case to a trustee.

first-priority liability under the Bankruptcy Act, although they are not provided for in the debtor's schedule of liabilities. These first-priority, administrative liabilities include obligations of the debtor-in-possession (or trustee or receiver), the judge's salary and expense fund, and such other expenses of administering the proceeding as attorneys', accountants', and appraisers' fees.

Another priority liability arises if the proceeding fails as the result of a formal challenge by creditors. As pointed out earlier, any creditor has the right to object to the debtor's proposal at the court's hearing on confirmation. Occasionally, creditors succeed in overturning a Plan of Arrangement by filing specifications of objection that lead to the debtor's being adjudicated a bankrupt. When this occurs, those creditors are entitled to recover their reasonable costs and expenses on a third-priority basis. That is, upon liquidation of the company, these expenses are paid after the costs of administering the proceeding and after the priority wages and commissions owed by the bankrupt estate, but before taxes or any other liabilities.

During insolvency examinations, accountants should naturally address themselves to any noteworthy aberrations or revealing developments. The examination report should include any indications of possibly preferential transactions, irregularities, and evidence of acts by the debtor that could bar the debtor's discharge. It should also include a comparison of the books and records with financial statements issued to third parties in connection with the extension of credit.

Section 60 of the Bankruptcy Act defines a preference and sets forth four elements:

1. A transfer of money or property was made in payment of an antecedent debt.

2. The transfer was made at a time when the debtor was insolvent, and *in addition,* the creditor involved knew, or had reasonable cause to believe, that the debtor was insolvent.

3. The transfer was made no more than four months before the petition was filed.

4. The transaction had the effect of enabling one creditor to recover a greater percentage of the amount owed that creditor than other creditors of the same class.

At first glance, these elements appear to be deceptively simple and clear-cut, but complications are legion. For example, if the debtor received some appropriately valuable consideration from a creditor in exchange for the payment, the exchange might not represent a preference. Again, a creditor who receives a preferential payment enjoys a setoff to the extent that the creditor extends additional credit to the debtor before the Chapter XI petition is filed. On the other hand, merely granting a lien to a formerly unsecured creditor has the same effect as a transfer of property, and so might create a preference.

Moreover, establishing the four elements of recoverable preference, particularly a creditor's knowledge of the debtor's insolvency or reasonable cause to believe it, can be extremely difficult. Frequently, the facts can be determined only in the course of litigation.

As a result, it is worth emphasizing here that *it is not the examining accountant's duty to determine whether or not a transaction has resulted in a recoverable preference.* Instead, the accountant's role is to develop complete, accurate information, which will enable counsel to recommend to creditors an appropriate course of action if a recoverable preference is suspected. (Not all preferential transfers are worth litigating, of course, but a convincing threat of lawsuit may be enough to trigger at least partial recovery.)

Turning now to acts that could bar a debtor's discharge (release from debt), it is interesting to note that any creditor has a right to bring on a hearing objecting to such discharge. Moreover, if reasonable grounds are demonstrated for believing that the debtor (or bankrupt) has committed any of these acts, the burden of proof immediately shifts to the debtor or bankrupt, who must prove that it has *not* committed any of these acts. Clearly, this is a matter with which anyone involved in an insolvency situation should be conversant, and the examining accountant must be alert throughout the investigations for evidence of such acts.

Section 14 of the Bankruptcy Act sets forth the acts of a bankrupt (or debtor, in a Chapter XI proceeding) which will serve to bar the debtor's discharge. As set forth in the act, the following constitute grounds for objection to the discharge of a business debtor:*

1. Destroying, mutilating, falsifying, concealing, or recklessly failing to keep (or preserve) books of account or records, from which the debtor's actual financial condition and business transactions might be ascertained. [Of course, the corner laundromat is not expected to maintain records of a caliber appropriate to IBM.]

---

*Discharge may also be denied a debtor who has committed any of the nine bankruptcy crimes, punishable by imprisonment, that are specified in the Federal Criminal Code—accepting bribes, making false entries, taking false oaths, concealing or transferring property, etc. Such offenses must have been committed knowingly and fraudulently. A detailed discussion of such criminal activity is beyond the scope of this book, and readers persuaded that they have encountered it are advised to seek legal counsel at once.

2. Obtaining money or property on credit, or extending or renewing such credit, with the aid of a materially false statement, in writing, concerning the debtor company's financial condition.

3. Transferring, removing, destroying, or concealing any of the debtor's property—with intent to hinder, delay, or defraud creditors—within the twelve months before the petition is filed.

4. Having already been granted a discharge, in a proceeding under the Bankruptcy Act, within the six years prior to filing the present petition.

5. Refusing to obey any lawful order or to answer any material question approved by the court in the course of a proceeding under the act.

6. Failing to explain satisfactorily any asset losses or deficiencies that prevent the debtor from meeting its liabilities. [One effect of this provision is that a profligate debtor, who squanders company assets on personal pleasure, may be denied discharge.]

Initially, it may appear that not all the "grounds for objection" just mentioned are the legitimate concern of an examining accountant. While items 1, 2, 3, and 6 obviously concern matters that should be covered in the course of the accountant's examination, what of items 4 and 5? Both lie well within the scope of the examination, and the astute accountant remains alert to their possible existence and their implications.

For instance, several years ago a Chapter XI petition was filed in the Southern District of New York. While reviewing credit-agency reports on the debtor, the examining accountants found that a debtor of virtually the same name had been through a Chapter XI proceeding just four years prior to the present petition. Further inquiry revealed that the company that filed the new petition had only recently been incorporated.

It developed that, in an attempt to evade the six-year limitation in the law, without attracting the attention of suppliers by an abrupt change in name, the recently "laundered" debtor, once more in financial trouble, simply transferred its assets to a newly formed corporation in a tax-free exchange. Shortly thereafter, the new corporation, posing as a fresh debtor, filed a Chapter XI petition. Apprised of this turn of events by the examining accountants, a creditor moved to block the discharge. The court ruled that the debtor's transaction was a sham, and the company was adjudicated a bankrupt.

The accountant's responsibility under item 5 arises from the nature of the proceeding. A debtor-in-possession is permitted to operate its business under a court order which imposes certain conditions, such as deposits in special tax accounts, filing monthly income and expense reports, reports of cash receipts and disbursements, payment of certain salaries to officers, and so forth. It is the duty of the examining accountant to ascertain if these conditions are being complied with. A debtor's ignoring or violating any order of the bankruptcy court would, in accord with item 5, constitute an act that could bar discharge. Accordingly, the accountant is obliged to reveal such findings to creditors or the court. (As a matter of courtesy, counsel to the debtor is normally notified also, so that corrective action can be advocated.)

PREPARATION OF CONVENTIONAL FINANCIALS

The procedures outlined here are directed at assembling the information that should be recorded in the accountant's work papers. As pointed out earlier, decisions regarding the scope and detail of information to be included in the special report to the debtor and creditors are matters of discretion of the examining accountants.

1. Assets
   a. *Cash—reconciled or counted.* In the event the account has been closed (as it would be in a formal Chapter XI proceeding), any checks outstanding on the statement date should be reversed for book purposes. New checks may be issued subsequently (with court approval) to relieve appropriate obligations. If the bank account has been overdrawn, any overdraft that has not been covered should be set forth as a liability.
   b. *Accounts receivable.* An aged list of accounts receivable should be prepared, and if the debtor is in liquidation, the address of each of these accounts should be furnished. Contra accounts receivable should be offset against the appropriate liabilities.

   Credit balances should be segregated and set forth separately on the balance sheet. Technically, credit balances with customers are general liabilities, but from a practical point of view, a debtor commonly has to satisfy customer credit balances by providing new merchandise or services in order to maintain customer goodwill. If the amounts involved are substantial, however, court permission and the permission of counsel should be secured.

Legal counsel may also be desirable if accounts with large balances have been turned over for collection; in any event, the examiners should review the book provision for uncollectible accounts.

Accounts receivable representing retainages, which are usually found in the construction industry, should be set forth separately, as should any significant amounts due from United States or other government agencies. Government receivables may be subject to offset by taxing authorities or to lien claims for progress payments made by other government entities. Accountants often present progress payments as a deduction from amounts due from government agencies. Alternatively, they may be presented as a secured liability, since the collateral may consist both of accounts receivable and inventory.

Two other special categories of accounts receivable should also be identified and set forth separately. These are any accounts receivable from affiliated or subsidiary companies, and any that have been pledged as security for loans, and which are therefore subject to liens by the lenders. (In the case of the latter, the associated indebtedness should also be set forth separately as a secured liability.)

c. *Inventories.* Physical inventories may be taken or observed, or inventories may be estimated or simply presented as recorded on the books. No single, generally acceptable procedure can be followed in every instance. If the inventory items are fungible and nonspecialized, a physical count may well be desirable. In many instances, though, time considerations or the highly specialized nature of the inventories makes physical confirmation impractical in time for use in the special report.

One alternative which may be acceptable, if no other means can be utilized, is an independent appraisal by knowledgeable auctioneers. In a liquidation, the proceeds of the trustee's auction sale may have to be used as the closing inventory.

Inventory in the hands of third parties (i.e., subcontractors) should be set forth separately, as it may be subject to counterclaims for unpaid balances due. Inventories of work-in-process that can be linked to specific contracts on the books should be used in the unaudited financial statements. In some cases, it may be desirable and useful to compute the cost of converting work-in-process to finished goods, or the cost of completing a government contract.

Some of the procedures suggested for inventories—count, appraisal, etc.—may also be used to gauge the value of fixed assets or intangibles for purposes of the accountant's report.

d. *Fixed assets.* Fixed assets should be scheduled by year of acquisition. The company's income tax returns are sometimes a handy tool for easily determining the year of acquisition. Normally, the current value of real estate can be determined readily, either from actual market transactions for comparable property or from appraisals. In addition, examination of real estate tax bills may yield key information regarding assessed value.

Confirming or estimating the value of other facilities often presents more of a challenge. In some cases, a knowledgeable, objective appraiser must be engaged, but the examining accountants should not overlook another valid and well-informed source of information: the debtor's creditors. One or more *au courant* representatives of the major creditor companies can normally provide dependable insights, after an unhurried tour of the debtor's facilities.

In certain industries, an active market for used equipment makes it relatively easy to determine market value. For example, in the plastic molding industry, generic descriptions of a debtor's molding equipment by year and type will give creditors a fast and reasonably accurate fix on its value. This would also be true of automotive equipment, the heavy equipment used in the construction industry, and characteristic facilities common in various other industries.

e. *Other assets.* Prepayments, sundry receivables, deferred charges, and the like should be evaluated from the best information available. Unless substantial and unusual, they are rarely taken into consideration by either the debtor or the creditors in formulating or presenting a plan.

The amounts anticipated from claims for income tax refunds as the result of carry-back losses should be recorded on the asset side of the balance sheet. However, these claims are always subject to audit, and should be evaluated with care unless they are unquestionably valid. Even then, they may be reviewed by the taxing authorities and at least partially offset against outstanding tax liabilities. Whenever such claims appear on the balance sheet, a footnote should clearly disclose that any recovery is subject to review, audit, modification, and possibly offset.

2. Liabilities
   a. *Secured liabilities.* Liabilities secured by pledged assets should be analyzed carefully to ascertain all the terms of the security agreements. Schedules should be prepared comparing the book value of the pledged assets to the secured debt, indicating, in each case, whether the obligations represent purchase money debts or new loans. All debts that have been cross-collateralized or guaranteed by a parent or other affiliated company should be described.
   b. *Priority liabilities.* Other liabilities must be segregated according to their priority under the bankruptcy statutes (see the sequence of liabilities explicit in the Appendix, Exhibit B). For instance, wages and commissions earned within three months of the date on which the petition was filed, totaling up to $600 per employee-creditor, carry priority status, and are so set forth on the balance sheet. (Owed compensation exceeding that amount is carried over as a general unsecured debt.)

   It is worth noting in this connection that compensation owed to managers and supervisors who own substantial stock in the company is not protected by this provision, but all severance pay, and up to $600 in sales commissions, even if earned by nonemployees, are to be included. Similarly, certain earned "fringe benefits," such as vacation pay earned within three months of the filing date, are entitled to priority treatment, while payments owed to union welfare funds are not. The accountants' report should call attention to any such priority wages or commissions that have been paid since the balance sheet date.

   Taxes should be scheduled according to the taxing authority involved. To aid analysis, the various tax classifications and taxing periods involved should be clearly indicated. With some well-defined exceptions, taxes due for periods extending back beyond three years from the date the petition was filed are dischargeable. Accordingly, these amounts should be classified separately under general liabilities. Here again, though, since all liabilities and claims relating to taxes are subject to review and audit by taxing agents, a footnote to the balance sheet should so indicate.

c. *General liabilities.* The debtor's general liabilities should be scheduled into an appropriate number of major categories: for instance, debts due to financial institutions or insurance companies, trade debt, amounts due for wages and commissions in excess of the amounts entitled to priority, amounts owed for back taxes no longer protected by priority, and so forth, depending on specific circumstances. Information regarding these liabilities should be detailed and listed in the examiner's work papers with sufficient backup information so that they may be adequately discussed, with all likely questions answered. It is particularly important to collect complete information regarding long-term debt, bank loans, and loans from others.

Amounts owed to officers, stockholders, and affiliated companies should be analyzed to inception, and a complete record of the details and descriptions of each such transaction should be prepared, including photostats of key payments that were made by check. In general, any liabilities arising as the result of journal entries, or other noncash or nontrading transactions, should be fully documented.

The examining accountant's report presents the debtor's assets in the usual form on a statement of assets and liabilities. However, a typical liability section, reflecting the priorities set forth in the Bankruptcy Act, would look like the one on the following page.

Before completing their report to the debtor and creditors, the examining accountants should try to reconcile the balance sheet they have prepared with the schedules that the debtor filed with the Original Petition under Chapter XI. Recent financial statements prepared by the debtor's accountant should be examined also, particularly footnote details that might affect the examining accountant's report.

Further, it is usually a good idea to get a copy of the claim docket, as maintained in the bankruptcy clerk's office, and compare it to the book liabilities. Claim dockets have been known to harbor misplaced decimal points and to disclose unrecorded liabilities (such as lawsuits and claims arising from executory contracts) as well as disputed items.

LIABILITIES

Secured Liabilities

(Presented normally, with explanations suggested above.)

Liabilities Having Priority

Wages and commissions entitled to priority
Taxes (categorized by taxing authority)
Other debts due to the United States and its instrumentalities
Other priority obligations*
(Wages or other obligations that have been paid are noted on
the statement, i.e., "Wages—Paid by the Debtor-in-Possession
(or Trustee) Pursuant to Court Order.")

General Liabilities

Amounts due to financial institutions
Amounts due to trade creditors
Other general liabilities
(Set forth within as many classifications as the examining
accountants consider necessary. Amounts of loans payable
to officers, directors, stockholders, or any related individual
or affiliated entity are generally presented as a separate
category.)

---

*See Appendix, Exhibit B, "Original Petition under Chapter XI," for a sequential list
of priorities and the relative position of nonpriority liabilities.

The examiner's schedules should list details of all such executory contracts, and touch on pertinent historical information relating to the
debtor. It is also important to examine individual claims, as typo-
graphical errors and incorrect designations of priority and nonpriority
status do occur.

Important as it is for helping all parties concerned in arriving at a
realistic assessment of the debtor's worth, either as a going concern or
under the auctioneer's hammer, the balance sheet does not normally
reveal much about how the debtor arrived at the present predicament.
Far more valuable in this connection are comparative financial statements, which should be prepared in great detail for at least the two
years preceding, plus the short accounting period immediately before,
commencement of the insolvency proceeding.

These comparative financials often include entries that suggest further review. A drastic change in the gross profit on sales, for instance,
or in any significant expense category, obviously warrants a closer look.
One purpose of this comparative analysis is to detect and investigate
any marked changes in the conduct of the debtor's business. It is not

unusual, unfortunately, to find a substantial number of large purchases in the months immediately preceding the petition date, coupled with a concurrent reduction of payments to creditors. This indicates bad faith on the part of a debtor who is secretly, but fully, aware of serious trouble ahead.

Comparative operating statements are prepared in the usual form, except that prime gross profit is usually set forth separately, to facilitate the identification of direct material and labor costs. While this procedure may create problems if overhead is included in inventory, it is, as a general rule, the most informative and useful approach.

The examining accountant is free to select any acceptable form of presentation, and the format used in the following illustration is only one of many possibilities. (As a matter of fact, the addition of key percentages, omitted here, is often of considerable value to the readers of such financial statements.)

	1974 in dollars	1973 in dollars	1972 in dollars
Sales (net)	1,500,000	2,000,000	1,750,000
Cost of sales			
Prime cost of sales			
Opening inventory	660,000	510,000	450,000
Purchases	810,000	820,000	660,000
Direct labor	660,000	710,000	410,000
Closing inventory	(310,000)	(660,000)	(510,000)
	1,820,000	1,380,000	1,010,000
Prime gross profit or (loss) on sales	(320,000)	620,000	740,000
Factory overhead	500,000	550,000	560,000
Gross profit or (loss) on sales	(820,000)	70,000	180,000
General and administrative and selling expenses	200,000	210,000	170,000
Net profit or (loss)	(1,020,000)	(140,000)	10,000

This is a typical example of what frequently occurs. The following questions, as a minimum, suggest themselves:

1. What caused the gross loss on sales in 1974?

2. Why was there such a marked increase in direct labor costs in 1973?

3. What is behind the significant increase in the cost of purchased material in 1973 and 1974?

Explanations are sought from management. Among many possible reasons for the aberrations are these:

The closing inventory at December 31, 1974 is incorrect, either because (*a*) there has been a concealment of assets, or (*b*) the closing inventory was not priced consistently with prior inventories, or (*c*) the closing inventory has been deliberately understated. Alternatively, the opening inventory at January 1, 1974, and therefore the closing inventory at December 31, 1973, has been overstated. Such overstatement may have been deliberate, to conceal from creditors, stockholders, or others losses sustained in 1973. (We describe in the next chapter an actual case in which a theoretical inventory shortage was calculated, leading to the conclusion that the opening inventory probably was overstated.)

Labor costs may have increased in 1973 because of new labor contracts, a major change in product, or changed manufacturing methods. Materials purchased may have increased because of a switch to more expensive materials, a supplier's price increase, or hedge buying by the debtor as protection from an impending strike at the supplier's plant.

The examining accountants may test the debtor's cost records or compute their own cost data to verify the prime gross loss on sales. On occasion, where the nature of the business lends itself to unit analysis of a basic component, this technique may represent a means of checking for concealment of assets. For example, fifteen to twenty years ago, many small concerns began manufacturing television and radio sets, usually unsuccessfully, and bankruptcies in that industry reached epidemic proportions. During that era examining accountants routinely made unit analyses of television tubes, which were critical, expensive, portable, and readily salable components.

POSSIBLE PREFERENTIAL TRANSFERS

All transactions with creditors during the four months preceding the statement or petition date should be examined for evidence of possible preferential transfers. Any large or unusual payments of debt or returns of merchandise to creditors should be recorded in detail. Similarly, any notes that have been anticipated or loans that were repaid before they were due should be appropriately documented. If the debtor's correspondence files or records indicate that actual or threatened litigation resulted in debt payments, or that checks were returned for insufficient funds and then replaced, the examiners should collect all supporting evidence.

Anything that leads the examining accountants to believe that a security interest may have been granted to a creditor during this four-month period should be documented in detail. Any consideration that the debtor received in exchange for the security interest should also be recorded. Remember, too, that a lien granted to a formerly unsecured creditor may constitute a preference. Counsel for the creditors should be given a list of all allegedly secured creditors, and should proceed to make lien searches under the Uniform Commercial Code. Sometimes liens are not filed properly, on time, or in the proper jurisdiction, in which case they can be challenged.

The examining accountants should always determine whether or not any debt was guaranteed by third parties or secured by third-party collateral. They should also review the minute books and stockbook of the company, and compare these findings with the books of account, to determine if all stock was issued for adequate consideration.

The most effective way to determine the possibility of preferential transfers is to make a detailed comparison of the individual balances of debts payable on the date of the petition and those payable four months earlier. A noticeable reduction in any particular debt between the two dates indicates a possible preferential transfer. As a practical matter, the size of the debt reduction is important, because the cost of litigating small transfers may not be worthwhile in light of the potential amount to be recovered.

In addition, it is very difficult, under normal circumstances, to prove that trade creditors knew, or had reasonable cause to believe, that the debtor was insolvent at the time the transfer was made. Such proof is necessary before a preference is recoverable. The most telling evidence of creditor knowledge, of course, is a clear background of unsuccessful collection efforts or of litigation, checks that were returned for insufficient funds, or other obvious indications of the debtor's financial instability.

Loan creditors who are repaid, and creditors who receive liens, are the most frequent source of litigation in preference actions. As a result, particular study should be made of all transactions of this kind. The debtor's anticipation of notes given for outstanding obligations may also indicate a possible preference. (However, to the extent that additional credit is granted *after* the transfer of property, there is no recoverable preference.)

The accounts for debts owed to financial institutions require especially close scrutiny. This class of creditors receives the most current financial information, and is apt to be the most knowledgeable regarding the affairs of debtors. Debtors in financial difficulty will almost always try to protect their institutional creditors. They know that institutional lenders have long memories; and in most cases, the corporate officers or stockholders have personally guaranteed the institutional debt, so they have a pressing desire to satisfy these obligations.

Not surprisingly, most preference litigation is against banks and other financial institutions.

SUPPORTING INVESTIGATION

As a general rule, the accountant's work-paper file should include details regarding such of the following as may be appropriate in the circumstances:

1. Officers' salaries

2. Other executives' salaries

3. Travel and other selling expense

4. Automobile rental or expenses

5. Professional expenses

6. Any other significant category of expenses which the examining accountant considers meaningful

Other matters to be inquired into, to the extent appropriate, would include long-term employment contracts, employees who are related to principal officers or stockholders, important stockholders on the payroll, compensation to former employees or stockholders for consulting services, and retirement payments to former employees, stockholders, or their relatives.

Occasionally, an alert review of invoices for legal or other professional services will reveal information regarding the affairs of the company that was not volunteered by the principals. Similarly, canceled check vouchers for at least six months should be examined for possible irregularities, double endorsements, and checks payable to cash.

Internal control should be reviewed to the extent the examiners consider necessary. Organization charts should be examined (or prepared), and the names, addresses, and compensation of all employees in key positions should be recorded. This list should include shipping and receiving clerks and others of similar responsibility, and it is worthwhile to learn something about the employees who supervise inventory counts and pricing.

If possible, a complete schedule should be prepared which summarizes sales, purchases, and payments to creditors for approximately two years. A summary schedule of cash receipts and disbursements for at least six months prior to commencement of the proceeding can also be very enlightening, and should be included in the examining accountant's report.

Careful inquiry should be made regarding contingent liabilities, lawsuits in which the debtor is either plaintiff or defendant, and pending tax examinations. Note especially the details of any long-term leases which have not yet been recorded on the books, and therefore have not been considered earlier in the examination.

Among the various other procedures that have proved to be helpful is the request for copies of at least two years' financial statements—including interim statements where available—at least two years' tax returns, and the most recent tax examinations. Copies of inventories, leases, agreements with lending institutions, employment and other significant contracts, and so on should also be reviewed.

A final, but very important part of the insolvency examination is a review of all recent financial statements filed with creditors or their representatives. Usually, creditors or trade agencies will readily furnish such statements, and they should be examined for evidence of culpable carelessness or possible fraud. The next chapter details a number of actual frauds that were detected by creditors' examinations, and a fraudulent financial statement is presented and discussed.

Chapter Seven

ACTUAL FRAUDS DETECTED BY THE EXAMINING ACCOUNTANTS

As we have pointed out elsewhere, a careful examination of the books and practices of an insolvent company serves a number of valuable functions. One is the regrettably necessary search for evidence of fraud. Many times, a businessman in distress will resort to desperate measures and expedients that he would not even consider in normal circumstances. When the gamble—and his business—fails, he commonly finds that he has compounded his problems by making it extremely difficult to regain the trust and patronage he needs to start over. Tragic as these situations sometimes are, the creditors' accountants necessarily must single-mindedly address themselves to protecting the interests of the creditors.

Unfortunately, too, some business people deliberately try to exploit their creditors' ignorance of a deteriorating financial situation. The ingenuity and variety of fraud that can precede an apparently innocent insolvency is remarkable, and investigators can minimize creditor losses only by being as astute and imaginative as were those who engineered the fraud. Perhaps in no other aspect of accounting is an alert skepticism more likely to pay off.

Here, drawn from actual insolvencies (all names disguised), are several typical examples of the more common types of fraud encountered, and how they were detected.

CASH DIVERSION

Cash, often in small denominations, is a relatively common commodity in the day-to-day affairs of many small and medium-sized enterprises. In addition, cash transactions are normally fairly easy to conceal, and of course, the cash itself is easily disposed of—everybody wants it. All this makes cash a tempting source of funds for a desperate or dishonest business person, and the ways in which it can be siphoned off are legion. In some cases, diversion is literally impossible to detect, after the fact.

A classic example of cash diversion is that of a wholesaler who sells merchandise at retail, for cash, to "properly introduced" customers and does not record the sale on the company's books. Especially if internal control is weak—either by oversight or design—cash is easily taken in, and no entry appears on the books and records. Some business people continue this practice for years, until financial difficulties impose a review of their accounts by outside accountants representing their creditors.

A small-appliance maker presents another case in point. During the 1960s the Anchor Manufacturing Company was the largest independent manufacturer of electric broilers for home use. The founder, Charles Davis, was in his late seventies, but remained active as the company's president and principal stockholder. His son and son-in-law also held executive positions in the company, which employed over 200 people in a four-story factory building on the west side of New York City.

Mr. Davis boasted that he never missed a day at the office, and he was intimately familiar with every aspect of the business. As a matter of fact, he even personally opened, sorted, and selected the mail—an apparently harmless eccentricity, the significance of which emerged later.

In response to heavy sales, Anchor Manufacturing overexpanded. This, coupled with limited working capital and poor management, resulted in serious losses. For example, in the year before it turned to the courts, Anchor Manufacturing recorded sales of about $6 million, on which it sustained losses in excess of $1 million. Finally, deepening debt forced the company to seek relief through a Chapter XI proceeding. When the petition was filed, Anchor Manufacturing owed more than $4 million to trade creditors.

During the course of an accountant's examination on behalf of the creditors, the examiner noted that Davis himself drew a very modest salary—about $15,000 a year—while the other executives earned substantially more. Yet, the president's life-style required a significantly higher income. The possibility of fraud suggested itself. All Anchor Manufacturing's accounts receivable were pledged to a finance company, and both the nature of the local customers and the company's internal accounting controls and procedures seemed to mitigate against there having been quiet cash sales of any consequence.

However, further investigation brought to light another source of temptation. The company packaged each of its broilers with a conventional guarantee card and a self-addressed envelope to encourage its return to the company. The guarantee card suggested that customers enclose $1, in exchange for which the company would send them a special electric broiler cookbook.

Hundreds of these reply cards came in every day, and in many cases the customer simply enclosed a dollar bill. As the company sold about 200,000 units per year, these enclosures brought in substantial cash—all of it in small bills. Interestingly, a significant increase in revenue from the sale of cookbooks was recorded after the Chapter XI petition was filed. Neither before nor after that date were accurate records kept of the number of cookbooks forwarded to customers. The smoke was getting dense.

Deciding to analyze recorded cookbook purchases over a three-year period, and to compare them with sales of the company's electric broilers, the auditors discovered that the company purchased approximately 150,000 cookbooks during the three-year period. About 10,000 copies were on hand at the time of the investigation. Total cash receipts reported by the company from cookbook sales during the thirty-six-month period were roughly $40,000.

An examination of the company's contemporary bank deposit tickets indicated that, typically, only about 5 percent represented cash from cookbook sales. This contrasted dramatically with the experience of the debtor-in-possession, which reported about 80 percent of cash receipts from this source.

Allowing a 10 percent inventory shrinkage factor, to account for cookbooks given away or otherwise lost, the auditors calculated the imputed discrepancy as follows:

Total cookbooks purchased in the three years preceding the inventory		150,000
Less: Inventory on hand	10,000	
10% allowance	15,000	
Sales reported @ $1 per copy	40,000	
		65,000
Estimated cookbooks unaccounted for		85,000

Apparently, during the three years reviewed, Davis had diverted some $85,000 in cash that had been sent in for cookbooks. How much cash he may have intercepted prior to that can only be guessed at. Told of this, the creditors refused to consider any proposal for reorganization unless it included repayment of the "missing" $85,000. Unfortunately, Davis either could not or would not comply, and the company was adjudicated a bankrupt.*

Although the diversion of assets was proved subsequently, the trustee in bankruptcy, considering Davis' age and failing health, decided not to pursue the matter. He reasoned that prosecution could hardly remedy things, and taking the old man's cherished company away from him was punishment enough.

Here is another example of cash diversion that destroyed an otherwise viable enterprise:

The Wishwash Company operated a laundry service to the retail trade, in connection with which it operated a fleet of over twenty trucks. Some customers paid by check directly to the company, but others paid their bills in cash to the route drivers who served them. These drivers kept a record of the customers' accounts in their route books. Internal control was excellent, and an exact accounting of all cash receipts was recorded in the books.

After prospering for some years, the company was sold, on terms, to several individuals with a talent for genteel larceny, who proceeded to bankrupt it for personal gain. The normal flow of cash turned in by the route drivers was the first target of opportunity. Every week, the new owners appropriated about $2,000 of the cash receipts before depositing the remainder in the company's bank account. The cash receipts journal recorded an allocation of these withdrawals as charges to a dozen expense accounts. From January to October, management siphoned off some $75,000 in cash.

The next ploy was to negotiate a second mortgage of more than $600,000 on the company's plant and real estate. Upon receipt of the mortgage proceeds, the principals promptly drew checks to their own order for a substantial portion of the loan and entered corresponding charges to construction costs.

If the company had been operated profitably, with its accounts payable under some control, these diversions might never have been revealed. However, the new owners were thieves in a hurry, and the company was rapidly driven into bankruptcy. In this case, the defrauded creditors were joined in their grief by the many former small stockholders, who never collected a substantial portion of their sales price. The company only survived for a year after they sold out.

---

*The relatively minor cash diversion, by itself, did not cause this company's failure, of course. The example is included to show a common type of cash diversion and the way the examining accountants went about uncovering it.

SALES AT LESS THAN FAIR VALUE

Darrell Dirkdaughter was a wholesale diamond merchant operating under a trade name as a sole proprietorship. A member of the Diamond Club, he was well known in the trade and was considered astute and of good reputation. Yet in the spring of 1971, he abruptly filed a voluntary petition in bankruptcy, listing liabilities of $620,000 and assets of only $12,000.

In the diamond trade, merchandise is customarily sold on consignment with the purchase actually consummated only after the diamonds have been resold. Dirkdaughter had suffered substantial losses on such sales. Moreover, certain of his customers had purchased many parcels of gems for cash, and on each transaction Dirkdaughter took a significant loss. He replenished his stock by taking more diamonds on consignment, for which he issued notes in exchange, a common practice in the diamond market. The merchants supplying these diamonds thereby became his creditors.

Suspicious of the size and regularity of Dirkdaughter's losses, the trustee in bankruptcy and the creditors' committee decided to retain an accounting firm to make a creditors' examination of his records. There were no funds in the bankrupt estate, so the creditors formed a pool of several thousand dollars and retained both an accountant and an attorney.

The accountant first prepared unaudited financials that included comparative operating statements for the previous two years, 1969 and 1970. To summarize the operating results:

	1970	1969
Sales	$ 833,000	$268,000
Cost of sales	1,137,000	248,000
Gross profit or (loss)	(304,000)	20,000
Expenses	59,000	16,000
Net profit or (loss)	($ 363,000)	$ 4,000

Clearly, a very poor year, followed by a catastrophe, despite his having handled four times as much merchandise as he customarily did.

Realizing how unlikely it was that an experienced diamond merchant would blunder into honest losses of this magnitude, the creditors' committee set about matching the purchase and sales slips of specific lots that could be identified. From these, the accountants were able to prepare detailed schedules of the sales to each customer, showing both cost and selling prices. The summary looked like this:

	Sales	Cost of sales	Gross profit or (loss)
Customer A	$ 65,415.08	$ 83,614.34	($ 18,199.26)
Customer B	272,649.34	359,816.76	(87,167.42)
Customer C	6,210.40	7,344.94	(1,134.54)
Customer D	1,520.40	2,324.04	(803.64)
Customer E	27,323.54	25,013.14	2,310.40
Customer F	8,589.90	10,010.55	(1,420.65)
Customer G	52,288.10	63,667.83	(11,379.73)
Customer H	1,160.00	1,363.00	(203.00)
Customer I	29,573.43	41,959.58	(12,386.15)
Customer J	2,040.43	2,218.72	(178.29)
Customer K	3,663.00	4,302.36	(639.36)
Customer L	9,011.50	12,057.92	(3,046.42)
	$479,445.12	$613,693.18	($134,248.06)

As the purchases were made on credit, while the sales were made in cash, the implication was obvious—Dirkdaughter was not merely an innocent incompetent. He had been systematically defrauding his creditors.

In the trustee's objection to Dirkdaughter's discharge under appropriate sections of the Bankruptcy Act, the trustee pointed out "that on or after May 29, 1969, the bankrupt transferred certain of his property, to wit diamonds, to . . . others for an inadequate consideration with intent to hinder, delay, or defraud his creditors." Other specifications were also charged, and at the resulting trial of objections to the bankrupt's discharge, the accountant for the trustee and various creditors testified as to their analysis of the sales and purchases.

The judge denied the bankrupt's discharge, noting, among other things, that Dirkdaughter had made personal withdrawals from his proprietorship in 1970 amounting to about $60,000. The trustee also filed a lawsuit against "Customer B" on the grounds that an apparent conspiracy existed.

THEORETICAL GROSS LOSSES ON SALES

James Spyder was another wholesale diamond dealer in New York, transacting an annual volume of about $500,000, and apparently prospering. Yet, in June 1972, he called a meeting of his creditors to announce that his corporation was insolvent. At that time, he turned over to his attorney his entire inventory, which consisted of 2,084 carats of diamonds. The attorney placed the gems in escrow in a vault.

Spyder had been carrying these diamonds in his inventory on a cost basis of $305,000. However, the creditors' committee counted and appraised them at a value of $250,000. Auditors retained by the creditors' committee then examined the debtor's books of account, and made some curious discoveries.

For one thing, the books of the corporation had not been closed on December 31, 1971. The company's last sale of diamonds took place in March 1972, but no entries whatever had been made in the general ledger in 1972. No information at all was available regarding the inventory on January 1, 1972, and there was no detailed inventory listing for January 1, 1971. Spyder had simply given his accountant a letter from the corporation, fixing the January 1, 1971, inventory at $485,000.

The accountants for the creditors' committee prepared a trial balance of the general ledger at December 31, 1971, unadjusted. Next, they journalized the original books of entry for 1972 and posted these entries to the trial balance. Financial statements were then developed from the trial balance. Finally, they prepared comparative balance sheets as of January 1, 1971, and as of June 30, 1972 (actually as of March 31, 1972, since no purchases or sales were recorded after that), spanning a period of eighteen months.

These financial statements are summarized below:

STATEMENT OF ASSETS AND LIABILITIES
(Unaudited)

ASSETS

	January 1, 1971	June 30, 1972
Cash	$ 6,600	$ 127
Inventory	485,000	250,000*
Other current assets	335,000	10,300
Other assets	700	47,000
Total	$827,300	$307,300

LIABILITIES

	January 1, 1971	June 30, 1972
Liability—notes payable—bank		$379,000
Liabilities—trade creditors	$704,000	381,300
Liability—loan creditors		27,000
Other liabilities	18,800	15,000
Total liabilities	722,800	802,300
Capital (deficiency) or Capital	104,500	(495,000)
Total	$827,300	$307,300

*Appraisal value.

COMPARATIVE STATEMENTS OF INCOME AND EXPENSES
(Unaudited)

	January 1, 1970, to December 31, 1970	January 1, 1971 to June 30, 1972
Sales	$1,381,000	$ 688,000
Cost of goods sold		
Opening inventory	528,000	485,000
Purchases	1,210,000	908,000
	1,738,000	1,393,000
Less ending inventory	485,000	250,000
	1,253,000	1,143,000
Gross profit (or loss)	128,000	(455,000)
Less expenses	119,000	138,000
Excess of costs and expenses over revenue 1971–1972 or revenue over expenses 1970	$ 9,000	($ 593,000)

Notice that the operating statement for the eighteen months ended June 30, 1972, indicating a gross loss of $455,000 on sales of $688,000.

The absence of a detailed inventory by carats at January 1, 1971, made it impossible to prepare a unit analysis of purchases and sales for the eighteen months ended June 30, 1972. Nevertheless, it was clear that sales by carats during the period exceeded purchases less closing inventory.

DEVELOPMENTS IN TERMS OF CARATS

Purchases 1971	5,711
Purchases 1972	1,104
	6,815
Less	
Inventory June 30, 1972	2,084
Imputed consumption in 1971 and 1972	4,731
Known sales in 1971 and 1972	5,923
Excess (presumably from inventory on hand at January 1, 1971)	1,192

Unfortunately, there was no way to determine the carats on hand at January 1, 1971. To be sure, one could assume that only the known 1,192 carats were on hand. However, the dollar value of the opening inventory on that date was $485,000. This assumption, therefore, would imply an average price per carat of about $400, whereas Spyder rarely paid more than $200 per carat, and his 1971–1972 purchases averaged about $150 per carat.

The calculations in dollars, therefore, indicate a theoretical inventory shortage, although without a detailed inventory at January 1, 1971, there is no way to be certain that the shortage arose during the eighteen-month period.

The shortage might have resulted from any of a number of causes. For example, the opening inventory (January 1, 1971) might have been overstated. Alternatively, Spyder might have made cash sales that were not recorded on the books. Finally, he might have withheld some diamonds before he placed his inventory in escrow, where the creditors' committee could count and appraise it.

Accountants tried to reconcile Spyder's purchases to specific sales by the diamond merchants on the creditors' committee, but were unable to derive any significant information. A review of the debtor's sales and purchases during the period indicated that most diamonds were sold at close to cost, except for one large lot disposed of in March 1972. These sales were amply profitable, of course, as the gems had been acquired on credit and not paid for.

Ultimately, the creditors' committee concluded that Spyder's 1971 opening inventory had been overstated and that probably he had overstated previous inventories as well. His objective, of course, was to present an image of financial strength, to induce other diamond merchants to extend him credit. As a practical matter, the defrauded creditors had to settle for a pro rata share of the money realized from selling the diamond inventory Spyder had surrendered. This course of action was chosen to save time and the costs of a full bankruptcy proceeding.

DELIBERATE PLUNDERING

In recent years, criminal elements have developed new techniques in insolvency fraud. One favorite tactic is to make available large sums, either as loans or as equity capital, to business people of good reputation who find themselves in distress. Such loans are made at exorbitant rates of interest, and often provide for the lender's participation in important management decisions.

As soon as intimidation or loan defaults have placed the legitimate business person under the control of these criminals, the business activity of the company—by now certainly a future bankrupt—is suddenly expanded. Sales are increased, purchases are increased even more rapidly, and in a period of a few weeks, perhaps a million dollars of credit can be extended by unsuspecting trade sources. The criminal element—by now owners or de facto managers of the business—simply liquidate the inventories, ignore their creditors, and quickly close out all bank accounts. Abruptly, the doors of the once-honorable business are closed, and the new "managers" disappear. Creditors are left with an empty shell.

Food processing businesses are very susceptible to this technique, because a large volume of their sales is characteristically condensed into short periods of time. As a result, suppliers are accustomed to periodic surges in the volume of goods ordered, and the whole sordid game is over before they suspect anything.

Another favorite technique of organized crime is a little more sophisticated and was popular for a number of years. A company—to all intents and purposes founded expressly to defraud suppliers—is started, often to specialize in the wholesale or retail sale of manufactured items. Frequently, the company sells only by mail order.

To build credibility, the new company initially places small orders and pays its bills promptly. After several months of this, the apparently prospering mail-order house progressively increases the size of its orders, and the elated suppliers happily fill them. Suddenly the criminals spring their trap: they rapidly dispose of the merchandise for cash, at distress prices, and then declare bankruptcy and go out of business. The principals, of course, immediately disappear, taking with them the cash proceeds of the merchandise sales.

While the FBI is obliged to look into a situation when a trustee in bankruptcy complains of a criminal violation of the Bankruptcy Act, officials make it clear that there must be good evidence that a fraud or concealment of assets has taken place. They will not take action based merely on the suspicions of creditors or a trustee in bankruptcy. This imposes a burden on the creditors' or trustee's accountant to provide documentation to support the claims of fraud. Even then, the FBI can hardly afford to give cases of commercial fraud the same attention it devotes to the violent, subversive, or spectacular crimes over which it has jurisdiction.

EMPLOYEE FRAUDS

Dramatic and tragic as they may be, examples of deliberate fraud by specialized criminals are less common than are instances of fraud by dishonest employees who respond to targets of opportunity. The following is an example:

The Somnolent Manufacturing Company was a division of a major industrial concern. Among other raw materials, Somnolent purchased

stainless steel and related components which were used in the manufacture of a highly specialized, patented machine used in the paper
industry. The company maintained a highly computerized inventory
control system which was programmed to alert management to shortages of any raw materials that fell below minimum stock-room requirements. Unfortunately, the computer did not alert management to excess
stockpiling.

Observing this oversight, Raymond Slye, the company's metals purchasing agent for twenty years, negotiated an arrangement with several
suppliers of stainless steel, under the terms of which Slye received a 10
percent kickback on all purchases. As a predictable result, the warehouse, at the end of three years, had a ten-year supply of stainless steel.

When management questioned the large purchases from these suppliers, Slye explained that the heavy steel purchases (which he pru-
dently neglected to identify as *stainless* steel) were required in connection with a multimillion-dollar building program on which the parent
company had embarked. Its curiosity satisfied, management returned
to its other concerns, and Slye returned to his lucrative purchasing.

Eventually, independent auditors called management's attention to
these huge inventories of stainless steel, and when confronted with the
facts, Slye promptly committed suicide. The company then sued the
culpable suppliers, some of whom were forced into bankruptcy. All
this proved small comfort to Somnolent. An employee fidelity insurance
policy covered only part of the loss the company sustained, and the
parent organization was forced to close down the operation and abandon the product line.

Here is another example:

Harvey Creetin was the office manager and credit manager for the
Hi-fun Manufacturing Corp.—"the company with dash"—which pro-
duced a sophisticated line of electronic sound equipment in kit form for
hobbyists. Hi-fun purchased wire, electronic parts, metals, wood cabi-
nets, and other components from a variety of sources, including
importers, jobbers, and manufacturers. It sold its kits both by mail
order and through hundreds of small retail outlets throughout the
country.

For a long period of time, Creetin found it very difficult to collect
from the host of small retail customers. At one point, more than $100,-
000 of a total of $300,000 of outstanding retail accounts was over six
months old. Frantic, Creetin hit upon an odd scheme that worked well
—temporarily. One of his duties as office manager was to approve and
direct the payment of suppliers' invoices. Recognizing that the total
lack of internal control enabled him to do just about anything he
desired, Creetin concluded that what he desired was to conceal his
flood of overaged accounts receivable.

Over a period of three years, he succeeded in doing just that, diverting funds that the company had ostensibly paid to many of its smaller suppliers. He simply held checks made payable to suppliers, canceled them, and recorded the canceled checks as receipts from customers.

The unpaid suppliers, of course, took a dim view of all this, but their complaints, initially at least, were directed to the office manager: Creetin. As a result, top management had no knowledge of these shenanigans until Hi-fun was deluged by collection letters and threatened lawsuits.

Creetin himself received no personal benefit from his manipulations, except that he saved his job—at least until the dam broke and the facts became known. Hi-fun's independent public accountants routinely prepared unaudited financials, and therefore the accounting services they rendered did not include a review of transactions, which would have disclosed the fraud several years before it erupted in a flurry of creditors' claims.

Initially, Hi-fun filed a petition under Chapter XI, but it was never able to recover from the financial disaster resulting from Creetin's lengthy machinations. Ultimately, Hi-fun went bankrupt and was liquidated. Creetin, out of a job at last, suffered less loss than any other party to the Hi-fun fiasco.

MANIPULATING THE BOOKS

Auditors have recently become aware of new opportunities for fraud involving the manipulation of electronic data processing records. The volume of paperwork entailed, and the sophistication of systems specialists, make effective auditing more difficult than ever before. The Equity Funding fraud, involving vast numbers of fictitious insurance policies, is a dramatic example of the possibilities for wide-ranging deception that attend computer-based record keeping.

Even without a computer, of course, a resourceful executive or employee with a taste for larceny or deceit can find ample ways of manipulating a company's books for his or her own purposes.

Fraudulent financial statements are often used initially as a temporary expedient, to conceal what the perpetrators hope will prove to be a transient problem. If the situation deteriorates, instead, the temptation to continue or even increase the deception grows apace. Here is an example of how this formalized fraud inevitably converts a financially embarrassing situation into a disaster:

The rules of the New York Stock Exchange require member firms to maintain a certain ratio of capital to aggregate indebtedness, and to periodically report their financial condition to the Exchange. The ratio, and the frequency of these reports, are established by the Exchange in light of prevailing trading conditions. In addition, member firms are subject to a surprise audit, conducted annually by independent public accountants. Finally, the Exchange itself can audit the books of a member firm when it is uneasy about the firm's financial health.

In computing its capital for reporting purposes, each member firm is permitted, within certain limitations, to include securities owned by partners of the firm as well as by the firm itself. It can also include cash, securities, and other property that has been borrowed, provided the lenders subordinate their positions to those of other creditors. The capital computation is therefore as follows:

1. Capital accounts of partners, plus

2. The value of securities contributed as capital, or loaned to the firm, by its partners, plus

3. The value of securities borrowed from subordinated lenders, plus

4. The value of money or other property borrowed from subordinated lenders, less

5. Debit balances in the partners' accounts.

Securities listed on public stock exchanges are recorded at market value, but issues traded over the counter, and *letter stock*—i.e., restricted securities held for investment, which cannot be sold on the open market except under certain strict rules—are assigned a value lower than what either listed or unrestricted shares would have. This procedure is known as *haircutting* the value of such securities.

Knickerbocker Investments was a limited partnership, functioning as a stockbroker and dealer, investment banker, and underwriter of securities. It was a member of the New York, American, and other public stock exchanges throughout the country. During the hectic market of the late 1960s, the firm began to have trouble meeting the net capital requirements of the New York Stock Exchange. Certain of the partners responded by manipulating the books of the firm, in order to conceal its disintegrating financial position. The two chief methods used to overstate capital and earnings were (1) the temporary repayment of partners' loans and debit balances, and (2) the temporary sale of securities which had been subject to haircutting.

In the summer of 1971, the regular surprise audit by the firm's independent auditors revealed that Knickbocker fell short of meeting the Exchange's capital requirements by several hundred thousand dollars. This triggered a detailed examination of the firm's accounts by the

Exchange's auditors, who also uncovered a number of other impro-
prieties.

The procedures described below were all directed at concealing the
shrinking capital position of the brokerage house. They were performed
just prior to each of several scheduled reporting dates, and each time
they substantially increased the amount of the capital reported to the
Stock Exchange.

The partners' loan accounts showed debit balances of about $150,000.
The partners routinely repaid these loans on the last day of the month
(statement date), and withdrew them again two days later, in time to
cover the personal checks used to repay the loans.

In a variation of this scheme, one new partner transferred securities
from his personal margin account, which then had a debit balance of
about $60,000, to the firm's capital shortly before the statement date. On
the last day of the month, he gave the firm his personal check in the
amount of $60,000 to cover the debit balance. This entire sum was with-
drawn immediately after the statement date.

Two of the other partners were obliged to make capital contributions
to the firm. They arranged to borrow the necessary $200,000 from a com-
mercial bank on their joint signatures. They deposited this money in
the firm's capital account, then proceeded to repay the loan, at the rate
of $20,000 a month over ten months, using systematic withdrawals from
the firm, which were charged to the drawing accounts of the two
partners.

Complicating matters further, these loans were collateralized by a
pledge of several securities which were in the firm's name. Nevertheless, the same securities were also included in the firm's reported capital on the statement date. Shortly after the statement date, other securities were substituted for those originally pledged to secure the loan.
Apparently, when the firm's independent auditors reported shortages
in the account, some means was found to switch collateral and free the
securities in question, so that the accountants were satisfied. The
market value of the pledged stock exceeded $200,000.

The firm also resorted to another deceptive practice, colloquially
known as "parking" securities; that is, temporarily selling them to
associates in order to enhance the financial situation as of a particular
reporting date. In the case under discussion, approximately $300,000
worth of securities were sold to various individuals connected with
members of the firm. These securities were subsequently repurchased
by the firm, after the statement date, and in some instances the co-
operating "customers" realized profits on the transactions at the expense of the firm.

The final gambit has never been fully unraveled. Two days after the
statement date, $100,000 in checks were drawn, payable to an indi-

vidual related to one of the partners. The checks were charged in part to the subordinated securities account of the payee, and in part to the capital securities account of the related partner.

The final disposition of these funds was not determined, but the pattern of conduct of the offending partners suggests that in some way these funds found their way back into the member firm to cover withdrawals (which impaired capital) that were made prior to the statement date.

To summarize the transactions:

1. Temporary repayment of partners' loans	$150,000
2. Temporary repayment of the unsecured debit balance in a partner's margin account	60,000
3. Company-owned stock pledged at the bank to secure partners' loans	200,000
4. "Parking" of various stocks (30 percent haircut)	90,000
5. Payments to relative of a partner	100,000

After the financial statements were issued in the fall of 1970, certain partners of the firm began a series of other financial transactions which affected the monthly reports that the company submitted to the other partners and to the Stock Exchange.

One of these transactions involved improper bank reconciliations. Approximately $200,000 in checks were deposited in the firm's bank account, and credited to the security accounts of an individual who was related to a partner. These checks were returned because of insufficient funds; however, instead of reducing the recorded cash in the bank account and charging the customer's margin account, the firm carried these sums as "deposits in transit." This fiction continued for a period of six months, until the next "surprise" audit by the firm's independent accountants.

The returned checks were covered by well-timed deposits and withdrawals overlapping the audit date, in much the same manner as described before. The resulting bank reconciliation looked like this:

Cash in bank per books	$1,000,000
Add: outstanding checks	350,000
Total	1,350,000
Less: deposits in transit	200,000
Balance per bank statement	$1,150,000

The large volume of transactions—involving millions of dollars per day —made it relatively easy to bury these transgressions.

The firm maintained a private, handwritten ledger in addition to its general ledger, which was maintained by a computer service. The private ledger contained the capital accounts (except for the capital securities accounts), the drawing accounts, and the profit and loss accounts for the partners. The general ledger contained a control account for the private ledger, and the private ledger had one for the general ledger.

This arrangement enabled the desperate partners to record a very complex series of transactions over a period of months to further inflate the reported capital on the monthly statement dates. Here is a typical example:

On July 9, 1971, the following journal entry appeared in the general ledger:

Private ledger control	$200,000	
R. Mandrake—capital securities account		$200,000

No entry was made in the private ledger, so there was naturally an imbalance between the "private ledger control" account in the general ledger and the "general ledger control" account in the private ledger. This is the way the two ledgers appeared:

	General ledger *Private ledger control*	*Private ledger* *General ledger control*
July 9, 1971	$200,000 debit balance	No entry

On July 30, 1971, a deposit of $200,000 was recorded in one of the firm's bank accounts, and credited to the private ledger control account in the general ledger. Therefore, the control accounts between private and general ledger were in balance.

Partner Mandrake's capital securities account in the general ledger had been increased by $200,000; therefore, the firm's reportable capital was inflated by the same amount. Three days later, on August 2, 1971, a check for $200,000 was drawn to Mandrake's order and charged to his drawing account. He used this check to cover one that he had written on his personal account on July 31 to cover the July 30 deposit to the firm's private ledger control account.

The net effect of this circuitous transaction was to overstate the firm's capital position on July 30, 1971, the critical statement date. This was one of several similar transactions, which together had the effect of bloating the firm's reported capital by more than $500,000 on that date.

The partners also employed still another method of deceptive book-keeping. This one took advantage of the fact that the transaction "cage" closed for the day promptly at 3 P.M. Any checks drawn after 3 P.M. were dated as of the following day, and entered on the following day's business. Margin accounts, however, were kept open until 5 P.M., the end of the normal business day.

The opportunity was obvious, and the partners took it. Checks were drawn on the cash or cage account after 3 P.M. and deposited in the margin account on the same day. For instance, a cash withdrawal dated on the first of one month could be deposited to the margin account as of the thirtieth or thirty-first of the preceding month. Here again, the result, depending on the accounts credited, was to overstate the firm's cash and capital as of a reporting statement date.

The cumulative effect of the various fraudulent practices just described was substantial. Between the fall of 1971 and the summer of 1972, the extent of capital overstatement alone increased by more than $500,000. When the firm's auditors discovered and reported the violation of the Stock Exchange's capital requirements, the Exchange terminated the firm's operation and launched a detailed examination.

In tandem, and while the firm was in liquidation, independent public accountants were retained by the firm's managing partners. These accountants brought to light the specific methods that had been used to conceal the capital shrinkage the firm had suffered as a result of large operating losses sustained in 1970 and 1971.

Fraudulent financial statements can be prepared in a number of ways. Sometimes, as we have seen, the perpetrators are not trying to divert company funds into their personal bank accounts. Instead, their objective is to deceive superiors, creditors, investors, partners, or others who rely on the doctored statements as representing the company's financial condition and earnings.

In one case, corporate officers systematically inflated a company's performance simply to exaggerate their own custodianship. This brought them praise, prestige, enhanced compensation, and very nearly a capital gain when a major corporation decided to buy out their employer. Unfortunately for them, the prospective purchaser spotted their game and backed away, which alerted their own board.

Here is how the fraud was perpetrated, and how it came to light:

MicroWave, Inc., manufactured microwave equipment which it sold to some of the largest industrial companies in the country. In most instances, MicroWave was a subcontractor to companies that incorporated its products into equipment supplied to the United States government. MicroWave also stocked a line of manufactured items that were sold via catalogs, but most sales were special orders, built to customer specifications.

The company was publicly owned and the stock was actively traded over the counter. The board of directors included the founder's widow, but was predominantly made up of outsiders, almost all of whom were large stockholders.

At the close of 1967, MicroWave owed a large commercial bank approximately $700,000, short term, including an inventory loan, an accounts receivable loan, and some unsecured debt. Early in 1968, management secured a $750,000 long-term loan from a Midwestern insurance company, and transferred the MicroWave accounts to another commercial bank. This bank made a total of almost $1 million of unsecured financing available to its new customer.

The company reported 1967 pretax earnings of over $500,000 on sales of about $3 million. Its reported stockholders' equity on December 31, 1967, amounted to about $950,000, which included approximately $300,000 of retained aftertax earnings. Current assets exceeded $2 million, divided about equally between accounts receivable and inventories, while current liabilities were roughly $1.4 million. In short, the financials depicted a small, well-operated company with considerable promise, but in need of additional working capital, which the insurance company and the bank provided early in 1968.

Predictably, all this attracted the attention of a large company listed on the New York Stock Exchange. Early in 1968, this company sent MicroWave a letter of intent, providing for MicroWave's acquisition in an exchange of stock. So eager was this prospective suitor that late in 1968 it guaranteed about $200,000 of new bank loans to MicroWave, and promptly sent its auditors over for a preacquisition review of the company's accounts. Shortly thereafter, the larger firm abruptly terminated both its audit and its interest.

In February 1969, the president of MicroWave, a professional manager brought in after the death of the founder and original president, told the board of directors that the company's reported 1968 sales and earnings were incorrect. He admitted to having followed a policy of prebillings, and that as of that date (February, 1969) between $600,000 and $700,000 of prebillings had been recorded as sales. Accordingly, accounts receivable and sales were overstated to that extent. He insisted, however, that all such prebillings had taken place in 1968, and that earlier figures were accurate.

Thunderstruck, and concerned about the company's reported performance in earlier years, despite the president's assurances, the board of directors decided to ask independent auditors to review the company's accounts and report their findings directly to the board. The new auditors began by reviewing the financial statements for the year 1967.

Initially, they were given a list of accounts receivable, dated December 29, 1967, which totaled $800,000. By contrast, the financial statement showed $1,300,000 in accounts receivable. Examining the accounts receivable ledger, the auditors noticed that on the last day of the year, very large sales entries were made to several customers' accounts. The sales journal reflected this, showing sales entries on December 31, 1967, in excess of $500,000.

As these records were being examined, the bookkeeper entered the room and said, "Mr. Smith [the controller] gave you the wrong list of accounts receivable. Here is the list we gave our accounting firm."* The total of this second list coincided with the amount set forth in the financial statements, and of course included the large sales entries made on the last day of the year.

Confronted with these findings, the controller and the president confessed that incoming orders were immediately entered on the books as sales—that is, completed transactions—even though deliveries were not made until as much as six months later. Moreover, the officials admitted that they had been doing this for several years.

Pursuing the investigation, the independent auditors next examined every invoice that the company issued in 1966, 1967, and 1968, and compared them with shipping records. The available copies of all inventories were also checked, and the original purchase invoices were compared to the values set forth in the inventory lists.

This exercise revealed another rather clumsy fraud. In many instances, the values set forth for both raw materials and purchased parts had been increased by simply adding a zero after the value. For example, $10 was converted to $100 and $250 became $2,500. It was obvious that the handwritten changes had been made by someone other than the person who originally prepared the inventory records.

Probing deeper, the auditors discovered that the work-in-process inventory included jobs that had not in fact been started as of December 31, 1967. In one instance, a job was included that never started. Furthermore, the same work-in-process inventory appeared on both the December 31, 1966, and December 31, 1967, records. In addition, the finished-parts inventory included units that resulted from overruns on jobs two and three years old.

Capitalized tools, leasehold improvements, and fixtures had not been properly amortized, and liabilities for unpaid real estate taxes had been overlooked. In addition, an examination of the records for the first part of 1968 indicated that expense invoices for 1967 were entered in 1968,

*The company's original independent auditors subsequently testified that they had simply used negative confirmations for accounts receivable, and had "backed into" their computation of the work-in-process inventory.

and had not been accrued as of December 31, 1967. The 1967 year-end payroll had not been recorded, either.

All told, the new auditors' review of MicroWave's extensively "doctored" books revealed that the company's December 31, 1967, balance sheet, as originally reported, included the following discrepancies, among others:

- Accounts receivable were overstated by $722,000

- Inventory was overstated by $430,000

- Equity was overstated by $750,000

- Liabilities were understated by $41,000

The picture that emerged from all this contrasted sharply with the situation originally presented to the outside world early in 1968. Far from being a profitable company with a net worth of about $950,000, MicroWave had in fact lost $230,000 on its operations during 1967, and the stockholders' equity had disappeared entirely. Even after allowing for about $300,000 in state and federal tax refunds that were eventually collected, the company's overall capital deficiency exceeded $400,000.

MicroWave suffered additional losses of about $767,000 in 1968, and the bankrupt company was liquidated at public auction in 1969. Proceeds reverted to the bank, which had converted MicroWave's unsecured debt into secured debt early in 1969, in connection with new loans made in a vain attempt to salvage the company. Subsequently, the company's original auditors (responsible for the misleading financials) settled out of court with the stockholders, who had begun a class action, and with the insurance company and bank.

Interested readers may find the details and revelations of the examining accountants' revised financial statements instructional, so they have been reproduced in toto and appended to this chapter.

THE PERENNIALS

The more common forms of bankruptcy fraud recur year after year in apparently endless variations on a few basic themes. These include padding expense accounts, padding payrolls, recording fictitious invoices from suppliers, opening bank accounts that are not recorded on the books, selling at substantial losses to customers who agree to secret kickbacks, and recording the proceeds of sales as loans made to the business by principals.

In most cases, a careful examination of the books and practices of an insolvent company will detect such fraud, where it exists, and an astute auditor can uncover invaluable evidence in many such cases. This lesson, alas, has not been lost on those who deliberately and systematically defraud their creditors via structured bankruptcy. Increasingly, arson is employed to destroy books, records, and any remaining inventory (which often has been fraudulently depleted). This prevents reconstructing inventory records and collecting other accounting evidence of the looting of the company. In a very real sense, arson represents a trial by fire that precludes a trial in fact.

But enough of villainy. The detection of fraud, where it exists, is only one of the objectives of the insolvency examination. A more pleasant goal is to provide the debtor and the creditors with the objective information they need in order to negotiate toward a mutually acceptable and workable plan for resolving the situation. The range of possibilities is illustrated in the next chapter.

APPENDIX TO CHAPTER SEVEN

EXAMINING ACCOUNTANTS' REVISED FINANCIAL STATEMENTS FOR MICROWAVE, INC.

Board of Directors
MicroWave, Inc.
Huntington, New York

We have been engaged by you to make a special examination of the affairs of MicroWave, Inc. In connection with which we submit herewith, the revised Balance Sheet of MicroWave, Inc. as at December 31, 1967 and a revised Statement of Income for the year then ended and Notes to the Financial Statements, prepared from the books and records of the Company, without any independent verification thereof.

We were not engaged until February 6, 1969 and therefore, were not present to observe the physical inventory taken at December 31, 1966 and December 31, 1967. We have not been able to satisfy ourselves concerning inventory quantities and the pricing of the work in process.

In addition thereto, as detailed in Note 1 to the financial statements, adjustments of $948,869 decreasing the net worth of the Company were made as at December 31, 1967.

For the reasons stated above, we do not express an opinion on the accompanying revised Balance Sheet as at December 31, 1967 and the revised Statement of Income for the year ended December 31, 1967.

Weiserman & Morris

New York, New York
June 27, 1969

MICROWAVE, INC.
BALANCE SHEET
December 31, 1967

ASSETS

	Original balance sheet		
Current Assets			
Cash in banks:			
First National Bank of Nowhere	$ 20,745.28		
Pseudo National Bank	200.00	$ 20,945.28	
Cash in office		400.00	
Receivables:			
Accounts receivable ($651,237.94 assigned			
to First National Bank of Nowhere)	1,057,412.30		
Retention on completed contract	71,796.83	1,129,209.13	
Inventories (at cost) (partially pledged to			
First National Bank of Nowhere)			
Raw materials	18,872.57		
Purchased parts	245,283.80		
Work in process	553,996.56		
Finished goods	120,133.45	938,286.38	
Prepaid insurance		4,147.77	
Claim for refund—income taxes			
Total current assets			$2,092,988.5

Fixed Assets	Cost	Accumulated Depreciation	Book Value	
Machinery	$151,500.05	$ 67,228.49	$ 84,271.56	
Testing equipment	138,073.35	76,273.71	61,799.64	
Shop fixtures	33,591.36	9,412.66	24,178.70	
Leasehold improvements	9,829.73	1,750.92	8,078.81	
Office furniture and equipment	47,327.20	17,013.16	30,309.04	
Tools, jigs, and fixtures	133,176.29	—	133,176.29	
Total fixed assets	$513,497.90	$ 171,683.94		341,814.0

Other Assets				
Security deposits (Note 2)				10,744.7
Total Assets				$2,445,547.3

The company notes are an integral part of these financial statements.

Adjustments (Note 1)		Revised balance sheet	
Debits	Credits		
		$ 20,745.28	
		200.00	$ 20,945.28
			400.00
	$772,200	285,212.30	
		71,796.83	357.009.13
	12,000	6,872.57	
	124,000	121,283.80	
	204,000	349,996.56	
	90,000	30,133.45	508,286.38
			4,147.77
$ 4,600			4,600.00
			$ 895,388.56
		Book Value	
		$ 84,271.56	
		61,799.64	
		24,178.70	
		8,078.81	
		30,309.04	
70,000	42,200	160,976.29	
			369,614.04
			10,743.99
			$1,275,746.59

MICROWAVE, INC.
BALANCE SHEET
December 31, 1967

LIABILITIES AND STOCKHOLDERS' EQUITY

		Original balance sheet	
Current Liabilities			
Accounts payable (Note 2)		$521,362.21	
Accrued taxes payable:			
Payroll and other	$ 19,388.47		
New York State Franchise	26,446.73		
Federal Income	232,262.80	278,098.00	
Payroll payable			
Notes payable to First National			
Bank of Nowhere			
Due May 16, 1968	6,240.50		
Due November 15, 1969 (current part)	52,600.00		
Inventory loan	100,000.00		
Accounts receivable loan	474,990.05	633,830.55	
Total current liabilities			$1,433,290.76
Long Term Liabilities			
Notes payable to First National Bank			
of Nowhere—due November 15, 1969			52,750.00
Deferred Federal Income Tax			
(related to depreciation)			3,521.70
Convertible subordinated debentures			—
Stockholders' Equity			
Capital stock:			
Common stock—par value $1.00 per share;			
authorized 2,000,000 shares;			
issued 390,461 shares		390,461.00	
Capital surplus		260,613.16	
Retained earnings:			
Balance—January 1, 1967	23,864.69		
Add: Net income for the year (Note 2)	281,046.01		
Balance—December 31, 1967 (Note 2)		304,910.70	955,984.86
Total Liabilities and Stockholders' Equity			$2,445,547.32

The accompanying notes are an integral part of these financial statements.

Adjustments (Note 1)		Revised balance sheet	
Debits	Credits		
	$ 24,700		$546,062.21
		$ 19,388.47	
$ 26,446		—	
232,263		—	19,388.47
	16,600		16,600.00
		6,240.50	
		52,600.00	
		100,000.00	
		474,990.05	633,830.55
			$1,215,881.23
			52,750.00
3,522			—
			—
		390,461.00	
		260,613.16	
435,900		(412,035.31)	
1,260,700	747,731	(231,923.49)	
		(643,958.80)	7,115.36
$2,033,431	$2,033,431		$1,275,746.59

MICROWAVE, INC.
STATEMENT OF INCOME
For the Year Ended December 31, 1967

		Original statement of income	
Sales			
Products	$2,992,845.01		
Less: Discounts, returns, and adjustments	104,217.18	$2,888,627.83	
Sale of license		2,977.73	
Other		1,382.17	
Total sales			$2,892,987.73
Cost of Sales			
Inventories—beginning		403,860.97	
Materials		1,076,626,23	
Shop		787,476.80	
Engineering		363,582.56	
Indirect costs		220,231.64	
Depreciation and amortization		29,151.19	
Payroll taxes and insurance		149,759.34	
Total		3,030,688.73	
Less: Capitalized to tools, jigs, and fixtures account		—	
Balance		3,030,688.73	
Less: Inventories—ending		938,286.38	
Cost of sales			2,092,402.35
Gross Profit			800,585.38
Selling Expenses			
Sales salaries	39,787.84		
Travel, meals, and hotels	15,850.47		
Auto	5,548.45		
Supplies and expenses	3,829.19		
Entertainment and business shows	3,336.23	68,352.18	
General and Administrative Expenses			
Officers' salaries	54,000.00		
Interest and bank charges	45,032.30		
Office supplies and postage	20,857.06		
Office salaries	12,757.85		
Telephone	9,904.53		
Professional fees	18,942.60		
Payroll taxes and insurance	7,882.07		
Auto	4,004.14		
Stockholders' expenses	821.92		
Rent	6,518.70		
Subscriptions and dues	2,303.72		
Depreciation	3,662.89		
Other	1,138.30	187,826.08	
New York State Franchise Tax		27,576.61	
Total expenses			283,754.87
Income before provision for Federal Income Tax			516,830.51
Provision for Federal Income Tax (including $3,521.70—deferred)			235,784.50
Net income for the year (Note 2)			$ 281,046.01

The accompanying notes are an integral part of these financial statements.

Adjustments (Note 1)		Revised statement of income		
Debits	Credits			
$772,200	$247,700	$2,468,345.01		
		104,217.18	$2,364,127.83	
			2,977.73	
			1,382.17	
				$2,368,487.73
	128,000		275,860.97	
20,200	16,100		1,080,726.23	
14,700	13,700		788,476.80	
1,600	400		364,782.56	
2,000			222,231.64	
17,200			46,351.19	
			149,759.34	
			2,928,199.73	
	70,000		70,000.00	
			2,858,188.73	
430,000			508,286.38	
				2,349,904.35
				18,585.38
		39,787.84		
	900	14,950.42		
		5,548.45		
		3,829.19		
		3,336.23	67,452.18	
		54,000.00		
		45,032.30		
	500	20,357.06		
300	300	12,757.85		
2,500	2,000	10,404.53		
	1,300	17,642.60		
		7,882.07		
		4,004.14		
		821.92		
		6,518.70		
		2,303.72		
		3,662.89		
		1,138.30	186,526.08	
	26,446		1,130.61	
				255,108.87
				(236,523.49)
	240,385			(4,600.00)
$1,260,700	$747.731			$(231,923.49)

MICROWAVE, INC.

NOTES TO THE FINANCIAL STATEMENTS

December 31, 1967

NOTE 1—Adjustments

The revised financial statements reflect a decrease of approximately $950,000 in the net worth of the Company as at December 31, 1967 computed as follows:

	Originally reported	As revised	Net adjustments
Retained earnings (Deficit) January 1, 1967	$ 23,865	$(412,035)	$435,900
Net income (Loss) For the Year 1967	281,046	(231,923)	512,969
Retained earnings (Deficit) December 31, 1967	$304,911	$(643,958)	$948,869

MICROWAVE, INC.
NOTES TO THE FINANCIAL STATEMENTS
December 31, 1967 (*Continued*)

NOTE 1—Adjustments (continued)

This decrease results from accruals or adjustments for the following:

	Account adjusted	
	Balance sheet	*Statement of income*
Sales	Accounts receivable	Sales
Inventory	Inventory	Cost of sales
Purchases and expenses	Accounts payable	Cost of sales and expenses
Payroll	Payroll payable	Cost of sales and expenses
Vacation Payroll	Payroll payable	Cost of sales and expenses
Amortization of tools, jigs, and fixtures—	Fixed assets: tools, jigs, and	
1966*	fixtures account	None
1967	''	
Tools, jigs, and fixtures— capitalized	Fixed assets: Tools, jigs, and fixtures account	Cost of sales
Totals		
Less: Provision for Federal and New York State Income Taxes	Federal Income and NYS Franchise Taxes payable	Provision for Federal Income Tax and NYS Franchise Tax
Claim for refund—Federal and New York State Income Taxes	Claim for refund—income taxes	Provision for Federal Income Tax
Balances		

*Amortization of Tools, Jigs, and Fixtures prior to December 31, 1966. This adjustment does not affect the statement of income for the year ended December 31, 1967.

| Accruals or adjustments to retained earnings | | Adjustments to the statement of income for the year ended December 31, 1967 |
December 31, 1966	December 31, 1967	
$247,700	$772,200	$524,500
128,000	430,000	302,000
24,500	24,700	200
3,100	5,200	2,100
7,600	11,400	3,800
25,000	25,000	—
—	17,200	17,200
—	(70,000)	(70,000)
$435,900	$1,215,700	$779,800
—	262,231	262,231
—	—	4,600	266,831	4,600	266,831
$435,900	$ 948,869	$512,969

MICROWAVE, INC.
NOTES TO THE FINANCIAL STATEMENTS
December 31, 1967 (*Continued*)

NOTE 1-A—Sales

The sales for the year 1967 had been overstated by $524,500. This amount represents the net difference of $772,200 of shipments made in 1968 and 1969, but recorded as sales in 1967, less $247,700 of shipments made in 1967 but recorded as sales in 1966.

The actual shipments were made in the month of:

	Invoiced in 1966 Shipped in 1967	Invoiced in 1967 Shipped in 1968 or 1969
	1967	*1968*
January	$116,933	$202,100
February	47,723	208,700
March	46,329	188,700
April	12,365	34,100
May	5,312	63,700
June	208	3,200
July	—	4,400
August	—	1,800
September	—	11,100
October	—	27,200
November	—	—
December	—	8,500
		1969
January	—	18,700
Undetermined	18,830	—
Totals	$247,700	$772,200

NOTE 1-B—Inventory

The beginning inventory as at January 1, 1967 was overstated by $128,000.

The differences as determined for the January 1, 1967 inventory are summarized as follows:

	As originally reported	As revised	Difference
Raw materials	$ 17,876	$ 17,876	—
Purchased parts	100,528	81,528	$ 19,000
Work in process	204,505	163,505	41,000
Finished goods	80,952	12,952	68,000
Totals	$403,861	$275,861	$128,000

The ending inventory as at December 31, 1967 was overstated by $430,000. The differences as determined for the December 31, 1967 inventory are summarized as follows:

	As originally reported	As revised	Difference
Raw materials	$ 18,872	$ 6,872	$ 12,000
Purchased parts	245,284	121,284	124,000
Work in process	553,997	349,997	204,000
Finished goods	120,133	30,133	90,000
Totals	$938,286	$508,286	$430,000

The differences resulted from the following:

(1) Changes in unit prices
(2) Exclusion of nonsalable units
(3) Exclusion of units belonging to customers
(4) Exclusion of units not in process

NOTE 1-C—*Purchases and Expenses*
   Payroll
   Vacation Payroll

No accruals were made at December 31, 1966 and December 31, 1967, by the Company for the following:

(1) Purchases delivered by December 31st, but entered subsequent thereto.
(2) Expense invoices for 1966 entered in 1967 and expense invoices for 1967 entered in 1968.
(3) Payroll—a portion of the last week in each of the years paid in the first week of the following year.
(4) Vacation payroll liability for six months.

NOTE 1-D—*Amortization of Tools, Jigs, and Fixtures*

Prior to 1968, the Company did not record amortization on capitalized tools, jigs, and fixtures. In 1968, the Company determined that it was improper accounting procedure not to record amortization on these assets. Accordingly, amortization of $17,200 has been recorded as an expense for 1967 and $25,000 charged to retained earnings as an adjustment to prior years' earnings. Tools, jigs, and fixtures are amortized from date of acquisition on a five-year basis.

MICROWAVE, INC.
NOTES TO THE FINANCIAL STATEMENTS
December 31, 1967 (*Continued*)

NOTE 1-E—Tools, Jigs, and Fixtures

> The ending balance, as reflected in the fixed asset account Tools, Jigs, and Fixtures, was understated by $70,000.

NOTE 1-F—Provision for Federal and New York State Income Taxes

> The provision for taxes as at December 31, 1967 has been reversed since the Company has no tax liability, resulting from the net loss for the year.

NOTE 1-G—Claim for Refund—Federal and New York State Income Taxes

> Refund claims resulting from the carry-back of the net loss of 1967 have been filed for income taxes paid in the prior years.

MICROWAVE, INC.
NOTES TO THE FINANCIAL STATEMENTS
December 31, 1967 (*Continued*)

NOTE 2—The financial statements do not reflect a liability to the landlord for unpaid security deposits of $8,800 and additional real estate taxes of approximately $4,200. The effect of these transactions would be a further reduction of $4,200 in the net worth of the Company as at December 31, 1967.

Chapter Eight

DEVELOPING PROPOSALS FOR REORGANIZATION

There is virtually no limit to the kinds of proposals that have been or could be made to creditors by insolvent debtors or debtors in financial difficulty. The final package of provisions that all parties agree to is hammered out in the course of negotiation. There are partial-payment cash plans, deferred-payment plans, stock plans, payment-from-future-earnings plans, and uncounted combinations of these.

The gap between what the debtor wants to settle for and what the unsecured creditors are willing to accept starts at 100 percent and ends at zero. It does, that is, unless all negotiations fail and the debtor is adjudicated a bankrupt, in which case the remaining assets are gathered and auctioned off. In that case, the creditors must content themselves with dividing any proceeds that survive after administrative expenses and priority claims have been paid.

Creditors generally impose certain controls over the operations of the debtor to protect their interests after the reorganization. Most proposals include provisions such as these:

1. The stock of the debtor corporation is placed in escrow until the full payment agreed upon has been made.

2. Resignations of officers, key employees, and directors may be held in escrow.

3. Stop-loss provisions are established that will terminate the plan and trigger the take-over of the debtor by creditors if the situation deteriorates instead of improving.

4. Limitations are imposed on the salaries and fringe benefits of the debtor's executives and stockholder-employees.

5. Dividends and other distributions are prohibited, or at least limited.

6. The acquisition or expansion of fixed assets is restricted.

7. Limitations are imposed on new borrowing, whether secured or unsecured.

8. The debtor may be required to retain accountants designated or approved by the creditors' committee, until full settlement has been made under the plan.

9. Financial reports may have to be made at specified intervals to the creditors' committee or its counsel.

Once the debtor and representatives of the creditors have evolved and agreed upon a proposal for reorganization, the terms of the agreement are reduced to writing in the Plan of Arrangement. A complete example of such a document is provided on the next several pages. In many ways, this actual Plan of Arrangement (with identifying details disguised) is typical. As we have emphasized, there is no "standard" plan; each is derived by negotiations and each has unique features.

SAMPLE PLAN OF ARRANGEMENT

United States District Court
Eastern District of New York

In the Matter	In Proceedings for an Arrangement No. 71 B 1010
of	
ALBERT MFG. CO., INC. 　　　　　Debtor.	DEBTOR'S PLAN OF ARRANGEMENT

ALBERT MFG. CO., INC., the
above-named Debtor, proposes the following arrangement:

I. ADMINISTRATION
CLAIMS

The Debtor proposes to pay all
administration claims in cash upon confirmation, or upon such
terms and in such other manner as may be agreed upon between the
administration creditors and the Debtor.

II. PRIORITY CREDITORS

The Debtor proposes to pay all
priority claims in cash upon confirmation, or upon such installments
as may be agreed upon between the Debtor and the priority
claimants.

III. GENERAL UNSECURED
CREDITORS

The Debtor proposes to divide
creditors into two classes, as follows:

A. To all general unsecured
creditors whose claims, as allowed or as reduced by such creditors,
are less than $400, the Debtor will pay 30 percent of the amount
of such claims in cash upon confirmation.

B. To all general unsecured
creditors whose claims as allowed amount to $400 or more, the
Debtor offers either of two options: a cash settlement and a stock
settlement.

1. To creditors who elect the
cash option, the Debtor will pay 30 percent of each allowed claim,
payable in three consecutive annual installments, without interest,
as follows: 5 percent of said claim three years from the date
of the order of confirmation to be entered herein (the Order);

10 percent thereof four years from the date of the Order; and 15 percent thereof five years from the date of the Order. Each such settlement shall be evidenced by the Debtor's non-negotiable promissory note, a specimen copy of which is attached hereto as Attachment A.

2. To creditors who, in lieu of the cash option described in paragraph III B(1) above, elect the stock settlement, the Debtor proposes to distribute—in exchange for, and in full satisfaction of, the claims of each such creditor—one share of common stock of the Debtor, par value $.05, for each $1 of allowed claim.

Each creditor must elect the stock settlement in writing at any time prior to the entry of an order of confirmation. Failure of any creditor to notify the Debtor of such election on time and in writing shall constitute that creditor's acceptance of the alternative cash payments described above. The Debtor shall not be required to issue fractional shares of Debtor Company stock, and each creditor shall receive the lowest whole number of shares to which he is entitled.

3. The shares of Debtor Company stock issued and delivered to such creditors shall bear an appropriate legend, in form satisfactory to counsel for the Debtor, to the effect that the shares have not been registered under the Securities Act of 1933 (the Act) and may not be sold or offered for sale in the absence of (a) an effective registration statement for the said shares under the Act, (b) a "no-action" letter from the Securities & Exchange Commission, or (c) an opinion of counsel satisfactory to the Debtor that such registration is not required.

4. In addition to the foregoing, and regardless of the settlement option selected by any creditor whose claims as allowed amount to $400 or more, the debtor shall distribute to such creditors, pro rata, 132,660 shares of stock of Multiplex Transmission, Inc. Said stock, which the Debtor owns and has heretofore held as an investment, shall be distributed on June 30, 1975, or thirty days after confirmation, whichever is later.

5. Starting no later than the date after the end of the third year after confirmation, the Debtor shall, at its own expense, and acting expeditiously, commence to qualify all shares of stock or securities it has issued to creditors for registration under the Securities Act of 1933 as then in effect. In addition, the Debtor shall, upon request by such creditors, qualify such shares under applicable "Blue Sky" or other state

securities law and obtain appropriate compliance with any other governmental requirements. The debtor, however, shall be obligated to effect such registration, qualification or compliance one time only. Moreover, the Debtor may delay compliance with this subparagraph until the requirement for certified financial statements to accompany such registration can be met by statements based upon the Debtor's regular year-end audit.

6. If the Debtor determines to register any of its securities for public offering under the Act, the Debtor shall promptly notify all holders of stock issued under paragraph III B(2) hereof, and at the request of any of such holders will, to the extent permissible under the Act and the rules and regulations thereunder, and at its own expense, include in such registration, any of the stock then owned by such holders; and will at its expense effect the qualification or compliance of such stock with any state law or government requirements, so that it may be so disposed of.

In the case of each registration, qualification or compliance pursuant hereto, the Debtor will keep such holders advised in writing as to the initiation, progress, and completion thereof; and at its own expense, will keep such registration, qualification and compliance effective until all sales and distributions contemplated in connection therewith are completed, but in no event longer than one year from the effective date of such registration.

The Debtor, at its expense, will supply such holders with prospectuses, offering circulars or other documents incident to such registration, qualification or compliance. The Debtor will indemnify each of such holders and each underwriter of the stock being sold (and any person who within the meaning of Section 15 of the Act controls such holders or underwriter) against all claims, losses, damages, liabilities and expenses resulting from any untrue statement of a material fact contained therein (or in any related registration statement, notification, or the like) or from any omission or alleged omission to state therein a required material fact or a fact necessary to make the statements therein not misleading; all except insofar as the same may have been based upon information furnished in writing to the Debtor by such holders, or any of them, or by such underwriter, expressly for use therein.

The holder or underwriter furnishing such information to the Debtor will indemnify the Debtor against all claims, losses, damages, liabilities and expenses resulting from any untrue or alleged untrue statement of material fact, or any omission or alleged omission to state a material fact required or necessary to make the information not misleading.

IV. DEBTOR'S COVENANTS

Until all Notes issued under the Plan are fully paid, or unless any of the following covenants are waived or modified by the holders of at least two-thirds of the balance outstanding on the Notes, the Debtor covenants that:

1. The Debtor will not purchase fixed assets in excess of $25,000 in the combined aggregate in each fiscal year following confirmation of the Plan of Arrangement;

2. The Debtor will not merge or consolidate with, or purchase the assets of, or an equity or similar interest in, any other business entity:

3. The Debtor will not pledge, mortgage or hypothecate any of its assets, excepting to secure payment of loans borrowed for its business operations;

4. The Debtor will not sell any assets except in the ordinary course of business;

5. The Debtor will not purchase any shares of its common stock, nor pay any cash dividends on its common stock;

6. The Debtor will not make any loans or advances to any officers, directors or shareholders;

7. The Debtor will maintain insurance on its real and personal property with responsible insurance companies, covering risks customarily insured against by similar businesses operating in the same area, in amounts not less than 80% of the depreciated replacement value of such property;

8. Messrs. A. Smith, R. Albert, and Fred Cone will devote their services full time to the Debtor and will not receive compensation for such services in excess of the following amounts:

A. Smith (President and General Manager)	$40,000 a year
R. Albert (Chief Engineer)	$23,000 a year
Fred Cone (Production Manager)	$23,000 a year

provided, however, that the voluntary or involuntary termination of the employment of any one of the foregoing shall not of itself constitute a default hereunder;

9. The Debtor will engage an independent public accounting firm from among the following:

Alexander Grant & Company
Arthur Andersen & Company
Haskins & Sells
S. D. Leidesdorf & Co.
Peat, Marwick, Mitchell & Co.;

and

10. The Debtor shall not guarantee, endorse, agree to purchase, or otherwise become liable upon, the obligations of any person, firm or corporation; except (a) endorsement by it of negotiable instruments for deposit or collection in the ordinary course of business, and (b) letters of credit, bills of exchange, or similar instruments necessary in the conduct of the business.

V. EVENTS OF DEFAULT

All of the said Notes shall become due and payable without notice or demand upon the occurrence of any of the following:

1. Failure in the performance of any undertaking by the Debtor, including failure to make payment of any of the Notes within fifteen days after the maturity thereof, or any installment thereof;

2. Default in the performance of any covenant which can be, but is not, cured within a period of thirty days after the receipt by the Debtor of notice thereof by registered or certified mail, return receipt requested, which notice shall specify the event of default;

3. Filing against the Debtor of a petition, under any of the provisions of the Bankruptcy Act, that is not dismissed within ninety days by an order of the court having jurisdiction;

4. The Debtor's petition for, or consent to, adjudication of bankruptcy;

5. Execution by the Debtor of an assignment or deed of trust for the benefit of creditors;

6. Failure of the Debtor to avail itself of any debtor-relief proceedings under any federal or state law;

7. Appointment of a receiver of all or substantially all of the property of the Debtor, unless such appointment is set aside or vacated within thirty days;

8. The attachment, levy of execution, garnishment or seizure by any judicial process, writ or order, of Debtor property in excess of $35,000 in the aggregate, unless vacated or discharged by bond, final order or otherwise, within thirty days;

9. Entry of judgments against the Debtor in excess of $35,000 in the aggregate, unless execution has been stayed or a security bond furnished within thirty days.

VI. RESERVATION OF RIGHTS

All creditors affected by this Plan shall be deemed to have reserved all of their rights, claims and remedies against any person, firm, or corporation, other than the Debtor, with respect to any act, transaction or occurrence.

VII. LOANS

Last National Bank, Inc. has agreed to lend the Debtor prior to confirmation not less than $50,000 repayable in sixty equal monthly installments, with interest at the rate of six per cent per annum, the first installment to be due and payable six months after the loan is made. Said loan shall be secured by a security interest in all of the Debtor's inventory, goods, work in process, machinery, equipment and automobiles, accounts receivable, contracts, contract rights, bank accounts and intangibles. This security interest shall be subject only to a prior security interest to the Collector of Internal Revenue if the same becomes necessary.

Prior to confirmation, Last National Bank, Inc. shall deliver to the escrow agent designated by the Court, said sum of $50,000 to be held by the escrowee subject to confirmation and subject to a Court order providing that in the event a confirmation of this Plan is not signed by the Court prior to (*date*) said sum of $50,000 shall be returned to Last National Bank, Inc.

VIII. MISCELLANEOUS

Each creditor who accepts stock of the Debtor in lieu of cash payments shall be deemed to have taken said stock for investment purposes.

IX. ANTI-DILUTION PROVISIONS

The Debtor covenants that, except for a consideration in money or property, at least equal to the net book value per share of the issued and outstanding common shares of stock of the Debtor, it will not issue additional shares of common stock which will aggregate more than the total of the following:

1. The number of its shares of common stock outstanding after confirmation;

2. The number of shares of common stock to be issued under paragraph III B(2) hereof; and

3. 100,000 shares of common stock optioned to Last National Bank, Inc. and 95,000 shares of common stock which may be optioned to employees of the Debtor. Said options to purchase common stock of the Debtor shall not be issued at a price less than $.20 per share.

Dated: _____
         (City or town, State)

_____
       (date)

               ALBERT MFG. CO., INC.

By _____
             A. Smith, President

ATTACHMENT A: NON-NEGOTIABLE NON-INTEREST BEARING PROMISSORY NOTE

$ _____   _____ 19___

    FOR VALUE RECEIVED, the undersigned promises to pay to

_____

at _____

the principal sum of _____Dollars

($_____), without interest, as follows: $_____

on _____, 19___; $_____ on

_____, 19___; and $_____ on

_____, 19___.

    This Note has been issued pursuant to the Plan of Arrangement,

dated _____, 19___, in an Arrangement Proceeding entitled "In the Matter of Albert Mfg. Co., Inc., Debtor," No.

71 B 1010, confirmed by an order of Honorable _____,

Bankruptcy Judge, dated _____, 19___, and all of the provisions of the Plan are hereby incorporated by reference.

    This Note shall mature and become due and payable without notice or demand upon the occurrence of any event of default described in paragraph V of the confirmed Plan of Arrangement.

    This Note shall be prepayable at the election of the Debtor, provided all other similar Notes issued pursuant to said Plan of Arrangement are simultaneously prepaid.

    IN WITNESS WHEREOF, Albert Mfg. Co., Inc. has caused this Note to be executed in its corporate name with the manual or facsimile signature of its President or a Vice President and a facsimile of its corporate seal to be affixed hereto or imprinted hereon, attested with the manual or facsimile signature of its Secretary or its Assistant Secretary.

ALBERT MFG. CO., INC.

By _____
              President

Attest:

_____
    Secretary

The plan used as an illustration on the preceding pages is very comprehensive. It contains a number of sophisticated provisions, some of which warrant further comment. Creditors have been divided into two classes. Those in the first class, consisting of all creditors whose claims are for less than $400, are to receive a flat percentage of their claims in cash, as full settlement. This provision serves two purposes. Primarily, it disposes of numerous smaller claims on which postconfirmation payments could be burdensome. Secondarily, the provision offers creditors with claims somewhat in excess of $400 an opportunity to reduce their claims to $400, and thereby receive cash settlement immediately upon confirmation.

Creditors of the second class, including all those with more substantial claims, are to receive in settlement the same percentage of their claims as is to be paid to the smaller creditors, but such payments are extended over a number of years. The idea, of course, is to conserve assets that the beleaguered debtor will need in order to recuperate.

The second category of creditors is offered an option, however: In lieu of settling for a three-year cash recovery equal to 30 percent of their claims, these creditors may accept shares of common stock in the debtor company, at the rate of one share per dollar of allowed claims. Hardly cash, but a 100 percent recovery, nevertheless—coupled with the possibility of profit if the debtor prospers.

Stock distributed in a Chapter XI proceeding is exempt from the registration provisions of the Securities Act of 1933, and for decades such shares were considered freely tradable. More recently, however, the Securities and Exchange Commission has taken the position that this was a misconception. As of this writing, the Commission has not seriously tried to enforce its interpretation, but it has indicated that it would crack down if large blocks of stock received by creditors were traded actively. Our sample Plan of Arrangement takes this prospect into account, and paragraphs III B and VIII are very specific about the status and disposition of creditors' holdings in the debtor company.

Notice that paragraph III B(3) refers to a "no-action" letter from the SEC or an opinion of counsel that registration is not required. In light of the publicly stated position of the SEC, it is highly unlikely that such a "no-action" letter would be issued. Moreover, Commission members have on several occasions cautioned publicly that lawyers who issue opinions regarding the exemption available to such shares do so at their own risk. Understandably, this has made such opinions harder to come by. Still, the plan illustrated acknowledges both of these possibilities. Our sample plan goes on to provide for registration of the debtor's stock three years after confirmation.

In recent years, bankruptcy judges have asked the Securities and Exchange Commission to review plans of arrangement that include a distribution of the debtor's stock to claimants in a reorganization proceeding. Generally, Commission staff members are content to participate as observers. In the actual case from which our illustration is drawn, however, the plan's most unusual feature—the additional distribution of stock in an unaffiliated company that the debtor had held for investment—led the SEC to intervene. As a result, the plan had to be amended to substitute shares of the debtor's own stock, before the plan could be confirmed. The provision is retained above as an example of the kind of bold resourcefulness that often emerges during debtor-creditor negotiations.

Paragraph IV of the plan illustrates the type of restrictions creditors often impose, including limitations on:

1. Fixed asset acquisition

2. Merger, consolidation, and acquisition of other companies

3. Mortgage or hypothecation of assets

4. Sale of assets

5. Acquisition of the company's own stock

6. Loans to interested parties

7. Executive salaries

8. Guarantees or endorsements

In addition, the paragraph contains two other fairly characteristic provisions:

9. The debtor's assets must be adequately insured

10. The debtor must engage public accountants acceptable to the creditors

Interestingly, though, this plan does *not* have two other characteristic safeguards. There is no stop-loss provision, and there is no specific requirement for the debtor to regularly report its financial results. The absence of these two routine stipulations was not an oversight in this case, but simply a pragmatic recognition that the debtor—a public company—had to regularly report its financial picture under the requirements of the Securities Act. Parallel reporting, specifically for creditors, would have been redundant. Most plans of arrangement, however, impose a strict financial reporting regimen.

In listing five major accounting firms (including the debtor's customary auditors) as acceptable options, this plan gives the distressed company reasonable latitude in selecting its auditors. Many plans simply require that the auditors engaged must be acceptable to the creditors, without naming any specific accounting firm.

Typically, this plan recites specific events that will constitute default and accelerate the amounts due under the plan (paragraph V). More unusual is paragraph VII, detailing arrangements for a loan which will make available the funds necessary to carry out the plan. The copy of the debtor's nonnegotiable, non-interest-bearing promissory note attached to this plan is a commonplace addendum. On the other hand, such plans frequently provide for continuing supervision of the debtor's performance by the creditors' committee. This one does not. The spectrum of customary, exceptional, and unique features found in this actual Plan of Arrangement underline the fact that there is no universal plan that one can turn to like a Blumberg Law form. Each one evolves out of a unique set of circumstances and is tailored to fit them exactly.

Here are sample provisions drawn from several other actual plans (true identities disguised):

PTL Corp. provided three alternatives:

1. A 15 percent cash settlement in full, 5 percent upon confirmation and two annual installments of 5 percent each; or

2. 5 percent in cash plus, for each $8 of claim, one share of the debtor's stock, which the debtor could optionally repurchase within three years at $6 per share; or

3. 100 percent of allowable claims, payable in cash over a period of ten years out of one-half of the debtor's annual aftertax profits.

This last provision was worded so that the company's auditors were not obliged to show the resulting liability accrual on the company's financial statements until, and to the extent that, the liability actually accrued as the result of realized earnings.

Like many other plans of arrangement, this one included supervision of the company's affairs by a creditors' committee, and permitted the committee to grant extensions of payments and to waive defaults under the plan.

S&E Corporation offered creditors two options:

1. 7 percent in cash upon confirmation, or

2. 5 percent in cash plus, for each $160 of claim, one share of stock in a corporation not a party to the Chapter XI proceeding. The plan further provided that the securities involved are exempt from registration, and then prudently hedged the exemption issue by adding that if, for any reason, the shares are *not* deemed exempt, the debtor shall forthwith provide for their registration.

LSC, Inc., like the debtor in our detailed sample plan, divided its creditors into two classes. Class A creditors—carefully described in the plan—were to receive 30 percent in cash on confirmation, payable out of a fixed sum of cash to be deposited under the plan. In the event this fund proved insufficient to pay the 30 percent settlement, the Class A creditors were entitled to collect an additional 5 percent of their claims in debtor's stock at the rate of $5 per share.

Another class of creditors, also defined in the plan, were to receive 25 percent of their claims in cash. A similar provision provided for the contingency issue of debtor stock to these creditors. This plan was silent with regard to the stock's possible exemption from registration under the Securities Act, and there were no restrictions imposed on the debtor, since it was a cash plan.

WDT Associates, Inc., provided for payment of 40 percent of each creditor's claim, 5 percent in cash upon confirmation, and the balance in monthly installments over a three-year period. The debtor issued notes secured by a chattel mortgage, and the plan imposed numerous restrictions. In addition, since the debtor was a private company, its stock was deposited with the creditor's committee as collateral for the payments due under the plan.

DRC Co. Inc., a case that resulted from the infamous "salad oil swindle," again divided its creditors into two classes. Class A creditors were those whose claims exceeded $50,000. All others were Class B creditors. The former were issued participation certificates entitling them to share in the proceeds of claims filed by the debtor in connection with other bankruptcy proceedings as well as in the proceeds of litigation against certain third parties and insurance companies. In addition, the debtor agreed to pay these creditors, pro rata, one half of its aftertax profits for a period of ten years. The total payments under this provision to any creditor could not exceed the total of allowed claims, and the total payments to all creditors as a group could not exceed $500,000. Class B creditors received 10 percent of their claims in cash on confirmation and 90 percent from the proceeds of a tax refund for which the debtor had applied.

BBC Corporation's Plan of Arrangement called for payments of 15 percent of creditors' claims, over a four-year period, with interest.* Convertible debenture holders were permitted, until confirmation, to convert their debentures under the original terms of the debenture. After confirmation, these debenture holders were entitled to convert at a different rate for a period of six months.

This plan had several interesting features, including an $800,000 maximum limit on the total amount to be paid to unsecured creditors. If the 15 percent recovery exceeded this amount, all payments were to be reduced pro rata. The plan also provided for a modification of the amounts to be paid if debenture holders did not convert.

Another unusual provision of this plan provided that the debtor was obliged to merge with a corporation having a net worth of at least $1,500,000.

HO Co., Inc., provided for payment of 30 percent, without interest; 10 percent in cash upon confirmation, and 20 percent over a three-year period. As an added inducement to creditors, the debtor's principal owner agreed to personally invest another $50,000 in the common stock of the company, to assure that adequate working capital was available.

EML Enterprises provided for payment of 35 percent to unsecured creditors over a two-year period. In addition, the debtor agreed to pay creditors a percentage of the amounts received under pending claims against the Department of Defense. In making this latter distribution, amounts due to the debtor's principal stockholders were subordinated.

Such subordination of legitimate interests, particularly on the part of a debtor company's officers, stockholders, and affiliates, is commonly a key element in gaining acceptance of a Plan of Arrangement. It can be an especially important gesture with respect to attracting a new infusion of working capital. These pivotal steps—getting the plan accepted by creditors and confirmed by the court, and raising the cash necessary to carry out the plan—are considered in the chapter that follows.

---

*Most of these plans did not provide for interest on the deferred payments. The notes in a Chapter XI proceeding are not issued for property, goods, or services, but rather are notes issued to evidence the liability remaining after giving effect to a reorganization under the bankruptcy statute. It would seem to be self-defeating if the debtor received a credit to income or surplus from the forgiveness of indebtedness, and thereafter a charge to operations for the imputed interest. Nevertheless, in June 1974 the Financial Accounting Standards Board released its Interpretation No. 2, which provides that interest should be imputed on these obligations. From a businessperson's point of view, it seems unfair to have to record interest income in years following a composition of debt, after having sustained a loss in an earlier year on the face value of the debt.

Chapter Nine

CONFIRMING AND FINANCING THE PLAN OF ARRANGEMENT

As the sampling of actual plans of arrangement in the preceding chapter illustrates, the scope and specific features and provisions of such plans are limited only by the ingenuity of those formulating them and by the competing objectives and relative bargaining position of the debtor and the unsecured creditors.

Only the debtor can propose the Plan of Arrangement in a Chapter XI proceeding. The plan must be accepted, however, by a majority, both in number and in the amount claimed, of all unsecured creditors whose claims have been proved and allowed. The mechanics of soliciting and challenging proofs of claim were presented in Chapter Three and need not concern us further here. Suffice it to say that the creditors' committee solicits the claims of debt and negotiates the terms of the Plan of Arrangement on behalf of all the unsecured creditors.

The committee, on behalf of the debtor this time, also solicits acceptances of the plan. As the committee characteristically includes the creditors with the largest claims, its members can be very persuasive. Creditors may either approve or disapprove of the plan. Those who do not return the Form of Acceptance are deemed to have rejected the plan.

When a majority of the unsecured creditors have accepted the Plan of Arrangement, the bankruptcy judge sets a date for the hearing on confirmation, which is required by statute. In order to confirm the plan, the court must satisfy itself that:

1. The plan is in the best interests of creditors.

2. The plan is feasible.

3. The debtor has not committed any acts that would be a bar to the discharge of a bankrupt.

A representative of the debtor, such as a corporate officer or the company's accountant, must appear at the confirmation hearing to testify with regard to these three points and to respond to any questions or objections raised by the creditors. (See Exhibit L in the Appendix for an example of characteristic testimony.)

Generally, the "best interests of creditors" criterion is satisfied by testimony to the effect that creditors will receive at least as much under the plan as they would if the debtor were liquidated. The debtor next establishes the feasibility of the plan by demonstrating that after confirmation of the plan, the debtor will be able to comply with all its provisions.

For instance, suppose the plan provides for a single cash payment to each creditor upon confirmation, in full settlement of each claim. In that case, the debtor must show that sufficient cash is immediately available to pay all the administrative costs of the proceeding, plus all priority claims, such as the liabilities of the debtor-in-possession, plus the proposed dividend for each creditor. (In addition, of course, the debtor would have to have sufficient resources after all such payments are made to enable it to continue in business with some hope of success. Otherwise, the company is doomed anyhow, and the Plan of Arrangement would be a futile exercise.)

Many plans call for subsequent payments to creditors as well as the initial "down payment" upon confirmation. In such cases, the debtor must convince the court and the creditors that the wherewithal to make those payments will be available when they fall due. (The debtor company will want to be thoroughly convinced of this itself, too, for if it is unable, for any reason, to carry out every provision of its plan, the company can immediately be adjudicated a bankrupt, and all is lost.)

The third criterion that must be met before the court will confirm a Plan of Arrangement is evidence that the debtor has not committed any of the six acts that would bar the discharge of a bankrupt. Section 14C of the Bankruptcy Act details those acts, any one of which will bar discharge. Briefly, they are that the debtor:

1. Destroyed, falsified, concealed, or failed to keep books and records.

2. Obtained credit by issuing a false financial statement.

3. Transferred, destroyed, removed, or concealed property, within twelve months of filing the insolvency petition, with the intent to defraud creditors.

4. Was granted a discharge or a confirmed Plan of Arrangement

in another insolvency proceeding, within six years of filing the petition for the present proceeding.

5. Refused to obey any lawful order of the court.

6. Failed to explain satisfactorily any asset losses or deficiency of assets that prevent it from meeting its liabilities.

If any of these acts can be proved, the plan will not be confirmed.

Any creditor who does not agree with the testimony of the debtor's representative during the confirmation hearing may raise questions or challenge the facts being adduced. The court may then adjourn the confirmation hearing until the parties work out their differences, as was done in the following case:

CHAP. XI PLAN FOR GILCHRIST CHALLENGED

PHILADELPHIA (FNS)—Charges made by a dissident creditor of Gilchrist Co. at a hearing Monday have put off confirmation of the Boston-based department store chain's 50 per cent Chapter XI plan.

National Union Electric Co., the creditor, charged that the plan was not in the best interests of creditors because Gilchrist's liquidation value is higher than the amount offered in the plan.

Other charges include that the debtor fraudulently transferred certain assets while insolvent and that a majority of creditors did not accept the plan.

On the latter point, Bankruptcy Judge Emil F. Goldhaber told FNS that according to his tally, the plan was accepted by the majority.

The judge set a hearing on the objections for Friday at 10 A.M. Gilchrist is a subsidiary of Uni-Shield International Corp., Cornwells Heights, Pa., which is also in Chapter XI proceedings here.

Alternatively, the bankruptcy judge may take testimony from both the debtor and the objecting creditor. In that event, the hearing becomes a trial on the objections. This can have serious consequences, particularly if the objecting creditor alleges that the debtor committed an act that would bar discharge.

Normally, however, the debtor and the creditors have come to terms on all issues prior to the hearing on confirmation, which is then a routine matter with no surprises in store. The accountant who is assisting the debtor in achieving the confirmation of its plan must prepare and submit cash flows, earnings projections, estimates of liquidation value vs. proposed payments to creditors, and the like. The accountant may be called upon to testify at the hearing or may simply furnish the detailed financial information and supporting exhibits to the company officer or other representative who will appear.

Financing is often a substantial impediment to the feasibility of a Plan of Arrangement. This is particularly true when one takes into account both the money needed immediately, to qualify the plan for confirmation, and the money needed to support the insolvent company's interim operations. Quite aside from the working capital the debtor company needs, the cash necessary upon confirmation can be formidable, even if the plan calls for a very modest initial payment to creditors.

For instance, in the example outlined below, the company would need approximately $1 million to confirm its plan.

Total general unsecured liabilities	$5,000,000
Funds required for confirmation:	
1. Cost of administration, including statutory court costs, attorneys and accountants for both the debtor and the creditors, appraiser's fees, and expenses of the creditors' committee	$ 200,000
2. Payments on priority tax liabilities	$ 250,000
3. 10% initial payment to unsecured creditors	500,000
Total	$ 950,000

In rare instances, a debtor may be able to internally generate enough working capital and cash to confirm and execute its plan. More often, though, outside financial resources must be brought to bear.

Most companies that initiate formal bankruptcy proceedings, or an out-of-court arrangement with creditors, are at a considerable financial disadvantage when they try to raise capital. This is especially true if they are forced into such action by lawsuits, threatened action by tax authorities, a crippling strike, a natural catastrophe, or some similar crisis.

They may be fortunate enough to have unencumbered assets, but more often distressed companies will have pledged their assets to financial institutions. This has become especially prevalent since the 1960s, when commercial banks acquired many of the country's commercial finance companies. Not surprisingly, these banks routinely encourage their corporate customers—particularly those in a weakened financial condition—to switch from unsecured financing, via the bank, to secured financing via the bank's affiliated finance company.

Therefore, one of the first tasks of a company in a Chapter XI or out-of-court proceeding is to make new financial arrangements for working capital. In this endeavor, the company in a formal Chapter XI proceeding has one advantage—all obligations incurred after an arrangement petition is filed have payment priority over obligations incurred prior to the filing. Further, creditors who have an important stake in the continuance of the debtor company may be persuaded to extend fresh credit to a debtor-in-possession.

In addition, the debtor-in-possession may be authorized by the bankruptcy court to issue debtor's certificates for fresh working capital from financial institutions, investors, or other lenders. These certificates may, if the order of the court so provides, have first priority over all other obligations of the debtor-in-possession. The debtor-in-possession may also borrow on any of its unencumbered assets—again if authorized by the bankruptcy judge. The court permitting these types of financing stipulates the terms of the financing and the collateral, if any, to be pledged to secure the new loans.

Another possible source of interim working capital is potential private or institutional investors in the company. That is, an investor interested in helping to salvage and reorganize the debtor company, in exchange for partial or complete ownership, may be induced to provide advances for working capital under the special court-authorized protections mentioned above.

Predictably, the banks and other lending institutions, aware that working capital is pivotal to the confirmation and prospects of a Plan of Arrangement, can be very difficult to negotiate with. In such circumstances, the debtor may find it necessary to supplement the payment, or "dividend," to creditors of this class in order to secure their cooperation. Characteristically, this is done by having this new debt guaranteed by other interested parties, such as stockholders, subsidiaries, or parent companies. Much might also be achieved by having other parties subordinate their own claims to those of the lending institutions. Either way, the net result is that the bank or other source of these critical new funds receives a larger "dividend" from the debtor than do other creditors.

However it is accomplished, the necessary financing must be arranged, in order to get the court's confirmation of the Plan of Arrangement. Sometimes, of course, this cannot be achieved. Sometimes, too, the debtor is successfully shown to have committed an act that, under the law, bars its discharge. Finally, sometimes, despite confirmation and the best of intentions all around, the Plan of Arrangement cannot be complied with. If any of these occur, the debtor company may find itself in court, either as an adjudicated bankrupt or as defendant in a suit by creditors seeking to bar discharge, or both. These eventualities —litigation and liquidation—are the subject of a subsequent chapter. Fortunately, most Chapter XI proceedings are more routine, and are concluded, as the law intends, with the debtor's discharge and a new start on the company's commercial life.

Chapter Ten

DEALING WITH GOVERNMENT AGENCIES IN AN INSOLVENCY PROCEEDING

Although the federal courts play a key role in any formal insolvency proceeding, various other government agencies may also take part. When they do, they can exert considerable influence. Their interests must always be taken into account, and can sometimes be turned to account, as well. Taxing authorities will make their presence felt in any insolvency situation, and a number of other federal, state, and local agencies may also get involved.

Interested parties could range from the Department of Defense, concerned about past progress payments and future deliveries, to a local economic development commission, concerned about losing jobs or a tenant for its subsidized industrial park. Accounting considerations do not predominate in many of these situations, however, and in any event, the accounting aspects are likely to be peculiar to a given set of circumstances. Accordingly, a detailed treatment of the practicalities of dealing with all the government agencies that might inject themselves into an insolvency proceeding is beyond the scope of this book.

In some cases, too, a government agency's involvement is confined to a particular kind of insolvency; so again, a comprehensive discussion would be inappropriate in a book of this sort. For example, the avalanche of bankruptcies among stock brokerage houses following the market debacles around the turn of the decade led Congress to establish the Securities Investor Protection Corporation (SIPC). This agency confines itself to regulating and supervising the liquidation of bankrupt brokerage houses, with a view to providing at least some protection for investors trapped by a broker's collapse.

As we have seen, the financial structure and practices of a brokerage house can lead, in the event of insolvency, to a number of challenges and circumstances unique to that industry. There are both attorneys and public accountants who specialize in dealing with the intricacies of winding up the affairs of bankrupt brokerage houses. Accordingly, the insolvency activities of SIPC can be disposed of, for our purposes, with a notation that SIPC functions, in general, through the administrative machinery of the bankruptcy courts, and directly compensates the specialized attorneys and public accountants who serve its purposes.

Whenever a publicly held company files a Chapter XI petition, the Securities and Exchange Commission may consider itself an interested party. This can complicate matters, particularly when, for reasons it considers valid, the SEC contends that the more complex Chapter X, rather than Chapter XI, is the proper form for a particular reorganization. In some instances, the courts have granted the SEC's motion to switch the proceeding, but more often than not, the motion has been denied.

Public companies in Chapter XI are theoretically subject to all the reporting provisions of the Securities Act. As a practical matter, though, most such companies cannot afford the accounting and legal expenses associated with complete compliance. The Commission has recognized this problem, and on June 30, 1972, it issued Release No. 9660, modifying the reporting requirements for companies in reorganization. The preamble to the release summarized the matter:

"A relaxation of reporting provisions may be available to an issuer whose operations have ceased or have been severely curtailed" provided the company keeps its shareholders, the investment community, and the SEC informed of its financial condition. The troubled company must continue to supply information comparable in character to that required by the conventional reporting forms. For example, suppose the company wants to forego the certification of its financial statements by an independent auditor. It must meet at least three criteria if it hopes to obtain SEC permission to modify this reporting requirement. First, it must mail copies of its unaudited financial statement to its shareholders with an explanation. Second, it must issue press releases to the financial community with similar information. Third, it must make the information available to stockbrokers and dealers who request it.

"The Commission will be more flexible in the modifications allowed to trustees operating a corporation under the Bankruptcy Act," the SEC release points out, but as soon "as conditions merit, the full requirements of the reporting procedure will apply."

With the exception of the bankruptcy court itself, the government agency that will most certainly participate in an insolvency proceeding is the Internal Revenue Service. Tax liabilities, as a group, carry third* priority under the Bankruptcy Act, but for many years they were never

---

*Fourth, if creditors successfully abort a Chapter XI proceeding. See page 53.

dischargeable. In 1966, the statute was amended to provide that certain tax liabilities, incurred at least three years prior to the Original Petition, are dischargeable. (This does not include trust fund taxes, such as income taxes withheld from employees' wages, state sales taxes, the employee's share of Social Security taxes, and the like.) As a result, it is now entirely possible for taxing authorities to be listed both as priority and as general creditors. Within the priority category, the federal government's claims come first, and other taxing authorities line up in descending order; i.e., states, cities and townships, school districts, etc.

The schedules filed in a Chapter XI proceeding should include a list of all taxing authorities within whose jurisdiction the debtor operated. The appropriate tax officials must be notified of the proceeding, and they are obliged to file claims for the amounts due them. The various taxing agencies have different methods for fixing liabilities. Generally, a U.S. Internal Revenue agent communicates with the debtor to ascertain if all returns have been filed, and if not, to secure personal delivery of any unfiled returns. The tax agent may also decide to audit the debtor's income tax returns.

At one time, Internal Revenue Service agents required one return covering the period up to the date of the filing and a subsequent one covering events from the filing date to the end of the taxable period. This has now been changed, and the Form 941* bracketing such a period needs simply to indicate on its face which portion of the taxes are prepetition and which are postpetition. The distinction is important because *the postpetition portions must be paid when due.*

As a result of abuses and delinquency by debtors-in-possession (and sometimes even by trustees and receivers), a debtor-in-possession is now obliged to file with the Internal Revenue Service, at the end of each pay period, a report of deposits made in a special tax account. These accumulated deposits are transferred, as required under the Internal Revenue statutes, to depository receipt accounts. Copies of the proof of deposit and payment must be furnished regularly to the bankruptcy court. On page 128 is a copy of the form used for notifying the tax authorities of these deposits (a copy of this form is generally attached to the report to the bankruptcy court).

The court order permitting a debtor to remain in possession specifies which tax accounts must be opened and the manner in which they must be maintained.

It often happens that a debtor is simply unable to pay its taxes in full upon confirmation of a Plan of Arrangement, as required by the statute.

---

*Quarterly payroll tax report for income tax withheld from employees' wages and Social Security taxes due.

NOTICE OF AMOUNTS REMITTED TO FEDERAL DEPOSITARY
ON ACCOUNT OF F.I.C.A. AND WITHHELD INCOME TAXES

NOTE *THIS FORM IS NOT TO BE ATTACHED TO YOUR TAX RETURN. SEE INSTRUCTIONS ON REVERSE*

TO: District Director, Internal Revenue Service, ... District
Attn: **Chief, Special Procedures Section**

Pursuant to the order of the United States District Court, ... **District, dated** ....
**you are hereby notified that the following amounts were remitted together with a Federal tax deposit form
(Department of the Treasury Form 501) to the**

....
(NAME & ADDRESS OF BANK)

on .... **for the payroll period** .... **to** ....
(DATE)   (DATE)   (DATE)

GROSS WAGES PAID TO EMPLOYEES .... $ _____

INCOME TAXES WITHHELD .... $ _____

F.I.C.A. *(Employees' and employer's share of Social Security Tax)* .... $ _____

TOTAL DEPOSITED ▶ $ _____

_____
(Debtor-in-Possession, Receiver, or Trustee)

BY _____
(Signature & title of person authorized in court order)

_____
(Address)

_____
(Date)

BANK CERTIFICATION

This certifies receipt of deposit described below covering Federal taxes as defined in Treasury Department Circular No.
1079 (Revised) to be transmitted or credited to the Federal Reserve Bank of .... as Fiscal Agent
of the United States, pursuant to provisions of Treasury Department Circular No. 1079 (Revised).

DEPOSITOR'S EMPLOYER IDENTIFICATION NO.	AMOUNT OF DEPOSIT	DATE OF DEPOSIT
	$	
NAME & ADDRESS OF BANK		RECEIVED BY-

THE ABOVE CERTIFICATION IS LIMITED ONLY TO THE RECEIPT OF DEPOSIT

NAR Form **2-13** (Rev. 6-74)   Department of the Treasury - Internal Revenue Service

---

Such a situation need not be as hopeless as it might seem. In the first
place, tax authorities, like other creditors, can generally be brought to
realize that they have more to gain in the long run by helping the debtor
company recover than by destroying it and taking pot luck under an
auctioneer's hammer.

In addition, the debtor might be able to turn to account an aspect of the law that normally works to the disadvantage of tax authorities. Ordinarily, interest and penalties on tax liabilities may be accrued only up to the date of the petition filing. However, in recent years, regional IRS commissioners have on a number of occasions worked a *quid pro quo* with debtors that enabled the government to collect interest on taxes that fall due after the commencement of the proceeding. That is, in exchange for an extended payout period, the debtor agreed to voluntarily accrue interest on the tax debt after confirmation of a Plan of Arrangement (for an example, see Exhibit K in the Appendix).

As the federal government is positioned ahead of other taxing entities with respect to recovering tax liabilities, an arrangement with the Internal Revenue Service can usually be used as a model when the debtor negotiates with tax collectors further down in the order of priority. Other taxing authorities will generally follow the lead of the IRS and accept agreements along similar lines.

It is important to recognize, however, that negotiations directed at working out partial payments or extensions of tax liabilities should get under way early in the reorganization proceedings. It sometimes takes several months to negotiate an agreement acceptable to both the debtor and the office of the regional Internal Revenue Service commissioner. Moreover, negotiations are becoming increasingly sophisticated.

Among the complicating factors is the regional commissioners' policy of requiring that the amount of cash paid to non-tax creditors under the Plan of Arrangement, either by down payment or in installments, cannot exceed the cash paid to the United States. That is, Uncle Sam must receive proportionately as much as other creditors, dollar for dollar. (Incidentally, astute debtors have found that this is a persuasive argument in marshaling the acceptance of small cash down payments to non-tax general creditors.)

In requesting a part-payment or payment-extension plan, a debtor should provide the Internal Revenue Service regional commissioner's office with a proposal including the following information, as specified in NAR Publication No. 26:

OUTLINE TO BE USED BY DEBTOR IN PREPARATION OF PROPOSAL FOR INSTALLMENT PAYMENT OF FEDERAL TAXES IN PROCEEDINGS UNDER CHAPTER X OR XI OF THE BANKRUPTCY ACT

1. Show amount and type of federal taxes, periods involved, and, if notice of tax lien has been filed, state type of tax, date, and place of filing.

2. State any credits, refunds, or abatements which the debtor claims or may contemplate claiming, indicating when and where claim therefor was filed and basis thereof.

3. State amount of loss to be carried forward, if known; if not known, give estimate.

4. State whether debtor has claims against any other agency or department of the United States; if so, show in detail nature and amount. If contractor or subcontractor, give full information.

5. State:
   a. Nature and amounts of priority claims (wages and other tax claims, including local and state taxes) and treatment proposed for each under the plan;
   b. Amount of secured claims and proposed treatment of such claims;
   c. Amount of unsecured claims and proposed treatment of such claims.

6. Show book or stated value, estimated liquidation value, and fair market value of debtor's assets, including receivables and all causes of action; show which assets are free of and which subject to liens.

7. Submit balance sheets and profit and loss statements for two years prior to proceedings and other data showing debtor's financial condition, also similar data for operations under jurisdiction of court by receiver or trustee or debtor-in-possession.

8. State:
   a. Number of employees, length of time debtor has been in business, and nature of business (wholesale, retail, garment, restaurant, etc.);
   b. Prospects of the debtor after approval of the plan or as reorganized, including reasons why the plan will be likely to succeed;
   c. Estimates of anticipated gross and net income;
   d. Reasons for financial difficulty of debtor;
   e. Whether debtor or any of its principal officers or principal stockholders (if a corporation) have been involved in any proceedings under the Bankruptcy Act or insolvency proceedings under state law within the past six years;
   f. Salaries drawn in past by principal officers and present salaries;

    g. The amounts of any repayments of loans by the debtor to its principal officers, stockholders, or its or their relatives within the past year;

    h. Amounts, if any, owed to the debtor by its officers;

    i. Whether debtor is being managed by same people under whom it got into difficulty. What steps have been taken to ensure a better operation and what assurance is there that there will not be the same difficulty as in the past?

9. Give full information as to the inability to make the deposit required by Section 337(2) of the Bankruptcy Act, including detailed estimate of administration expenses and how they are to be paid, i.e., in full on confirmation or in some other manner.

10. State:

    a. Whether it is contemplated to organize a new corporation or to dispose of or in anywise encumber all or any part of debtor's assets;

    b. Amount of cash that will be required to carry out plan;

    c. Whether this cash will be supplied from outside sources and is it intended to encumber the debtor's assets to obtain it or any part of it;

       (1) If from outside sources, name them;

       (2) Terms of repayment;

       (3) How it is expected to make enough to repay such debt and to make payments required under the plan.

11. Present installment proposal for payment of taxes due the United States, i.e., amount of down payment and weekly or monthly payments (proposal should contemplate a substantial down payment and weekly or monthly payments over as short a period of time as the financial condition of the debtor permits), and explain the source from which such deferred payments will be made.

12. What security will be given to guarantee payment of the taxes due to the government?

THE FOREGOING SHOULD BE SUBMITTED BY LETTER, IN DUPLICATE, SIGNED BY THE DEBTOR OR PRINCIPAL OFFICER OF THE DEBTOR. IF DEBTOR HAS COUNSEL, COUNSEL'S NAME SHOULD ALSO BE AFFIXED. IF A CONFERENCE IS DESIRED PRIOR TO A FINAL DETERMINATION, KINDLY SO ADVISE. PROMPTNESS IN THE SUBMISSION OF THE ABOVE INFORMATION WILL EXPEDITE ACTION UPON YOUR PROPOSAL OF SETTLEMENT.

As a practical matter, the debtor's proposal requesting IRS agreement to a partial- or extended-payment plan need not take the form of a separate document. For example, the letter on the following pages combines a detailed challenge of the taxes claimed by the IRS with all data necessary to support the debtor's proposed installment-payment plan. Like the other illustrations in this book, the letter is essentially identical to one actually used in a recent Chapter XI proceeding.

Regional Counsel
Internal Revenue Service
26 Federal Plaza
New York, New York 10007

Re: Chapter XI—docket 72B885

Sir:

This letter relates to your proof of claim in the amount of
$104,937.38 dated November 3, 1972 filed in the above-named pro-
ceeding. Details of the claim are annexed hereto.

This claim is excessive because it includes $49,754.19 representing
income tax assessments arising from a revenue agent's report
dated November 2, 1972 covering an alleged audit of the taxpayer's
records for the years 1964 to 1969. The revenue agent came to
these conclusions without completing his audit of the books and
records for the years in question; and in fact has an appointment with
representatives of the taxpayer on January 11, 1973 to resolve
the open questions. A copy of the taxpayer's Protest to the revenue
agent's findings is attached. In addition we enclose a copy of
the Federal income tax returns for the year ended June 30, 1972 and the
year ended June 30, 1971. These returns in toto indicate, before
any net operating loss deduction, losses of ($678,128). It should
be obvious therefore that even if the revenue agent's findings were
correct, these losses, when carried back, would have the effect
of abating the proposed deficiency assessment. In fact, immediately
after confirmation of the plan of arrangement, the taxpayer intends to file a quick carry-back claim for these years.

If the income tax assessments were abated, the maximum tax
liability based upon the proof of claim would be $50,743.19.

No tax liens were filed for any portion of this claim.

Following are the answers to NAR Publication #26(8-65) which
have not already been provided:

Paragraph 3. The net operating loss for the year ended June
30, 1971 is ($616,283). The net operating loss deduction for the
year ended June 30, 1972 is ($61,845). It is not possible to determine
the amount of the loss which can be carried forward until the
items set forth in the opening paragraphs in this proposal are
resolved.

Paragraph 4. The debtor has no claims against any other agency
or department of the United States Government.

Paragraph 5. a) All priority claims will be paid in the same
proportion as the amounts due to the Internal Revenue Service
except for claims of less than $1,000, which will be paid in full. The
total amount of such priority claims for taxes, exclusive of the

claims of the Internal Revenue Service, is approximately $8,000. Commissions and wages payable, which total approximately $9,000, also will be paid in full on confirmation.

b) There are no secured claims.

c) The amount of unsecured claims is $502,935. Upon confirmation $8,000 will be paid to these creditors as a group with other installments, without interest, as follows:

5% of the claim three years from the date of confirmation

10% thereof four years from the date of confirmation

15% thereof five years from the date of confirmation

In addition, 227,700 shares of stock are to be issued at $1.00 per share, in settlement of $227,700 worth of debt.

Paragraph 6. Schedule attached hereto.

Paragraph 7. Federal income tax returns are attached hereto. The debtor-in-possession is now operating profitably.

Paragraph 8. a) 27 employees, 11 years in business, manufacturer of electronic modules.

b) Debtor has been profitable prior and subsequent to the Chapter XI proceedings. The loss was caused by two subsidiaries, one of which is bankrupt and the other of which was sold for a loss, resulting in a total loss of approximately one million dollars.

c) Estimated gross income for the following twelve month period is $750,000, with a net income of $75,000.

d) As previously stated, one subsidiary, KSW Electronics, is bankrupt, with a loss of approximately $450,000. Another, Power Phase Machine Tool, was disposed of at a loss of approximately $500,000.

e) No.

f) Salaries drawn in the past by principal officers totaled $35,000 (presently $40,000) per annum.

g) None.

h) None.

i) Previous officers have been replaced by new management. Overhead has been reduced, procedures tightened, and no acquisitions are presently under consideration.

Paragraph 9. The company requires working capital to continue the existing operation and to demonstrate financial stability.

Its customers, who are national companies, will not do business with the company unless it is financially stable.

The estimated administration expenses and cash required for confirmation are as follows:

Counsel to the Debtor	$30,000
Counsel to the Official Creditors' Committee	20,000
Accountant to the debtor-in-possession	4,000
Other expenses	3,000
Total	$57,000

Other amounts required for confirmation:

Taxes	15,000	
Wages & Commissions	9,000	
Unsecured creditors	8,000	33,000
Creditors to be paid in full*	1,000	
Total		$90,000

Paragraph 10. a) Corporation will continue to exist as it is now.

b) $89,000.

c) $89,000, payable over five years starting three years after confirmation. It is anticipated that earnings will be sufficient to accomplish the Company's objectives.

Paragraph 11. It is proposed to make a tax payment of $10,000 on confirmation, leaving a balance of approximately $40,000. Debtor proposes to pay the $40,000 balance in equal monthly install-ments over a period of thirty-six months, subsequent to confirmation. These payments will come from the earnings of the corporation. In this manner, the entire debt due to the Internal Revenue Service will be paid prior to any further payments to trade creditors.

Paragraph 12. It is proposed to pledge the fixed assets of the debtor corporation as security for the indebtedness due to the Internal Revenue Service.

Very truly yours,

*Small general creditors.

DEBTOR-IN-POSSESSION
SUMMARY ESTIMATE OF BOOK AND LIQUIDATION VALUE OF ASSETS
June 30, 1973

	Book value	Liquidation value
Cash	79,299	79,299
Accounts receivable	106,425	50,000
Prepayments and advance	2,942	–0–
Inventory	76,260	20,000
Fixed assets	148,258	30,000
Other assets	5,101	–0–
Total	418,285	179,299

The bankruptcy statute provides that income from the discharge of indebtedness under the bankruptcy statute is not taxable income to the beneficiary of the discharge. The book value of the taxpayer's property (other than money) must be decreased by the amount of the canceled debt, but it need not be decreased below fair market value. Notice, though, that taxable income may arise from the cancellation of indebtedness in an out-of-court settlement with creditors, to the extent that the debtor's assets exceed its liabilities after giving effect to the composition of debt, less expenses.

At the time of this writing, the use of net operating loss deductions as tax carry-backs or carry-forwards is not affected by the cancellation of indebtedness. Readers are cautioned, however, that there is no assurance that the Internal Revenue Service will continue to maintain this posture indefinitely. In fact, there are some indications to the contrary, although existing case law is silent on this point.

By and large, government agencies are cooperative and easy to deal with in connection with insolvency proceedings, consistent with protecting their legitimate interests. In fact, it is a matter of public policy, as expressed both in the statutes and in court decisions affecting bankruptcy proceedings, that the honest debtor who seeks relief will find a sympathetic reception at the agencies of the United States government —including the tax collection agency.

Nevertheless, a debtor may be simply unable to placate everyone involved, or, having done so, may find the business itself unsalvageable. The accountant's role in such cases is the subject of the next chapter.

ACCOUNTING SERVICES IN LITIGATION AND LIQUIDATION

As we have noted throughout this book, corporate insolvencies result from management errors or unanticipated financial drains much more often than from dishonesty. We have acknowledged, too, that by and large creditors have more to gain by helping a distressed customer survive and recover than by pressuring the debtor over the brink and into the hands of a trustee and an auctioneer. That said, however, a debtor and its creditors remain fundamentally in an adversary relationship with regard to unpaid bills; and the people involved on both sides are vulnerable to greed and the temptation to exploit a chain of events that neither knowingly initiated.

As a result, insolvency proceedings can and do trigger lawsuits, criminal prosecution, and straight bankruptcies. Insolvency accountants are regularly drawn into these developments, and should be prepared to render appropriate services in connection with litigation and liquidation.

The accountant's role in litigation normally involves either providing expert testimony, preparing special schedules and exhibits for attorneys or for other parties who will testify, or both. Litigation stemming from, or associated with, an insolvency proceeding usually relates to:

1. Challenged claims filed by creditors with the bankruptcy court

2. Establishing or attacking the feasibility of a proposed Plan of Arrangement or the notion that it is in the best interests of creditors

3. Attempts to recover alleged preferential transfers

4. Trying objections to a bankrupt's discharge

5. Collecting a debtor's accounts receivable

6. Trying claims that a debtor prepared and used false financial statements to induce others to extend credit

When an accountant will be called upon to testify personally, the attorney will generally consult with him or her in advance, to discuss the objectives of the testimony and to preview the general line of questioning that the attorney anticipates. Probably, the attorney will prepare a list of the questions he or she plans to ask when the accountant takes the stand, and will go over the accountant's replies. Just such a list of questions appears on pages 140–141 along with an accompanying letter (page 139) submitted to an accountant prior to an actual trial. At this trial, the IRS was suing the owners of a group of companies that had been liquidated in a bankruptcy proceeding about a decade earlier (actual names disguised).

Accountants who find themselves called upon to provide direct testimony in connection with litigation can generally depend on receiving this kind of guidance and support from the attorneys who will question them in court. Further, the accountant's preparation of special schedules, reports, and exhibits for use in litigation does not differ significantly from similar services provided in other connections. Accordingly, let us turn our attention to the accountant's role in liquidations.

When a debtor company files a petition in straight bankruptcy, the court immediately puts the company in the hands of a trustee in bankruptcy, who presides over its liquidation.* A trustee in bankruptcy is also appointed to take over from the debtor-in-possession and liquidate the company if the debtor is adjudicated a bankrupt. This can occur for any of a number of reasons, specifically:

1. Failure of the debtor to persuade its creditors that its proposed Plan of Arrangement is feasible and in the "best interests of creditors" (see definitions in Chapter Nine).

2. Failure of the debtor to provide the financing necessary to confirm the Plan of Arrangement.

3. Failure of the debtor to stem its losses, establish a positive cash flow, or otherwise successfully reorganize itself so that

---

*A trustee in bankruptcy, who is a kind of mortician as far as the bankrupt company is concerned, is not to be confused with the managing trustee whom the courts nearly always put in charge of distressed companies in a Chapter X proceeding (rarely, a debtor is permitted to remain in possession). The latter is counterpart to the receiver sometimes appointed, in lieu of a debtor-in-possession, in a Chapter XI proceeding. A receiver's or managing trustee's role is more analogous to that of a doctor to the insolvent company.

Address any reply to: 26 Federal Plaza, New York, N.Y.   10007

Department of the Treasury

Regional Counsel
Internal Revenue Service
North-Atlantic Region
Date: **MAY 1 6 1973**   In reply refer to:
         | CC:NY-TC-FLB

Mr. Robert Wiener

        In re: John & Mary Doernitz
                    Docket Nos. 5650-71 & 5832-72

Dear Mr. Wiener:

     I am sending you the enclosed list of questions for
your direct testimony in the Tax Court trial involving
John Doernitz. These questions are tentative and there
may be deletions and additions as a result of other
testimony in the trial.

     I request that you do not bring this list of
questions to the Tax Court. If you have any questions
concerning this list, please call me.

     The trial has been tentatively set for Tuesday,
September 4, 1973 at 11:00 a.m. Therefore, it will be
possible for you to testify at 3:00 on Tuesday. Please
call me on Monday afternoon to confirm the time for
trial and your testimony, because there is always a
possibility that the trial could be reset for a different
time.

                 Very truly yours,

                 Regional Counsel

         By:
             Attorney

Enclosure

DIRECT EXAMINATION -- ROBERT WIENER

1. What is your present occupation?

2. When did you become a Certified Public Accountant?

3. How long have you been involved in the insolvency accounting field?

4. Have you held any teaching positions in the field of accounting?

5. Were you the accountant for the trustee in bankruptcy in the bankruptcy proceedings for Doernitz Air Products, Inc., Industrial Gas Services, Inc. and Doernitz Medical Gases, Inc.? (Hereinafter these corporations will be referred to as the "Doernitz Corporations.")

6. Were you the accountant for the Doernitz Corporations, as debtors in possession, when they were in Chapter XI proceedings?

   (Chapter XI, October 24, 1961 to May 3, 1963)

7. As accountant for the debtors in possession, were you approved by the Creditors Committee?

   (Yes)

8. Have the books and records for the Doernitz Corporations been destroyed? (Bankruptcy case was closed on May 19, 1972. Order May 3, 1963 adjudicated corporations as bankrupt as of October 24, 1961)

9. In the Chapter XI bankruptcy proceedings, did you file financial statements for the Doernitz Corporations in the year 1962?

10. Did you also file a supplemental report for these corporations in 1962?

    (Identification of Financial Statements and Supplemental Report)

11. Were those reports prepared from the books and records of the Doernitz Corporations?

12. I refer you to page 10 of your report containing the financial statements of the Doernitz Corporations. On the balance sheet for Doernitz Medical Gases, Inc., what amount is listed as an amount due from John Doernitz to Doernitz Medical Gases, Inc.?

    ($16,929.00)

13. On page 12 of your report, could you read the liabilities owing from Doernitz Medical Gases to J.M. Trading Co., 58-20 Maspeth Avenue Corp. and Arrow Trading Co.?

14. Making reference to page 21 of your report, what amounts are listed as due from Doernitz Air Products, Inc., to affiliated companies and individuals?

15. In your supplemental report dated July 12, 1962, what are items referred to as "John Doernitz' withdrawals"?

    (Page 2. Supplemental report amounts changed on account books of debtors which were not in agreement with the payees designated on the checks.)

16. Is the list on page 3 of the supplemental report a list of payees on checks?

17. On Page 3, does the reference to "home phone" refer to Mr. Doernitz' home phone?

18. Does the reference to "mother's convalescent home" refer to Doernitz' mother's convalescent home?

19. Do the other items listed on page 3 relate primarily to Mr. Doernitz' personal expenses?

20. On Exhibit A for Doernitz Air Products, Inc., Exhibit B for Industrial Gas Services, Inc. and Exhibit C for Doernitz Medical Gases, there are listed so-called "previously agreed items." Could you explain how those figures were determined?

21. Do the payees listed on Schedules A-2 and A-3 relate to the personal expenses of John Doernitz?

22. Exhibit B of your report concerns Industrial Gas Services, Inc. Do the payees listed on Schedule B-2 relate to the personal expense of John Doernitz?

23. Exhibit C of your supplemental report concerns Doernitz Medical Gases, Inc. Do the payees listed on Schedule C-2 relate to the personal expenditures of John Doernitz?

24. What do Schedules A-1, B-1 and C-1 indicate?

25. Regarding the account of Industrial Gas Services, Inc. were there any large checks payable to Arrow Trading Company as "Leasehold Improvements"?

    (see page 4)

26. Was an automobile recorded as property on the books of Doernitz Medical Gases, Inc.?

    (Yes. 1960 Cadillac.)

27. Under whose name was the car registered?

28. What were the total payments to General Motors for the Cadillac?

it becomes a viable entity. Notice that throughout the duration of a Plan of Arrangement, any failure of the debtor-in-possession to meet any of the plan's payments or other terms can result in bankruptcy or termination of the business in accordance with the provisions of the plan.

4. The existence of some statutory defect that prevents consummation of an arrangement. For example, the debtor may already have been through a proceeding in the bankruptcy courts within the six years prior to the present petition. The debtor's commission of any of the other acts that would bar the discharge of bankrupt also results in the company's adjudication as a bankrupt.

Under any of these circumstances, the court appoints a trustee in bankruptcy to take over the bankrupt company, now called the *estate,* and to liquidate it, with, it is hoped, a dividend in some amount flowing to the unsecured creditors. The adjudicated bankrupt is required to file appropriate schedules and an up-to-date Statement of Affairs, as directed by the bankruptcy court.

The duties of the accountant serving a trustee in bankruptcy are twofold. First, he or she assists the trustee and the trustee's counsel in the housekeeping function; i.e., marshaling the assets of the estate and converting them into cash for distribution. Second, the accountant may be called upon to render assistance in litigation instituted on behalf of the trustee.

The first step in carrying out these duties is to visit the company premises and make a list of the books and records on hand, including tax reports, canceled checks, paid and unpaid invoices, copies of inventory lists, pertinent correspondence, sales invoices, shipping documents, and the like.

After ascertaining what records are on hand and what condition they are in, the accountant should consult with the trustee and the trustee's counsel to determine which records are to be removed to the accountant's office and which are to be stored in a public or private warehouse. Subsequently, the trustee and the counsel should be furnished with a list of the books and records, showing separately those in storage and those at the accountant's office.

The determination of which records should be kept readily available for further accounting work depends upon the condition of the accounts receivable records and the amount of work required to make the entries in the books necessary to record all transactions up to the date of the bankruptcy adjudication. A bankrupt company's books are often months behind.

The accountant should bring the estate's books up to date, either by continuing the original records or by opening up a new set of books. Either way, entries made by the trustee's accountant should be clearly distinguishable from the entries made earlier by the bankrupt's personnel. We suggest using a different ink for the new entries.

Some authorities contend that the trustee's accountant should make no entries in a bankrupt's books and records, insisting that an entirely separate set of books and records be maintained. This is a judgmental matter for each trustee and trustee's accountant to decide. Certainly, if the case has some elements of irregularity, either known or suspected, it is best not to touch the bankrupt's books and records, except for entries to bring accounts receivable or payable up to the date of the bankruptcy adjudication.

The accountant should prepare a report of findings, which is basically the same as the report an investigating accountant makes to the creditors' committee in a Chapter XI proceeding (see Chapter Six and Exhibit I in the Appendix). The information in the report should be expanded by including reproductions of appropriate canceled checks, invoices, or other material that will help the trustee and counsel to decide upon any courses of action, including litigation, that might be indicated to protect the interests of creditors.

Immediate attention should be given to the preparation and filing of all tax reports. This will avoid penalties for late filing and also ensure that the bankrupt estate receives credit for all tax deposits. Generally, the most critical returns are payroll tax and excise tax reports for all agencies, including Forms 940, 941, and any others that are appropriate.

Federal income tax reports should also be filed, if only to preserve net operating loss carry-forwards or to apply for tax refunds arising from the application of such carry-forwards or carry-backs. A trustee in bankruptcy must file an annual tax return for the bankrupt estate to report interest earned while the estate is being administered. The trustee applies the tax loss carry-forwards to the interest income earned by funds that the trustee has deposited in properly authorized, interest-bearing bank accounts.

In this connection, whenever net operating loss carry-forwards are not available or will expire before the estate is finally settled, the accountant should request estimates of the total cost of administering the estate, i.e., legal, accounting, and appraiser's fees, court costs, etc. These expenses may be accrued and charged to the interest income.

A bankruptcy case complicated by litigation can take a decade or more to settle. The accountant for the trustee should collect information relating to the estate's earnings on deposited funds and prepare annual income tax reports. These returns should be filed on the same form, such as 1120, that would be used if the company were still an operating business. However, the following statement, or one to the same effect, should be attached:

> This tax report is being filed on behalf of a Trustee in Bankruptcy (or an assignee for the benefit of creditors). The interest income reported arises from funds collected in the course of the liquidation of the estate. The trustee or assignee is not operating or conducting a business, so does not believe the income here reported is taxable. In any event, as the estate's final administrative costs cannot be known until the end of the proceeding, no tax liability can now be determined.

The trustee's accountant is also responsible for preparing W-2 forms for the company's employees for the year of bankruptcy (those for prior years were the responsibility of the debtor's staff, of course). We suggest that these be prepared early in the proceeding, because questions may arise regarding unpaid wages which require information from former employees. Notice that unpaid wages should not be included in the W-2, as these are reported when final distribution of the estate is made, at the conclusion of the bankruptcy proceeding.

Late in 1974, in the matter of Otte, Trustee in Bankruptcy of Freedomland (SCt) affirming CA-2, 480 F2d 184, the Court held that a trustee in bankruptcy must withhold income taxes and FICA taxes. In meeting both obligations, the IRS has agreed to accept a flat 25 percent of gross wages, together with the proper tax forms. Commerce Clearing House reported this decision as follows:

TRUSTEE MUST WITHHOLD ON PRE-BANKRUPTCY WAGE CLAIMS

A bankruptcy trustee must withhold, and pay, those taxes on wage claims which are earned by employees prior to the employer's bankruptcy, but which are unpaid at the inception of the bankruptcy proceeding. The U.S. Supreme Court has ruled that it agrees on this point with the four circuits that have decided the question.[1]

Legal Points Involved

The Code, of course, requires every employer making payment of wages to deduct and withhold income tax upon such wages. The Court decided that the bankruptcy trustee could be considered the "employer" because Code Sec. 3401(d)(1) provides that, if the person for whom the services were performed by the employee does not have control of the payment of the wages for such services, the term "employer" means the person having control of such payment. Moreover,

---

[1]*Otte, Trustee in Bankruptcy of Freedomland, Inc.*, (SCt) aff'g CA-2, 73-2 USTC ¶9504, 480 F2d 184. See also *Fogarty*, (CA-8) 47,2 USTC ¶9383, 164 F. 2d 26; *Curtis*, (CA-6) 50-1 USTC ¶9108, 178 F. 2d 268, cert. den. 339 U.S. 965; *Lines*, (CA-9) 242 F. 201, rehearing den. 246 F2d 70, cert. den., 355 U.S. 857.

it was decided that the payment of wage claims under the Bankruptcy Act constitutes the "payment of wages."

Nor did the Court feel that the withholding requirement would unduly burden the trustee, even though 413 former employees had filed wage claims in this case. The burden was the same that any employer would have to bear, according to the Court, and the Internal Revenue Service has endeavored to lighten the load by its alternative 25% combined bankruptcy withholding rate for income and FICA taxes. This would facilitate computation.

Withholding Claims as Wages

The Court also decided two issues that arose under the Bankruptcy Act. Payment of the taxes was not excused merely because the government had failed to file a proof of claim. The taxes were not in the nature of debts of the bankrupt, because its liability came into being only during bankruptcy. Moreover, the taxes to be withheld were entitled to a second priority of payment; the Court felt that they were part of the wage claims themselves and should be treated in the same manner as the wages. Back references: ¶4939.587, 5017.5565, 5641.085, 5789.38 and 5836.013.

Fairly early in the course of the bankruptcy proceeding the trustee and trustee's counsel publish a notice setting forth instructions and a time limitation for creditors filing proofs of claims. This is the first step toward the eventual distribution of the assets of the estate. Known creditors will be contacted directly, but in addition a notice will be published in the court's official newspaper of record, to alert any creditors not recorded in the bankrupt's books and records. Here is an example of such a public notice:

NOTICE

UNITED STATES DISTRICT COURT, Southern District of New York. Order directing filing of claims against debtor-in-possession in superseded Chapter XI proceeding. In the Matter of QUALITY ELECTROTYPE CORP., Bankrupt. In Bankruptcy No. 70 B 872.

A proceeding under Chapter XI of the Bankruptcy Act having been superseded by this bankruptcy proceeding and an order having been entered on February 11, 1972 adjudging the debtor a bankrupt and directing that bankruptcy be proceeded with, and the debtor-in-possession in said superseded proceeding having filed a sched-

ule listing unpaid obligations incurred by him (it), and a statement of all contracts, executory in whole or in part, assumed or entered into by him (it) in said superseded proceedings, it is

ORDERED, that all claims against the said QUALITY ELECTROTYPE CORP. as debtor-in-possession including all claims of the United States, any State, or any subdivision thereof, be filed in the office of the undersigned Bankruptcy Judge, Room 230, U.S. Court House, Foley Square, New York City, within 60 days after the date hereof, and it is further

ORDERED, that the proofs of such

claims shall be in the form of proofs of claim prescribed by §57 of the Bankruptcy Act and the rules and General Orders applicable thereto and shall contain a written statement signed by the claimant setting forth the claim, the consideration therefor, what security, if any, is held therefor, and what payment, if any, has been made thereon, and that the claim is justly owing from the debtor-in-possession to the creditor or his assignor, or otherwise constitutes an allowable claim which arose during the aforesaid proceedings superseded by this bankruptcy proceeding. All proofs of claim filed pursuant hereto shall be entitled in these proceedings, shall clearly indicate the period in which the claim arose, and shall designate the address to which all notices to the creditor shall be mailed, and it is further

ORDERED, that pursuant to §378b of the Bankruptcy Act, any contract which was entered into or assumed by the said debtor-in-possession which was executory in whole or in part at the aforesaid date of entry of the order directing that bankruptcy be proceeded with shall be deemed to be rejected unless expressly assumed by the trustee in bankruptcy on or before June 11, 1973, and it is further

ORDERED, that all claims against said debtor-in-possession not included in the aforesaid schedule filed by said QUALITY ELECTROTYPE CORP., if any, shall be filed herein in form and manner as hereinabove provided, on or before July 10, 1973, and it is further

ORDERED, that claims arising from the rejection by the trustee in bankruptcy as aforesaid of executory contracts entered into or assumed by said debtor-in-possession shall be filed herein in form and manner as hereinabove provided, on or before July 10, 1973, and it is further

ORDERED, that the trustee in bankrupty herein shall, on or before April 17, 1973, mail to all creditors listed in the said schedule, and all the other parties to the executory contracts listed in the statement heretofore filed herein by the said debtor-in-possession at their addresses as they appear in said schedule and statement, postage prepaid, a copy of this order, and by publishing a copy of this order in the Daily News Record on or before April 20, 1973, and it is further

ORDERED, that any claims directed to be filed by the terms hereof, but not filed within the times herein provided, shall not be allowed and shall be barred and the said QUALITY ELECTROTYPE CORP., debtor-in-possession, shall be forever discharged from any liability with respect to such claims.

DATED: New York, New York
　　　　April 10, 1973

　　　　　　　　EDWARD J. RYAN
　　　　　　　　Bankruptcy Judge

While the creditors' claims upon the bankrupt estate are being collected, the trustee proceeds to convert into cash all the bankrupt's assets that are to be administered for the benefit of unsecured creditors. (Meanwhile, secured creditors will naturally press their claims against whatever assets were pledged for their protection.)

Among other things, the trustee in bankruptcy will collect the estate's accounts receivable, and will pursue to completion any promising litigation such as that aimed at recovering preferential transfers or at setting aside any illegal acts of the bankrupt company's owners, officers, or stockholders. Remaining inventories, supplies, real estate, equipment, and other salable assets, whether tangible or intangible, are then sold at auction. This auction must be held promptly after appropriate public announcement, which usually takes the form of a notice in the court's official newspaper of record. Here is a typical example of such an auction announcement:

NOTICE

UNITED STATES DISTRICT COURT, Southern District of New York. In the Matter of: TUBOTRON INC., Bankrupt. No. 72 B 563.

<u>NOTICE OF SALE.</u>

Pursuant to an order of this Court, Notice is hereby given that the Assets of the above-named Bankrupt, consisting of Inventory, Machinery and Equipment, will be sold at Public Auction on Wednesday, April 18th, 1973, at 11:00 A.M., at premises, Somerset Valley Industrial Campus, Somerset, New Jersey.

WILLIAM N. OTTE,
Trustee

LEVIN & WEINTRAUB, Co-Attorneys for Trustee, 225 Broadway, New York, New York.

ARUTT, NACHAMIE, BENJAMIN & RUBIN, Co-Attorneys for Trustee, 11 West 42nd Street, New York, New York.

MARTIN FEIN & CO., INC., Auctioneers, 40A East 33rd Street, New York, New York 10016, Telephone (212) 683-7742.

HON. ASA S. HERZOG,
Bankruptcy Judge

In some cases, the trustee in bankruptcy, who has considerable latitude in disposing of a bankrupt company's assets, so long as the maximum benefit of creditors predominates, may entertain and select private bids for specialized assets of potential value to a relatively narrow population of buyers. Here is the outcome of one such instance:

NOTICE

UNITED STATES DISTRICT COURT, Southern District of New York. In the Matter of: GILMORE CAFETERIA, INC., Bankrupt. No. 74 B 1880. <u>ORDER</u>

Upon the annexed application of LAWRENCE SARF, the trustee herein dated July 17, 1975 and upon the offering letter of BINA REALTY CO., INC., annexed thereto and no adverse interest being represented, it is

ORDERED, that a special meeting of creditors be held before this Court at the Courthouse located at Foley Square, New York, N.Y., Room 201, before HONORABLE ROY BABITT on the 20th day of August, 1975 at 11:30 A.M. of that day to consider whether or not LAWRENCE SARF, as Trustee herein shall be authorized to accept the offer of BINA REALTY CO., INC. to purchase all of the physical assets of the bankrupt's estate contained and situated in premises 115-2nd Avenue, New York, N.Y., consisting of bakery equipment and fixtures for the sum of $2,000 or such other and better offer that may be made; and it is further

ORDERED, that Philip D'Amore, 142 Drake Ave., New Rochelle, N.Y. a disinterested person is hereby appointed as appraiser of the property being offered herein and he file his written appraisal in writing with this Court before the return date of this application and receive a maximum of $65.00 per day as his compensation, the exact amount of which shall be fixed by this Court upon application therefor.

DATED: New York, N.Y.
　　　　July 29, 1975

　　　　　　　ROY BABITT
　　　　　　　Bankruptcy Judge

Such sales must be approved of in advance by a court order, but they may take place without notice to creditors.

Another example of the disposition of assets without resort to the auctioneer is the sale to any interested party of the probably uncollectible accounts receivable remaining after the trustee has collected all those deemed worth pursuing. An offer of such tag-end receivables may be included in the notice of final meeting of creditors.

With the bankrupt's salable assets converted into cash, the trustee and trustee's counsel proceed to collect any remaining assets. Characteristic examples of such assets are performance deposits held by the telephone and local utility companies, rent deposits and advance payments, unearned insurance premiums, and any unencumbered bank deposits.

When the trustee in bankruptcy decides that he or she has done everything feasible to realize the greatest benefit for creditors of the estate, the trustee will direct the accountant for the estate to review the claims filed with the bankruptcy court. The accountant will examine the claims, in light of the bankrupt's books and records and in comparison with the schedules of assets and liabilities that the bankrupt has filed with the court.

In making this examination, the accountant should first secure a copy of the estate's claim docket, which is kept at the office of the clerk of the bankruptcy court. Generally, counsel will supply a copy of the docket, which lists all claims filed with the bankruptcy court in chronological order. Each claim is assigned a number, and the last claim filed by any creditor is called the final claim. Claims may include both debts that arose prior to the Chapter XI proceeding (if one was filed) and claims against the debtor-in-possession (the latter have priority over prefiling claims, as we have seen).

All claims should be compared with the Schedule of Liabilities that the debtor or bankrupt filed in the original proceeding. Duplicate claims should be noted, and if any claims do not agree with the schedules they should be compared with the bankrupt's books and records. Usually, the claims will have arrived with statements or copies of invoices attached, with proof of delivery.

All these indicia should be studied and considered by the accountant in making a report to the trustee and counsel. Counsel may move to object to claims that seem improper or excessive, on the basis of the accountant's report. The accountant may also be required to testify as to the comparison between the claims and the company's books and records, so that the bankruptcy judge can rule on the validity of any challenged claims.

Particularly troublesome are tax claims, which may include interest or penalties that have been improperly charged. A common problem arises in connection with the annual Federal Unemployment Insurance report. The federal unemployment insurance tax is calculated after applying credit for payment to state unemployment funds. Therefore a claim for unpaid state unemployment insurance taxes will usually be duplicated in the Federal Unemployment Insurance report. The accountant should furnish the trustee's attorney with detailed information concerning these taxes, so that the Internal Revenue Service can grant proper credit for payments made to the state as part of the final distribution of the estate's assets.

If the trustee has filed claims for refunds of income or other taxes, these too must be reviewed to make sure that proper credits are received. From time to time, there also may be assessments arising from income tax audits. If so, it is especially important to determine that net operating loss carry-forwards or carry-backs have been properly applied to offset the audit assessment.

As pointed out earlier, the litigation and out-of-court pulling and hauling that accompany settlement of a complex bankruptcy case can take a number of years. Meanwhile, the trustee must file with the court regular reports of the status of the proceedings and of the trustee's stewardship of the estate's cash and other assets, if any.

UNITED STATES DISTRICT COURT

for the _____ EASTERN _____ District of _____ NEW YORK _____

In re

HYGRADE PACKAGING CORP.
55 Motor Avenue
Farmingdale, New York   **Bankruptcy No** _68 B 1296_

Bankrupt*

ORDER FOR FINAL MEETING OF CREDITORS AND
NOTICE OF FILING OF FINAL ACCOUNT[S] OF TRUSTEE ~~AND RECEIVER~~
AND OF FINAL MEETING OF CREDITORS ~~AND OF HEARING ON~~
~~ABANDONMENT OF PROPERTY BY THE TRUSTEE~~

To the creditors:

The final report[s] and account[s] of the trustee [if appropriate and of the receiver] in this case having been filed,

It is ordered, and notice is hereby given, that the final meeting of creditors will be held
at The Courtroom of the undersigned Bankruptcy Judge, 900 Ellison Ave.

Westbury, New York   , on December 17, 1974, **at** 10:30 **o'clock**
ª .m., for the purpose [**as appropriate**] of examining and passing on the report[s] and account[s], acting on applications for allowances, and transacting such other business as may properly come before the meeting. Attendance by creditors is welcomed but not required.

The following applications for allowances have been filed:

Applicants	Commissions or Fees	Expenses
Receiver	$ _____	$ _____
William Otte	$ 5,449.88	$ _____
Trustee		
Attorney for Bankrupt	$ _____	$ _____
Attorney for Receiver	$ _____	$ _____
Jacob F. Gottesman	$ 82,500.00	$ _____
Attorney for Trustee		
Robert S. Linwood	$ 660.00	$ _____
Attorney for Petitioning Creditors APPRAISER		
Robert A. Wiener	$ 5,000.00	$ _____
Accountant		

Creditors may be heard before the allowances are determined.

508,616.88
The account of the trustee shows total receipts of $ _____ , and total disbursements of $ 236,868.09 . The balance on hand is $ 271,748.80

In addition to expenses of administration as may be allowed by the court, liens and priority claims totaling $ 13,745.62 must be paid in advance of any dividend to general creditors.

Claims of general creditors totaling $ 1,640,076.55 have been allowed.
ADM-$16974.84

~~[If appropriate] The trustee's application to abandon the following property will be heard and acted upon at the meeting:~~

Offers will be considered to purchase the Trustee's right, title
& interest in and to Accounts Receivable in the amount of $13,453.70.

The bankrupt has [not] been discharged.

Dated: Westbury, New York
December 4, 1974

_____ BORIS RADOYEVICH _____
Bankruptcy Judge

*Include all names used by bankrupt within last 6 years.

When all claims that were not accepted as filed have been adjudicated and either corrected, rejected, or approved, the trustee in bankruptcy files a final report with the court. Fundamentally, this consists of a statement of the trustee's receipts and disbursements.

At this point all those who have rendered services on behalf of the estate—attorneys, accountants, appraisers, and any others—file their applications for allowance. (Exhibit N in the Appendix is an example of such an application.) The bankruptcy judge then gives notice to all creditors of the status of the estate, and announces a date for the final hearing in connection with closing the estate. An actual and typical example of such an announcement is shown on page 150. This particular example appears on the form used by the Eastern District of New York. Those generated in other districts might vary in format and other details, but the thrust and purpose will be the same. Note that the order directing the final meeting of creditors includes the court's statement of the filed fees and expenses.

Separately, the bankruptcy judge sees to the preparation of a final schedule of all allowable claims, in order of payment priority. At the final meeting of creditors, the court directs the trustee to pay the costs of administration and priority claims, and to distribute the balance of the estate, pro rata, as a dividend to creditors.

Generally, the accountant for the trustee in bankruptcy does not participate in these windup activities (except to collect the fee approved for the accountant's services). On the other hand, the accountant may be specifically asked to assist further in particularly large or complex cases. These "extra" services may range from handling incidental details to assisting the bankruptcy court in its final report to the Federal Administrator of Bankruptcies in Washington, D.C. No two bankruptcy cases are exactly alike, and the accountant may be called upon to do anything within his or her realm of expertise, as long as the services rendered are properly recognized and compensated. By and large, though, the accountant's duties end when all creditors' claims are either approved or objected to.

The remainder of this book consists of exhibits selected to familiarize the reader with the chief forms and other documents encountered in connection with insolvency cases.

APPENDIX CONTENTS

Data Required for Chapter XI Petition

A typical form used by insolvency counsel to solicit information at the outset of a chapter XI proceeding.

Complete the answers on these pages where possible. If additional space is required for any answer, set forth on a separate page. The data on these pages is required *in addition to* the material to be set forth in the schedules and accompanying papers. If there are any questions in connection with any of these items, please call immediately.

**SET FORTH THE FOLLOWING
INFORMATION REGARDING DEBTOR.**

1. Debtor's name: _____.

2. Debtor's principal address: _____.

3. Debtor's IRS I.D. number: _____.
4.   a. Type of business operated by Debtor: _____.
     b. State of Debtor's incorporation: _____.
     c. Date of Debtor's incorporation: _____.

5. Has Debtor used any other trade name in the last six years? If so, set forth the name used: _____.

6. Debtor's President: (Name and Address)_____
   Debtor's Secretary: (Name and Address)_____
                               _____

7. Attach an alphabetized typewritten list of Debtor's creditors to this form. Full exact corporate names are required plus addresses. Amounts are not necessary but will have to be supplied when appropriate.

8. Summary of Debtor's assets and liabilities (state whether accurate or estimated, in whole or in part):

Real Estate	$_____	Priority wages	$_____
Cash on hand	$_____	Federal taxes	$_____
Inventory	$_____	State taxes	$_____
Automobiles	$_____	Local taxes	$_____
Machinery & Equip.	$_____	Secured claims	$_____
Accounts Receivable	$_____	Unsecured claims	$_____
Ins. policies	$_____	Other (specify)	$_____
Deposits	$_____		
Other assets (specify)	$_____		

9. Location of Debtor's physical assets. If any assets are not in Debtor's premises, give name and address of each additional location and describe assets located at such location.

10. Debtor's ten largest creditors in order of largest amount due, with full names, addresses, and amounts. Do not include tax or other priority creditors, secured creditors, creditors who are now in your employ or who are stockholders, officers, or directors, or creditors whose claims are substantially disputed.

Name	Address	Amount due
1.		
2.		
3.		
4.		
5.		
6.		
7.		
8.		
9.		
10.		

11. Attach a list of suits pending against Debtor. In each case, set forth the following:

Name of plaintiff:
Amount:
Court:
Index No.:
Name and address of
   plaintiff's attorney:
Nature of action:

12. Is any of Debtor's property in the possession or custody of a public officer, receiver, trustee, assignee for the benefit of creditors, mortgage pledge, or assignee of rents? If so, set forth the following:

Name and address of officer: _____
Property: _____
Attach copy of document authorizing same or describe in detail.

13. For premises occupied by Debtor under lease, set forth the following:

Address:
Landlord:
Date of lease:
Month, date and year of commencement of lease:
Month, date and year of termination of lease:
Rent:
Statement of any pending negotiations for
   modification of the lease:
Attach a copy of all leases.

14. Set forth the names and addresses of Debtor's stockholders. If Debtor is publicly held, set forth the classes of stock held publicly and the proportion of each class held publicly:

Name	*Address*	*No. of shares*	*% of class*

15. Estimated weekly payroll other than for Debtor's officers, directors, or stockholders, within the next 30 days: $_____.

16. Names and titles of Debtor's officers, directors and stockholders now being paid salaries to whom it is proposed to continue salaries in the next 30 days indicating amounts of present and proposed salaries in each case, and functions of each:

Name	*Title*	*Function*	*Current salary*	*Proposed salary*

17. Debtor's estimated additional operating expenses within the next 30 days, such as:

Rent:	$
Utilities:	$
Trucking:	$
Repairs and miscellaneous:	$
Interest:	$
Insurance:	$
Cleaning, etc:	$
Other:	$
Total:	$

18. Debtor's estimated gain or loss within the next 30 days: $_____.

19. Brief history of Debtor's business, including date of organization, reason for present circumstances, statement of future prospects, and a description of related business entities, such as parent or subsidiary corporations.

20. Are any of the Debtor's assets the subject of any liens, security interest, mortgages, etc.? If the answer is affirmative, set forth the following:

    Name and address of lienor or secured party:
    Amount of lien or security interest:
    Description of subject property:
    Nature of underlying transaction:
    Attach copy of all security agreements etc.

21. Is any of the Debtor's equipment, machinery or items of personal property under lease? If so, set forth the following:

Name and address of lessor:
Terms of lease:
Description of leased property:
Attach a copy of all personal property leases.

22. Set forth the name and address of the Debtor's bank or banks.

23. Is the Debtor in any way indebted to any of the banks which it has listed? If so, set forth the details.

24. Assuming that Debtor's current funds, and receipts which it anticipates will be collected within a reasonable time, can be made available for working capital, i.e., for current payroll, rent, purchases, etc., will Debtor still be in need of working capital? If so, what collateral can Debtor offer to a potential lender (e.g., real estate, receivables, inventory etc.) and how much working capital does the Debtor require?

25. Does Debtor have any agreements, contracts, leases etc. which are burdensome and which Debtor would like to cancel? If so, attach a copy of each such agreement.

26. Has Debtor made any transfers of its property for inadequate consideration or made payment for or on account of any pre-existing indebtedness within the past 4 months? Within the past year? If so, set forth the details:

27. Has Debtor done any of the following?
    a. Destroyed or failed to keep books and records;
    b. Issued a false financial statement;
    c. Transferred, removed, destroyed or concealed any of its property within the past year;
    d. Obtained a discharge or confirmed a Plan of Arrangement under the Bankruptcy Act within the past 6 years;
    e. Fraudulently concealed property from a receiver, custodian, trustee, marshal, or other court officer, or from creditors;
    f. Concealed, mutilated, falsified or made a false entry in any document relating to Debtor's affairs;
    g. Withheld any documents from any court officer;
    h. Made a false oath in any bankruptcy proceeding.
    If so, set forth details.

28. Does Debtor have a tax loss carry-forward and if so, what is its extent?

29. Are any of Debtor's principals liable to Debtor on account of loans, unpaid subscriptions, salary carried as loans, or otherwise? If so, give details:

30. Are Debtor's principals personally liable on any of Debtor's obligations by way of guaranty, endorsement, or otherwise, and if so, set forth the details and attach a copy of all relevant instruments:

31. Have any of Debtor's obligations on which Debtor's principals are personally liable been repaid in whole or in part within the past four months, and if so, set forth the details:

32. Is any of Debtor's stock the subject of options, warrants or related claims, and if so, set forth the details:

33. Is Debtor bound by any collective bargaining agreements, and if so, set forth the details:

34. Is Debtor liable to any of its principals, and if so, set forth the details:

35. Does Debtor have any credit cards in use, and if so, set forth the details:

36. Has Debtor had any problems with any governmental agencies (S.E.C., IRS, etc.) and if so, set forth the details:

37. Has Debtor issued any financial statements within the past few years and if so, attach copies or set forth the details:

38. Are any of the following in arrears, and if so, set forth the details: (a) wages, (b) fringe benefits to employees (pension, welfare, vacation, medical, severance etc.), (c) union payments (pension, welfare, medical, vacation, severance etc.), (d) withholding taxes, (e) sales taxes.

39. Does Debtor have any leases or contracts which must be preserved? If so, attach copies and specify whether they contain bankruptcy clauses.

UNITED STATES DISTRICT COURT FOR THE   Southern   DISTRICT OF   New York

In re

X Y Z Corporation

Include here all names used by debtor within last 6 years.   Debtor

ARRANGEMENT NO. 75 B 234
(Note - Number is affixed
by Clerk of the
ORIGINAL PETITION Court)
UNDER CHAPTER XI

1. Petitioner's post-office address is

No. One Broadway, New York, New York

2. Petitioner has[1] its principal place of business within this district
for the last six months.

3. No other case under the Bankruptcy Act initiated on a petition by or against petitioner is now pending.

4. Petitioner is qualified to file this petition and is entitled to the benefits of Chapter XI of the Act.

5. Petitioner is *insolvent   unable to pay his debts as they mature.*

6. A copy of petitioner's proposed plan is attached.[2]

Petitioner intends to file a plan pursuant to Chapter XI of the act.

Wherefore petitioner prays for relief in accordance with Chapter XI of the Act.

Signed: ....   Address: ....
☐ *Attorney for Petitioner*   ☐ *Petitioner*
(Petitioner signs if not represented by attorney.)

We have read the foregoing petition and consent to the filing thereof.

.... *Partner*   .... *Partner*

.... *Partner*   .... *Partner*

VERIFICATION

State of   County of   ss.:

INDIVIDUAL: I   the petitioner named in the foregoing petition, do hereby
swear that the statements contained therein are true according to the best of my knowledge, information, and belief.

CORPORATION: I   the[3]
of the corporation named as petitioner in the foregoing petition, do hereby swear that the statements contained therein are true
according to the best of my knowledge, information, and belief, and that the filing of this petition on behalf of the corporation
has been authorized.

PARTNERSHIP: I   *a member*
— *an authorized agent* — of the partnership named as petitioner in the foregoing petition, do hereby swear that the statements
contained therein are true according to the best of my knowledge, information, and belief, and that the filing of this petition
on behalf of the partnership has been authorized.

Subscribed and sworn to before me on   ....
Petitioner

....

....
Official Character

OF 11-F1: Original petition under Chapter XI: verifications   © 1974 BY JULIUS BLUMBERG, INC., 80 EXCHANGE PL., N. Y. C. 10004

[1] Insert appropriate allegations — resided [or has had his domicile or has had his principal place of business or if a partnership, or corporation, has had its principal assets] within this district for the preceding 6 months [or for a longer portion of the preceding 6 months than in any other district.]
[2] Or, strikeout and insert *Petitioner intends to file a plan pursuant to Chapter XI of the Act*. If Petitioner is a corporation insert paragraph 7 as follows: *7. Exhibit A is attached to and made a part of this petition.*
[3] Insert president or other officer or an authorized agent of the corporation named as petitioner in the foregoing petition.

UNITED STATES DISTRICT COURT FOR THE   Southern   DISTRICT OF   New York

In re

    X Y Z Corporation

                               Debtor

Include here all names used by debtor within last 6 years.

EXHIBIT "A"

1. Petitioner's employer's identification number is   13-15834092

2. If any of petitioner's securities are registered under section 12 of the Securities and Exchange Act of 1934, SEC file number is   Not registered

3. The following financial data is the latest available information and refers to petitioners condition on
    June 15, 1975 .

    a. Total assets: $.0.0.0.0.0.0.0.0.0.0.0.0 (Should agree with Summary of Debts and
    b. Liabilities: The financial information should follow   *Approximate* Property)
    the detailed Statements and the Summary of Debts   *Number of Holders*
    & Property

	Approximate (Property)	Number of Holders
Secured debt, excluding that listed below	$ 00000000000	One
Debt securities held by more than 100 holders	$ None	None
Secured	$ 00000000000	0000
Unsecured	$ 00000000000	0000
Other liabilities, excluding contingent or unliquidated claims	$	
Number of shares of common stock	Two	Two

Comments, if any:

4. Brief description of petitioner's business:

        Manufacture and sale of gadgets

5. The name of any person who directly or indirectly owns, controls, or holds, with power to vote, 25% or more of the voting securities of petitioner is
        Raymond Geltzer

6. The names of all corporations 25% or more of the outstanding voting securities of which are directly or indirectly owned, controlled, or held, with power to vote, by petitioner are
        None

UNITED STATES DISTRICT COURT FOR THE Southern   DISTRICT OF   New York

In re

        X Y Z Corporation

                                         Debtor

ARRANGEMENT NO.

Include here all names used by debtor   within last 6 years.

Schedule A — STATEMENT OF ALL DEBTS OF DEBTOR

Schedules A-1, A-2, and A-3 must include all the claims against the debtor or his property as of the date of the filing of the petition by or against him.

SCHEDULE A-1 — CREDITORS HAVING PRIORITY

Nature of Claim	Name of creditor and residence or place of business (if unknown, so state)	Specify when claim was incurred and the consideration therefor; when claim is contingent, unliquidated, disputed, or subject to setoff, evidenced by a judgment, negotiable instrument, or other writing, or incurred as partner or joint contractor, so indicate; specify name of any partner or joint contractor on any debt	Amount of claim
(a) Wages and commissions owing to workmen, servants, clerks, or traveling or city salesmen on salary or commission basis, whole or part time, whether or not selling exclusively for the debtor not exceeding $600 to each, earned within 3 months before filing of petition.	Alphonse Jones 1800 Fifth Avenue New York, New York 10020	Week ended June 30, 1975	$ 600
(b) Taxes owing (itemize by type of tax and taxing authority:) (1) To the United States (2) To any State (3) To any other taxing authority	Internal Revenue Service Holtsville, NY New York State Income Tax Bureau Albany, New York	FICA and withholding taxes For the 2nd Quarter of 1975 Income Taxes withheld from employee's wages 2nd Quarter of 1975	
(c) (1) Debts owing to any person, including the United States entitled to priority by laws of United States (itemized by type) (2) Rent owing to a landlord who is entitled to priority by the laws of any State accrued within three months before filing the petition, for actual use and occupancy.	(Could include Dept. of Defense, etc.)		
		Total	

OF 11-F5: Schedule A-1: (1)

Schedule A-2 — Creditors Holding Security

Name of creditor and residence or place of business (if unknown, so state)	Description of security and date when obtained by creditor	Specify when claim was incurred and the consideration therefor; when claim is contingent, unliquidated, disputed, subject to setoff, evidenced by a judgment, negotiable instrument, or other writing, or incurred as partner or joint contractor; so indicate; specify name of any partner or joint contractor on any debt	Market value	Amount of claim without deduction of value of security
Bank and Trust Company	Accounts Receivable	Continuing Accounts Receivable Financing	$ 00000000	$ 00000000
		Total	00000000	00000000

Schedule A-3 — Creditors Having Unsecured Claims Without Priority

Name of creditor (including last known holder of any negotiable instrument) and residence or place of business (if unknown, so state)	Specify when claim was incurred and the consideration therefor; when claim is contingent, unliquidated, disputed, subject to setoff, evidenced by a judgment, negotiable instrument, or other writing, or incurred as partner or joint contractor, so indicate; specify name of any partner or joint contractor on any debt	Amount of claim
		$
Jones Company, Inc. 185 South Street NY, NY 10012	Goods Sold and Delivered	00000000
Raymond Geltzer, CPA 1550 Avenue of the Americas New York, New York 10023	Accounting Services Rendered	00000000
	Total	00000000

OF 11-F5: Schedule A-2 & A-3: (2)   © 1974 BY JULIUS BLUMBERG, INC., 80 EXCHANGE PL., N. Y. C. 10004

Schedule A-3 — Creditors Having Unsecured Claims Without Priority

Name of creditor (including last known holder of any negotiable instrument) and residence or place of business (if unknown, so state)	Specify when claim was incurred and the consideration therefor; when claim is contingent, unliquidated, disputed, subject to setoff, evidenced by a judgment, negotiable instrument, or other writing, or incurred as partner or joint contractor, so indicate; specify name of any partner or joint contractor on any debt	Amount of claim	
		$	

Continuation Sheet for Schedule A-3

These sheets may be typed on paper of a similar size and attached as a schedule supporting A-3.

| | | Total | | |

SCHEDULE B — STATEMENT OF ALL PROPERTY OF DEBTOR

Schedules B-1, B-2, B-3, and B-4 must include all property of the debtor as of the date of the filing of the petition by or against him.

Schedule B-1 — Real Property

Description and location of all real property in which debtor has an interest (including equitable and future interests, interests in estates by the entirety, community property, life estates, lease-holds, and rights and powers exercisable for his own benefit)	Nature of interest (specify all deeds and written instruments relating thereto)	Market value of debtor interest without deduction for secured claims listed in schedule A-2 or exemp-tions claimed in schedule B-4
		$
Land and Building located at 65 Junes Street New York, New York	Deed	0000000000
	Total	

Schedule B-2 — Personal Property

Type of Property	Description and location	Market value of debtor interest without deduction for secured claims listed on schedule A-2 or exemp-tions claimed in schedule B-4
a. Cash on hand	Petty Cash Fund	$ 000000000
b. Deposits of money with banking insti-tutions, savings and loan associa-tions, credit unions, public utility companies, landlords, and others	Schedule attached showing nature of deposit and location of deposit	000000000
c. Household goods, supplies, and furnish-ings		
d. Books, pictures, and other art objects; stamp, coin, and other collections		
e. Wearing apparel, jewelry, firearms, sports equipment, and other personal possessions		
f. Automobiles, trucks, trailers, and other vehicles	1975 Cadillac Fleetwood located at the debtor's place of business	000000000
g. Boats, motors, and their accessories	(Attach schedule and description of vehicles)	00000000
	Total	000000000

Schedule B-2 — Personal Property (Continued)

Type of property	Description and location	Market value of debtor's interest without deduction for secured claims listed on schedule A-2 or exemptions claimed in schedule B-4
h. Livestock, poultry, and other animals		$
i. Farming supplies and implements		
j. Office equipment, furnishings, and supplies	Desks, typewriters, chairs, and other office equipment at debtor's place of business book value	0000000
k. Machinery, fixtures, equipment, and supplies (other than those listed in items j and l) used in business	Machinery, & equipment at book value used at debtor's place of business	0000000
l. Inventory	Tools and dies either at debtor's place of business or at subcontractor's place of business	0000000
m. Tangible personal property of any other description	Inventory of finished goods, work in process, or raw materials	0000000
n. Patents, copyrights, franchises, and other general intangibles (specify all documents and writings relating thereto)		
o. Government and corporate bonds and other negotiable and nonnegotiable instruments		
p. Other liquidated debts owing bankrupt or debtor	Various loans receivable- schedule attached	
q. Contingent and unliquidated claims of every nature, including counterclaims of the bankrupt or debtor (give estimated value of each)	Lawsuit for damages against a supplier Damages of $1,000,000 are sought	Unknown
r. Interests in insurance policies (itemize surrender or refund values of each)	Various policies of insurance covering debtor's property	Unknown
s. Annuities		
t. Stocks and interests in incorporated and unincorporated companies (itemize separately)		
u. Interests in partnerships		
v. Equitable and future interests, life estates, and rights or powers exercisable for the benefit of the bankrupt or debtor (specify all written instruments relating thereto)		
	Total	000000000

Schedule B-3 — Property Not Otherwise Scheduled

Type of property	Description and location	Market value of debtor interest without deduction for secured claims listed in schedule A-2 or exemptions claimed in schedule B-4
a. Property transferred under assignment for benefit of creditors, within 4 months prior to filing of petition (specify date of assignment, name and address of assignee, amount realized therefrom by the assignee, and disposition of proceeds so far as known to debtor)	None	$
b. Property of any kind not otherwise scheduled	None	
	Total	

Schedule B-4 — Property Claimed as Exempt

Type of property	Location, description, and so far as relevant to the claim of exemption, present use of property	Reference to statute creating the exemption	Value claimed exempt
	None		$
		Total	

OF 11-F5: Schedule B-3 & B-4: (7)   © 1974 BY JULIUS BLUMBERG, INC., 80 EXCHANGE PL., N. Y. C. 10004

This statement should track with the previous
schedules and statements. Each total should
agree with total on each schedule.

SUMMARY OF DEBTS AND PROPERTY

(From the statements of the debtor in Schedule A and B)

Schedule	Debts and property	Total
	DEBTS	
A—1/a	Wages having priority	
A—1/b(1)	Taxes owing United States	
A—1/b(2)	Taxes owing States	
A—1/b(3)	Taxes owing other taxing authorities	
A—1/c(1)	Debts having priority by laws of the United States	
A—1/c(2)	Rent having priority under State law	
A—2	Secured claims	
A—3	Unsecured claims without priority	
		Schedule A total
	PROPERTY	
B—1	Real property (total value)	
B—2/a	Cash on hand	
B—2/b	Deposits	
B—2/c	Household goods	
B—2/d	Books, pictures, and collections	
B—2/e	Wearing apparel and personal possessions	
B—2/f	Automobiles and other vehicles	
B—2/g	Boats, motors, and accessories	
B—2/h	Livestock and other animals	
B—2/i	Farming supplies and implements	
B—2/j	Office equipment and supplies	
B—2/k	Machinery, equipment, and supplies used in business	
B—2/l	Inventory	
B—2/m	Other tangible personal property	
B—2/n	Patents and other general intangibles	
B—2/o	Bonds and other instruments	
B—2/p	Other liquidated debts	
B—2/q	Contingent and unliquidated claims	
B—2/r	Interests in insurance policies	
B—2/s	Annuities	
B—2/t	Interests in corporations and unincorporated companies	
B—2/u	Interests in partnerships	
B—2/v	Equitable and future interests, rights, and powers in personality	
B—3/a	Property assigned for benefit of creditors	
B—3/b	Property not otherwise scheduled	
B—4	Property claimed as exempt	
		Schedule B total

OATHS TO SCHEDULES A AND B

State of   County of   ss.:

Individual: I   do hereby swear that I have
read the foregoing schedules, consisting of   sheets, and that they are a statement of all my debts and all my property in accordance with the Bankruptcy Act, to the best of my knowledge, information, and belief.

Corporation: I   the [*insert president or other officer or an authorized agent*]
                                                  of the corporation as bankrupt in this proceeding, do hereby
swear that I have read the foregoing schedules, consisting of   sheets, and that they are a statement of all the debts and all the
property of the corporation in accordance with the Bankruptcy Act, to the best of my knowledge, information, and belief.

Partnership: I   a [*insert member or an authorized agent*]
                                                  of the partnership named as bankrupt in this proceeding, do hereby swear
that I have read the foregoing schedules, consisting of   sheets, and that they are a statement of all the debts and all the property of the partnership in accordance with the Bankruptcy Act, to the best of my knowledge, information, and belief.

                                                  Signed:

Subscribed and sworn to before me on

                                                  official character

* In the opinion of the bankrupt-debtor the net value of the non-exempt assets will not exceed $150.00.

OF 11-F5: Summary of debts & property: oaths: (8)   (*To be signed if applicable*)
© 1974 BY JULIUS BLUMBERG, INC., 80 EXCHANGE PL., N.Y.C. 10004

* *Massachusetts District requires this statement, if applicable. Other Districts may require this or similar statements.*

UNITED STATES DISTRICT COURT FOR THE   Southern   DISTRICT OF   New York

In re   ARRANGEMENT NO.

X Y Z Corporation   STATEMENT OF AFFAIRS
                                        Debtor   FOR BANKRUPT
Include here all names used by debtor within last 6 years.   ENGAGED IN BUSINESS

Each question should be answered or the failure to answer explained. If the answer is "none," this should be stated. If additional space is needed for the answer to any question, a separate sheet, properly identified, and made part hereof, should be used and attached.

If the debtor is a partnership or a corporation, the questions shall be deemed to be addressed to, and shall be answered on behalf of, the partnership or corporation; and the statement shall be verified by a member of the partnership or by a duly authorized officer of the corporation.

The term "original petition," as used in the following questions, shall mean the petition filed under Rule 11-6 or, if filed in a pending case, the first petition initiating a case under the Act.   (Unofficial)

1. Nature, location, and name of business.

a. Under what name and where do you carry on your business?

X Y Z Corporation   One Broadway, New York, 10012

b. In what business are you engaged? (If business operations have been terminated, give the date of such termination.)

Manufacture and Sale of Gadgets

c. When did you commence such business?

July 1, 1970

d. Where else, and under what other names, have you carried on business within the 6 years immediately preceding the filing of the original petition herein? (Give street addresses, the name of any partners, joint adventurers, or other associate, the nature of the business, and the periods for which it was carried on.)

None

e. What is your employer identification number? Your social security number?

13-15834092

2. Books and records.

a. By whom, or under whose supervision, have your books of account and records been kept during the 2 years immediately preceding the filing of the original petition herein? (Give names, addresses, and periods of time.)

Alphonse Jones- 1970-1975
Eight Fifth Avenue, N.Y.N.Y.   10023

b. By whom have your books of account and records been audited during the 2 years immediately preceding the filing of the original petition herein? (Give names, addresses, and dates of audits.)

Our books have not been audited but we have frequently engaged Raymond Geltzer, CPA of 1550 Avenue of the Americas, New York, New York, 10023 to perform various accounting and tax services in the years 1970 to 1975.

c. In whose possession are your books of account and records? (Give names and addresses.)

The books and records are at the offices of the debtor

d. If any of these books or records are not available, explain.

No

e. Have any books of account or records relating to your affairs been destroyed, lost, or otherwise disposed of within the 2 years immediately preceding the filing of the original petition herein? (If so, give particulars, including date of destruction, loss, or disposition, and reason therefor.)

3. Financial statements.

Have you issued any written financial statements within the 2 years immediately preceding the filing of the original petition herein? (Give dates, and the names and addresses of the persons to whom issued, including mercantile and trade agencies.)

To various banks and credit agencies at December 31, 1974 and December 31, 1973

4. Inventories.

a. When was the last inventory of your property taken?

December 31, 1974

b. By whom, or under whose supervision, was this inventory taken?

Bruce Jackson

c. What was the amount, in dollars, of the inventory? (State whether the inventory was taken at cost, market, or otherwise.)

000000000 at the lower of cost or market

d. When was the next prior inventory of your property taken?

December 31, 1973

e. By whom, or under whose supervision, was this inventory taken?

Same

f. What was the amount, in dollars, of the inventory? (State whether the inventory was taken at cost, market, or otherwise.)

000000000 at the lower of cost or market

g. In whose possession are the records of the 2 inventories above referred to? (Give names and addresses.)

At the offices of the debtor-Bruce Jackson

5. Income other than from operation of business.

What amount of income, other than from operation of your business, have you received during each of the 2 years immediately preceding the filing of the original petition herein? (Give particulars, including each source, and the amount received therefrom.)

None

6. Tax returns and refunds.

a. In whose possession are copies of your federal and state income tax returns for the 3 years immediately preceding the filing of the original petition herein?

At the offices of the debtor and Raymond Geltzer, CPA

b. What tax refunds (income or other) have you received during the 2 years immediately preceding the filing of the original petition herein?

None

c. To what tax refunds (income or other), if any, are you, or may you be, entitled? (Give particulars, including information as to any refund payable jointly to you and your spouse or any other person.)

None

OF 11-F7: Statement of affairs: engaged in business: (1)   © 1974 BY JULIUS BLUMBERG, INC., 80 EXCHANGE PL., N.Y.C. 10004

7. Bank accounts and safe deposit boxes.

a. What bank accounts have you maintained, alone or together with any other person, and in your own or any other name, within the 2 years immediately preceding the filing of the original petition herein?
(Give the name and address of each bank, the name in which the deposit was maintained, and the name and address of every person authorised to make withdrawals from such account.)

Bank & Trust Company,
New York, New York Account #------
Signatory- Albert Smith

b. What safe deposit box or boxes or other depository or depositories have you kept or used for your securities, cash, or other valuables within the 2 years immediately preceding the filing of the original petition herein?
(Give the name and address of the bank or other depository, the name in which each box or other depository was kept, the name and address of every person who had the right of access thereto, a description of the contents thereof, and, if the box has been surrendered, state when surrendered or, if transferred, when transferred and the name and address of the transferee.)

Same

8. Property held for another person.

What property do you hold for any other person?
Give name and address of each person, and describe the property, the amount or value thereof and all writings relating thereto.)

None

9. Prior bankruptcy proceedings.

What proceedings under the Bankruptcy Act have previously been brought by or against you?
(State the location of the bankruptcy court, the nature and number of proceeding, and whether a discharge was granted or refused, the proceeding was dismissed, or a composition arrangement, or plan was confirmed.)

None

10. Receiverships, general assignments, and other modes of liquidation.

a. Was any of your property, at the time of the filing of the original petition herein, in the hands of a receiver, trustee, or other liquidating agent?
(If so, give a brief description of the property and the name and address of the receiver, trustee, or other agent, and, if the agent was appointed in a court proceeding, the name and location of the court and the nature of the proceeding.)

None

b. Have you made any assignment of your property for the benefit of your creditors, or any general settlement with your creditors, within the 2 years immediately preceding the filing of the original petition herein?
(If so, give dates, the name and address of the assignee, and a brief statement of the terms of assignment or settlement.)

None

11. Property in hands of third person.

Is any other person holding anything of value in which you have an interest?
(Give name and address, location and description of the property, and circumstances of the holding.)

None

12. Suits, executions, and attachments.

a. Were you a party to any suit pending at the time of the filing of the original petition herein?
(If so, give the name and location of the court and the title and nature of the proceeding.)

None

b. Were you a party to any suit terminated within the year immediately preceding the filing of the original petition herein?
(If so, give the name and location of the court, the title and nature of the proceeding, and the result.)

c. Has any of your property been attached, garnished, or seized under any legal or equitable process within the 4 months immediately preceding the filing of the original petition herein?
(If so, describe the property seized or person garnished, and at whose suit.)

Lien filed by Internal Revenue Service

13. Payments on loans and installment purchases.

What repayments on loans in whole or in part, and what payments on installment purchases of goods and services, have you made during the year immediately preceding the filing of the original petition herein?
(Give the names and addresses of the persons receiving payment, the amounts of the loans and of the purchase price of the goods and services, the dates of the original transactions, the amounts and dates of payments, and, if any of the payees are your relatives, the relationship; if the debtor is a partnership and any of the payees is or was a partner or a relative of a partner, state the relationship; if the debtor is a corporation and any of the payees is or was an officer, director, or stockholder, or a relative of an officer, director, or stockholder, state the relationship.)

None

14. Transfers of property.

a. Have you made any gifts, other than ordinary and usual presents to family members and charitable donations, during the year immediately preceding the filing of the original petition herein?
(If so, give names and addresses of donees and dates, description, and value of gifts.)

None

b. Have you made any other transfer, absolute or for the purpose of security, or any other disposition which was not in the ordinary course of business during the year immediately preceding the filing of the original petition herein?
(Give a description of the property, the date of the transfer or disposition, to whom transferred or how disposed of, and state whether the transferee is a relative, partner, shareholder, officer, or director, the consideration, if any, received for the property, and the disposition of such consideration.)

None

15. Accounts and other receivables.

Have you assigned, either absolutely or as security, any of your accounts or other receivables during the year immediately preceding the filing of the original petition herein? (If so, give names and addresses of assignees.)

To the Bank & Trust Company

16. Repossessions and returns.

Has any property been returned to, or repossessed by, the seller or by a secured party during the year immediately preceding the filing of the original petition herein? (If so, give particulars, including the name and address of the party getting the property and its description and value.)

Held as part of a routine
Accounts Receivable Financing Operation

17. Business leases.

If you are a tenant of business property, what are the name and address of your landlord, the amount of your rental, the date to which rent had been paid at the time of the filing of the original petition herein, and the amount of security held by the landlord?

Not applicable

18. Losses.

a. Have you suffered any losses from fire, theft, or gambling during the year immediately preceding the filing of the original petition herein? (If so, give particulars, including dates, names, and places, and the amounts of money or value and general description of property lost.)

b. Was the loss covered in whole or part by insurance? (If so, give particulars.)

None

19. Withdrawals.

a. If you are an individual proprietor of your business, what personal withdrawals of any kind have you made from the business during the year immediately preceding the filing of the original petition herein?

b. If the debtor is a partnership or corporation, what withdrawals, in any form (including compensation or loans), have been made by any member of the partnership, or by any officer, director, managing executive, or shareholder of the corporation, during the year immediately preceding the filing of the original petition herein? (Give the name and designation or relationship to the debtor of each person, the dates and amounts of withdrawals, and the nature or purpose thereof.)

None

None

20. Payments or transfers to attorneys.

a. Have you consulted an attorney during the year immediately preceding or since the filing of the original petition herein? (Give date, name, and address.)

b. Have you during the year immediately preceding or since the filing of the original petition herein paid any money or transferred any property to the attorney, or to any other person on his behalf? (If so, give particulars, including amount paid or value of property transferred and date of payment or transfer.)

c. Have you, either during the year immediately preceding or since the filing of the original petition herein, agreed to pay any money or transfer any property to an attorney at law, or to any other person on his behalf? (If so, give particulars, including amount and terms of obligation.)

(If the debtor is a partnership or corporation, the following additional question should be answered.)

Yes- A.Fish, Esq.,5th Avenue NY,NY

Retainer Fee = $5,000

None

21. Members of partnership; officers, directors, managers, and principal stockholders of corporation.

a. What is the name and address of each member of the partnership, or the name, title, and address of each officer, director, and managing executive, and of each stockholder holding 25 per cent or more of the issued and outstanding stock, of the corporation?

b. During the year immediately preceding the filing of the original petition herein, has any member withdrawn from the partnership, or any officer, director, or managing executive of the corporation terminated his relationship, or any stockholder holding 25 per cent or more of the issued stock disposed of more than 50 per cent of his holdings? (If so, give name and address and reason for withdrawal, termination, or disposition, if known.)

c. Has any person acquired or disposed of 25 per cent or more of the stock of the corporation during the year immediately preceding the filing of the petition? (If so, give name and address and particulars.)

Albert Smith, New York, New York

No

No

State of   County of   ss.:

I,   do hereby swear that I*

have read the answers contained in the foregoing statement of affairs and that they are true and complete to the best of my knowledge, information, and belief.

Subscribed and sworn to before me on

....

....
                                                    Debtor

....
                                            Official character

OF 11-F7:   Statement of affairs: engaged in business: (3)   © 1974 BY JULIUS BLUMBERG, INC.. 80 EXCHANGE PL.. N. Y. C. 10004

* Person verifying for partnership or corporation should indicate position or relationship to debtor

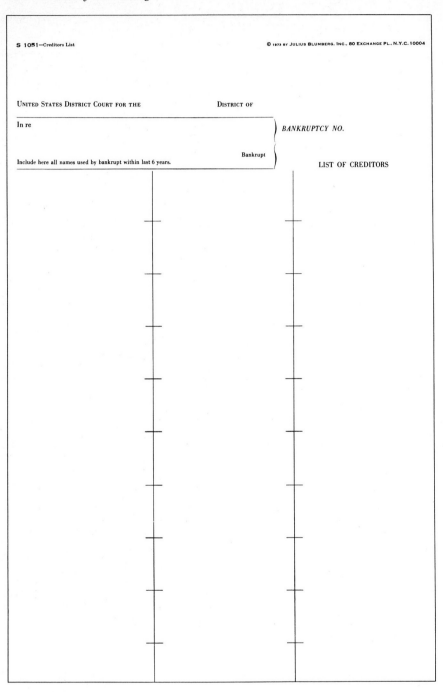

S 1051—Creditors List

© 1973 BY JULIUS BLUMBERG, INC., 80 EXCHANGE PL., N.Y.C. 10004

UNITED STATES DISTRICT COURT FOR THE

DISTRICT OF

In re

BANKRUPTCY NO.

Bankrupt

Include here all names used by bankrupt within last 6 years.

LIST OF CREDITORS

UNITED STATES DISTRICT COURT FOR THE Southern   DISTRICT OF New York

In re

ARRANGEMENT NO.

XYZ Corporation

Debtor

STATEMENT
OF
EXECUTORY CONTRACTS

Include here all names used by debtor within last 6 years.

The debtor has the following executory contracts:

Lease of five typewriters from I B M Corporation for two years at $ 1,200 per annum.

Etc. etc.

Dated

....
Debtor

State of   County of   ss.:

INDIVIDUAL: I   the debtor named in the above captioned case, do hereby swear that I have read the foregoing statements, that the statements contained therein are true according to the best of my knowledge, information, and belief.

CORPORATION: I   the of the corporation named as petitioner in the above captioned case, do hereby swear that I have read the foregoing statement, that the statements contained therein are true according to the best of my knowledge, information, and belief, and that the filing of this statement on behalf of the corporation has been authorized.

PARTNERSHIP: I   *a member* — *an authorized agent* — of the partnership named as petitioner in the above captioned case, do hereby swear that I have read the foregoing statement, that the statements contained therein are true according to the best of my knowledge, information, and belief and that the filing of this statement on behalf of the partnership has been authorized.

Subscribed and sworn to before me on

....
Debtor

....

....
Official Character

Exhibit C
Order Continuing the Debtor-in-Possession, and Staying Creditors

UNITED STATES DISTRICT COURT
SOUTHERN DISTRICT OF NEW YORK
_____x

In the Matter

of

BOWIE INSTRUMENT CORP.,
BOWIE INTERNATIONAL, INC.,
BOWIE/ARIZONA, INC.,
BOWIE TECHNOLOGY, INC.

Debtors.
_____x

ASA S. HERZOG
BANKRUPTCY JUDGE
In Proceedings for an Arrangement
No. 75 B 217, 221, 222, 223
APPLICATION & ORDER
AUTHORIZING DEBTORS-IN-
POSSESSION TO OPERATE
BUSINESS, ETC.

At New York, New York, in said District, on the 11th day of February, 1975.

Upon the annexed application of the debtors-in-possession, and no adverse interest being represented, and it appearing that no notice thereof need be given, and sufficient cause appearing therefor, it is

NOW, on motion of LEVIN & WEINTRAUB, attorneys for the debtors-in-possession,

ORDERED:

1. The debtors shall continue in possession of their property and shall have all the title and may exercise consistently with the provisions of Chapter XI of the Bankruptcy Act all the powers of a trustee appointed pursuant to Section 44 of the said Act.

2. The debtors-in-possession are authorized to operate their business and manage their property pursuant to Section 343 of the Bankruptcy Act and Bankruptcy Rule 11-23 until the further order of this court.

3. The debtors-in-possession are authorized to buy and sell merchandise, supplies and other property, and to render services in the normal course of their business for cash or on credit; and to purchase or otherwise acquire for cash or on credit, such materials, equipment, supplies, services or other property as may or shall be necessary and advisable in connection with the operation of such business and the management and preservation of said property and to pay for their purchases made on credit, when due; to employ, discharge and fix salaries and compensation of all employees and to enter into any contracts incidental to the normal and usual operation of said business and the management and preservation of said

Exhibit C   **175**

property; to receive and collect the income, revenue and profits of said business and to collect outstanding accounts receivable.

4. The debtors-in-possession shall open new books of account as of the opening of business on the day of the filing of said petition under Chapter XI, in which new books of account the debtors-in-possession shall cause to be kept proper accounts of their earnings, expenses, receipts, disbursements and all obligations incurred and transactions had in the operation of their business and the management, preservation and protection of the property within the estate; and said debtors-in-possession shall preserve proper vouchers for all payments made on account of such disbursements.

5. The debtors-in-possession are authorized to pay their employees entitled to priority, pursuant to Section 64a(2) of the Bankruptcy Act, wages earned by them *within two weeks* preceding the filing of the petition for arrangement herein.

6. The debtors-in-possession are authorized to institute, prosecute, defend, intervene in or become a party to any action or proceeding at law or in equity in any state or federal court as may be necessary for the protection, maintenance and preservation of their assets.

7. The debtors-in-possession are authorized to omit the requirements of Rule XI-5, Subd. 1, requiring weekly statements of cash receipts and disbursements, and subdivision 2(d) thereof, requiring a detailed inventory on hand at the beginning and at the end of each month.

8. The debtors-in-possession shall not sell any of their assets, except in the regular course of business, and shall not borrow nor hypothecate any of their assets without an order of this court.

9. The debtors-in-possession are authorized to make deposits of monies received by them in a designated depository and in the banks set forth in the schedule annexed hereto and made a part hereof and said debtors-in-possession are authorized to withdraw monies by check signed by any duly authorized officer of the debtors-in-possession or any other party designated by the debtors-in-possession.

10. All banks be and they hereby are directed to transfer to the account of the debtors-in-possession, all monies now on deposit in the name of the debtors, whether special or regular account; provided, however, that all banks are authorized and directed to honor all checks issued by the debtors on their payroll account.

11. The debtors-in-possession are authorized to maintain their present magnetic ink coding account numbers (if any) on their payroll checking account.

12. The debtors-in-possession are authorized to retain such attorneys as may be necessary for the purpose of collecting customer trade receivables and pay such attorneys the usual rates promulgated by the Commercial Law League of America.

13. (a) The debtors-in-possession and president, vice-president, secretary and treasurer, and any other person set forth in Section 7b of the Bankruptcy Act are hereby directed and required to segregate and hold separate and apart from all other funds all moneys deducted and withheld from employees or collected from others for taxes under any law of the United States during the pendency of the proceeding and to forthwith deposit the amounts so withheld or collected in a separate tax account. Such amounts shall be used and disbursed only for the particular purposes for which they are set aside or as more specifically set forth below.

(b) All federal income taxes required to be withheld and all social security taxes required to be contributed or deducted as herein above stated shall be remitted by the debtors-in-possession together with a federal depository receipt, to the debtors-in-possession bank of deposit not later than the end of the second business day next succeeding the day upon which taxes were required to be deducted or withheld.

(c) All federal excise taxes listed on quarterly federal excise tax return form 720 which the debtors-in-possession are required to collect or for which liability is incurred shall be deposited in the tax account on or before the end of the calendar week next succeeding the week during which such amounts are required to be collected or liability for them is incurred; and all such excise tax funds on deposit at the end of said second calendar week which represent amounts collected or incurred during the preceding calendar week shall forthwith be remitted by the debtors-in-possession to their bank of deposit, together with the federal depository receipt for said amount.

(d) The debtors-in-possession shall within one calendar week after making any remittances to a depository for federal taxes furnish the appropriate District Director of Internal Revenue with evidence that it has made the same, on forms furnished by, and under the conditions as may be prescribed by, the District Director of Internal Revenue.

(e) Each verified report which the debtors-in-possession are required to file with the court shall state the amounts and dates of payments transmitted by federal depository receipts, and, if applicable, a copy of such report shall be transmitted promptly to the creditors' committee or its duly authorized representative.

(f) The debtors-in-possession or their legal representative shall immediately transmit by mail one copy of this order to the Regional Counsel, Internal Revenue Service, and one copy to the District Director of Internal Revenue, where the debtors-in-possession normally file their tax returns, for the attention of the Chief, Special Procedures Section. Proof of such service should be forthwith filed with this court.

(g) The provisions of the foregoing paragraphs shall be effective as of the date the debtors-in-possession filed the petition in this proceeding and the debtors-in-possession are hereby directed to immediately comply with such provisions.

Exhibit C **177**

14. The debtors-in-possession be and they hereby are authorized to either return or pay for merchandise for which a proper and timely demand has been made to reclaim by the particular supplier under the provisions of Section 2-702 of the Uniform Commercial Code.

15. All persons, firms and corporations, including all creditors and landlords of the said debtors, and the representatives, agents, attorneys and servants of all such creditors and landlords and all sheriffs, marshals and other officers, and their deputies, representatives and servants, are hereby jointly and severally enjoined, restrained and stayed from removing, transferring, disposing of, or attempting in any way to remove, transfer or dispose of, or in any way to interfere with any property, assets or effects in the possession of the said debtors-in-possession, or owned by said debtors-in-possession, and in the possession of any officers, agents, attorneys or representatives of said debtors-in-possession or with the debtors' possession of any premises; and all said persons are further enjoined, stayed and restrained from executing or issuing or causing the execution or issuance or the suing out of any court of any writ, process, summons, attachment, replevin, execution or any other proceedings for the purpose of impounding or taking possession of or interfering with any property owned by or in the possession of the said debtors-in-possession or with any premises occupied by it; and each and all of said persons, firms or corporations having process against the debtors or having instituted arbitration proceedings are hereby jointly and severally restrained, stayed, and enjoined from proceeding with arbitration proceedings, or taking any steps, measures, proceedings, doing any act or thing in any action wherein the said debtors may be either plaintiff, defendant, petitioner or respondent, and from causing, procuring, suffering or permitting the same to be done until final decree herein.

16. All persons, firms and corporations be and they hereby are enjoined from disturbing, interfering with, cutting off or disconnecting the furnishing of gas, telephone service, heat, electrical service, water supply or any other utility of like kind furnished to said debtors-in-possession on account of any unpaid past due bills due from the debtors, until further order of this court.

_____
Bankruptcy Judge

Counsel's Letter of Instruction To the Debtor

Homann, Brainerd and Maltz
Counsellors at Law

Dear Mr. _____

This letter is in recapitulation of instructions given to you in our conferences, and also comprises a record of proceedings to date and a guide with respect to your conduct of the business as the debtor-in-possession.

It is imperative that all officers and all employees concerned with finances be completely familiar with, and completely understand, the contents of this letter and the provisions of the enclosed court orders. The procedures described must be followed rigidly, and the limitations set forth upon the operation of the business of the debtor-in-possession must be observed strictly.

I suggest that a copy of this letter be provided to all concerned officers and employees and that these copies be kept accessible for continuing reference until I advise you in writing that the procedures and limitations described are no longer in effect.

The petition was filed in the United States District Court, _____
District of New York on _____*(date)*_____, and the proceeding
has been referred to the Honorable _____*(name)*_____,
Bankruptcy Judge, whose office and Courtroom address is:

(data)

By order of the court, and pursuant to provisions of the Bankruptcy Act, your corporation is constituted, as of the filing date of the petition, as debtor-in-possession, authorized to operate its own business. The debtor-in-possession is a separate legal entity under the Bankruptcy Act, and has all the powers and many of the obligations of a trustee in bankruptcy. The debtor-in-possession, and the officers of the corporation individually, are legally accountable to the court as trustee for the operation of the business of the corporation. Strict adherence to the procedures and limitations prescribed in this letter will discharge that responsibility.

Pursuant to the provisions of the rules of the court, there will be a hearing, on notice to the ten largest creditors, before the Bankruptcy Judge at a time and place to be announced, to determine whether or not you as debtor-in-possession shall be permitted to operate the business without posting indemnity. As president of the corporation, you are required to appear with me at this hearing, the full purpose of which has been explained to you.

Pursuant to order of the court, the time to file schedules, statement of affairs and the statement of executory contracts required by the Bankruptcy Act has been extended to _____*(date)*_____.

I have already provided you with a check list to assist you in assembling the data required. I must receive answers to all items on this check list no later than four business days prior to the time fixed for filing the schedules in order to allow sufficient time for their preparation in final form, execution, and filing in court. The instructions for preparing these data must be followed strictly. If for any reason these data cannot be delivered to me at that time, it is imperative that you promptly advise me, so that an application may be prepared and submitted for a further extension.

The following orders have been sent to you under separate cover:

1. Certified photocopies of the order dated _____, of the United States District Court, temporarily authorizing operation of the debtor's business and staying proceedings by creditors.

2. Conformed copy of the order of the Judge directing procedures with respect to payment of federal withholding and social security taxes.

I particularly direct your attention to the following matters, which are included in the subject matter of these orders:

1. The prior books of account are to be closed as of the close of business on _____*(date)*_____, and new books of account are to be opened on behalf of the debtor-in-possession as of the opening of business on _____*(date)*_____.

2. All creditors, attorneys, marshals, sheriffs, and other officers are restrained by the court order from taking any steps or proceedings except before the United States District Court. The certified photocopy of this order is to be kept available so that it may be exhibited to any sheriff or other officer who calls at your premises and attempts to make a levy upon property of the debtor. Any summons hereafter served upon you or letter mailed to you by an attorney is to be mailed to my office on the day of its receipt. If any problem arises in connection with such matters, call my office immediately.

3. The same order restrains the disconnection or termination of gas, telephone, heat, electric service, water supply or any other utility by reason of non-payment of any indebtedness incurred prior to the filing of the

petition. The provisions of this order should be made known, and the order exhibited, to any utility that threatens to discontinue service. If there is a past indebtedness to a utility, the utility has the right to require a security deposit for future (not past) service. The deposit generally required is the average of two months billings, as ascertained with reference to the billings of the preceding year. If such security deposit is requested, the debtor-in-possession will be required to post it. Again, communicate with me immediately if there are any specific problems.

4. Your business may not in any way, either by display or advertisement, mention or use the name of the United States District Court.

5. The following salaries are authorized to be paid to officers, stockholders and directors:

> (Often, NONE until authorized later by
> court order.)

No other compensation, except as provided in the enclosed order of the Bankruptcy Judge, may be paid to officers, stockholders and directors. No expense account advances or reimbursements may be made, except reimbursement of specific expenses actually disbursed, supported by a statement of expenses and proper receipts or vouchers. Any salaries authorized for officers, stockholders, and directors may not be accumulated. Any such salaries not paid upon the regular payroll dates are deemed, by the terms of the Judge's order, to be waived.

6. The bank set forth below has been designated as the sole depository of the funds of the debtor-in-possession: (*bank name, branch and address*). New bank accounts are to be opened immediately in this bank, which are to be entitled as follows:

> (1) (Debtor company), debtor-in-possession
> General Account

> (2) (Debtor company), debtor-in-possession
> Tax and Trust Account

Checks drawn against said accounts are to be signed by the debtor-in-possession by authorized signatory.

To open the debtor-in-possession bank accounts, you will be required to deliver to the bank one of the certified photocopies of the order of the Bankruptcy Judge authorizing the debtor-in-possession to operate the business. All balances on deposit in any prior accounts in the same bank are to be immediately transferred to the general account of the debtor-in-possession, and the attention of an officer of the bank must be immediately directed to this requirement. If there are any funds or deposits in any bank other than that designated in the Judge's order, full details are to be supplied to my office immediately, so that proper steps can be taken to arrange for withdrawal and transfer of such deposits.

7. All monies and receipts of whatever nature are to be immediately

deposited in the debtor-in-possession general bank account. Transfers
are to be made from the general bank account to the tax and trust account,
or any other account, as required, in order to comply with the provision of the
enclosed court order and the instructions of this letter. Every check issued
by the debtor-in-possession must be so indicated. The printed statement
"(Debtor company), Debtor-in-Possession" is sufficient. Each check
must state on its face the purpose of the disbursement (e.g., invoice number,
transfer to payroll account, rent, etc.).

8. All monies deducted and withheld from the wages of employees
for federal taxes, specifically including withholding and social security
taxes, must be deposited in the debtor-in-possession tax account within 24
hours of the date of such withholding.

9. Federal income withholding taxes and all social security taxes,
including employees' deductions and employer's contributions, are to
be remitted, together with a federal depository receipt, via your bank no later
than the end of the second business day after the date of withholding
or deduction.

10. If the debtor-in-possession is required to collect any federal
excise taxes, you must specifically comply with paragraph 3 of the enclosed
order for payment of federal taxes.

11. One week after remittance of federal payroll taxes, together
with federal depository receipt as above, the debtor-in-possession is required
to complete and mail form NAR 2-13 to the Internal Revenue Service,
Special Procedures Section, New York City. You will receive a supply of these
forms directly from the Internal Revenue Service. Meanwhile use the
enclosures. If you have paid any federal payroll taxes by depository receipt
to date, complete one form NAR 2-13 for each such payment and mail
it immediately to the I.R.S. Special Procedures Section.

12. All other taxes, including other payroll taxes and taxes collected
from others, and all trust funds, must be deposited in the debtor-in-
possession tax and trust account. These deposits must be made as soon as
possible. Payroll taxes withheld from employees, union dues check off,
hospitalization deducted from employees' salaries and similar payroll
deductions must be deposited immediately upon distribution of the payroll.
Other required deposits in the tax and trust accounts are to be made
immediately upon completion of the computation of the tax or of the trust
fund, but in any event no later than one calendar week from the transaction
giving rise to the tax. This means that you must compute and deposit sales and
excise taxes within one week of the respective transactions, and in no
event later than once every week. You must compute employer contributory
payroll taxes (New York State Department of Labor, Unemployment
Insurance), and trust funds (union pension and welfare contributions and any
other funds which are to be held in trust) and deposit them within one
week of the transaction, and in any event at least once every week. Any
required taxes other than those which have been specified should be deposited

as soon as they are computed. All taxes, including federal payroll taxes, are to be reported to the respective taxing authorities on the regular tax return form, which must be filed on the regular due date. Form 941 for federal payroll tax will indicate thereon payment by federal depository receipt. Payment of all taxes other than federal payroll taxes is to be made with the return, when due, by checks drawn on the tax and trust account.

13. No obligations incurred prior to the filing date may be paid without an appropriate court order of authorization. This includes taxes, utilities, and debts of any character, excluding only wages entitled to priority that were earned within the seven days preceding the date of the filing of the Original Petition under Chapter XI.

14. Pursuant to rules of the court and the order of the Bankruptcy Judge the debtor-in-possession is required to file, by the 15th of each month, a verified statement of operations for the preceding calendar month, prepared on an accrual basis. The statement must include:

1. A balance sheet showing in detail all the assets and liabilities of the debtor-in-possession at the end of the calendar month.

2. A statement of income and expenses for the month, together with accumulated statements of operations, commencing with the date of the filing of the Original Petition.

In the preparation of the operating statement, no charge should be made for depreciation or interest on debts accrued prior to the filing of the petition.

The first monthly report must be filed on or before _____ *(date)* _____ for operations from _____ *(date)* _____ through _____ *(date)* _____, both dates inclusive. The reports are to be prepared in quadruplicate and three copies are to be signed and notarized as originals. I must receive the three executed copies no later than the thirteenth of next month and on the thirteenth of each succeeding month. A form is enclosed for your convenience.

15. I specifically direct your attention to the paragraphs enumerated 1 through 8 in the Judge's order authorizing the debtor-in-possession to operate its business. These paragraphs have in part been treated in detail in this letter. I repeat, however, that it is essential that these enumerated paragraphs, as well as every other provision of the enclosed orders, must be completely understood by all concerned officers and employees. I specifically direct your attention to the limitation on weekly purchases contained in paragraph 1, the requirement of maintenance of insurance, and the limitations upon the maintenance of the petty cash fund contained in paragraph 2.

16. The following transactions may not be engaged in by the debtor-in-possession unless specifically authorized in writing by the court:

(a) Borrowing money, (including accepting loans from employees and officers).

(b) Selling inventory or assets in bulk, as contrasted with sales in the regular course of business.

(c) Giving a security interest in assets for any purpose (security interest includes mortgage, pledge, assignments of accounts receivable, or actual physical transfer).

(d) Selling machinery, tools, fixtures, or equipment, except in certain specified cases approved by me.

Other than as limited by the provisions of the enclosed orders and the instructions of this letter, you as the debtor-in-possession are authorized to conduct the business in regular course; to purchase such merchandise, supplies and equipment, and to contract for such services, as are necessary; to pay for them in cash or on whatever credit terms can be arranged with the creditor; and to sell to, or perform services for customers.

Any sales made to, or services rendered to, the debtor-in-possession create administration expense claims, pursuant to Section 64 of the Bankruptcy Act. Such administration expense claims stand in first priority ahead of all claims incurred prior to the filing of the Original Petition under Chapter XI, including antecedent priority tax and wage claims. This should be made known to suppliers for their own protection, and your benefit in attempting to obtain credit for the debtor-in-possession. Purchases made by the debtor-in-possession must be paid when due, according to the terms of the purchase. The significance of this statutory priority to suppliers is that they are assured that in the event that the Chapter XI proceeding is not successful, they will be paid ahead of prior creditors, including antecedent priority tax and wage claims

If now or at any time there is any question in connection with the foregoing, or with the provisions of the enclosed orders, or with any other matter relating to the court proceedings, it is urgent that you call me immediately. If in doubt as to whether any specific proposed transaction is permissible, the details must be explained to me in advance.

Sincerely,

(name)

Attorney

Order, Petition and Accountant's Affidavit for Retention of Accountants to Perform an Insolvency Examination for a Creditors' Committee

UNITED STATES DISTRICT COURT
SOUTHERN DISTRICT OF NEW YORK
_____x

<table>
<tr><td>In the Matter</td><td>ORDER</td></tr>
<tr><td>of</td><td>No. 72 B 343</td></tr>
</table>

MILLER MECHANICAL DEVICES, INC.

_____Debtor.
_____x

   Upon reading and filing the annexed petition of the debtor-in-possession and upon the affidavit of Raymond T. Galen, duly sworn to the 30th day of May, 19--; it is on motion of Wolfson & Fisher, attorneys for the debtor-in-possession,

   ORDERED, that the debtor-in-possession be and it hereby is authorized to retain the services of Raymond T. Galen and company, CPAs, at compensation to be fixed upon application to this court.

Dated: New York, New York
   June 5, 19--.

              _____
                BANKRUPTCY JUDGE

UNITED STATES DISTRICT COURT
SOUTHERN DISTRICT OF NEW YORK

———————————————————————x

In the Matter	PETITION
of	No. 72 B 343

MILLER MECHANICAL DEVICE, INC.

Debtor.

———————————————————————x

TO THE HONORABLE ASA S. HERZOG, BANKRUPTCY JUDGE:

The petition of the debtor respectfully shows to this Court and alleges:

1. Petitioner filed a Chapter XI proceedings herein on March 30, 19--, pursuant to Section 322 of the Bankruptcy Act.

2. The debtor is engaged for the most part in the manufacture of fuzing and armament devices and acts as a general contractor for government defense contracts.

3. Annexed hereto and made a part hereof is an affidavit for retention of Raymond T. Galen & Co. as accountants for the debtor. The said Raymond T. Galen has never represented the debtor prior to the filing of its Chapter XI petition herein. The former accountants retained by the debtor prior to the filing of the petition have been terminated and it is necessary for the debtor to have independent certified accountants.

4. The Creditors' Committee has agreed to the retention by the debtor of Raymond T. Galen & Co. The amount to be paid for services to be rendered to the debtor is to be fixed upon application to the court.

5. The debtor is a publicly held corporation listed on the American Stock Exchange and is required to file reports with the Securities and Exchange Commission on a regular basis. It is necessary for the accountants to be retained by the debtor to review all financial statements and documents required to be submitted to the Securities and Exchange Commission.

6. The Court's attention is respectfully called to the fact that the Creditors' Committee has agreed to accept the accounting firm's report of its findings, in connection with the Chapter XI investigation which is normally required by a Creditors' Committee before it will negotiate a plan of settlement with the debtor.

7. The debtor verily believes that the retention of Raymond T. Galen & Co. is in its best interests.

WHEREFORE, the debtor respectfully prays for the relief set forth in the annexed Order.

Dated: New York, New York
     June 2, 19--.

Attorneys for Debtor
225 Broadway
New York, New York 10007

UNITED STATES DISTRICT COURT
SOUTHERN DISTRICT OF NEW YORK
_____x

<table>
<tr><td>In the Matter</td><td>AFFIDAVIT OF THE
ACCOUNTANT FOR THE</td></tr>
<tr><td>of</td><td>DEBTOR-IN-POSSESSION</td></tr>
<tr><td>MILLER MECHANICAL DEVICES, INC.</td><td>No. 72 B 343</td></tr>
<tr><td>Debtor.</td><td></td></tr>
</table>

_____x

STATE OF NEW YORK
CITY OF NEW YORK   } ss.:
COUNTY OF NEW YORK

Raymond T. Galen, being duly sworn, deposes and says:

That he is a Certified Public Accountant and a Partner of the firm of Raymond T. Galen & Co., Certified Public Accountants, maintaining offices at 420 Park Avenue South, New York City, New York.

That he was duly licensed to practice the profession of Certified Public Accountancy by the State of New York, on May 15, 1950.

That the members of deponent's firm are not related to and have no business relationship to, nor business association with any attorney, creditor, the debtor or any party to these proceedings and represents no interest adverse to the creditors or to this estate.

That your deponent has been retained on numerous occasions to investigate and make examinations of the affairs of insolvent debtors in various proceedings in the District Court for the Southern District of New York, and therefore has a wide familiarity with the scope of services to be rendered in this type of examination and investigation.

Your deponent has made a preliminary survey of the books and records in order to determine the extent and nature of the services to be rendered herein.

The services to be rendered include monthly reviews of the books and records of the debtor-in-possession and the supervision of the preparation of the monthly reports required under the rules of the Federal Court for the Southern District of New York.

In addition thereto, your deponent's firm will supervise the preparation of all tax reports and render whatever assistance is required by counsel and the officers of the debtor-in-possession in connection with the proposed arrangement proceeding.

Services will also include examination of the debtor's books and records from December 31, 19--, the date of a prior certified audit and will report the results of such investigation to the Creditors' Committee of the above captioned debtor.

The debtor is a public corporation listed on the American Stock Exchange. It is required to file various reports with the Securities and Exchange Commission which requires financial information. As part of the services to be rendered the firm will review all financial statements and documents required to be submitted to the Securities and Exchange Commission.

WHEREFORE, your deponent requests an Order of Retention providing for the above mentioned services.

_____

Sworn to before me this
    day of May, 19--.

Exhibit F

Authorization of Monthly Accounting Services

UNITED STATES DISTRICT COURT
EASTERN DISTRICT OF NEW YORK
_____x

In the Matter	PETITION, AFFIDAVIT AND
	ORDER FOR RETENTION OF
of	ACCOUNTANTS TO DEBTOR-
	IN-POSSESSION FOR MONTHLY
PEERLESS MANUFACTURING CORP.	ACCOUNTING SERVICES

Debtor.
_____x

     At Mineola, New York, in said District, on the 28th day of February, 1975.

     UPON the annexed petition of PEERLESS MANUFACTURING CORP., Debtor herein, dated February 24, 1975, and the affidavit of Stephen Stevens, of Stevens, Cary, & Williams, Certified Public Accountants, sworn to January 31, 1975, annexed hereto and made a part hereof, and upon all proceedings had and taken herein, it is

     ON MOTION of Smith & Duber, attorneys for the Debtor and Debtor-in-Possession,

     ORDERED, that PEERLESS MANUFACTURING CORP., as Debtor-in-Possession, be and it is hereby authorized to retain Stevens, Cary, & Williams, Certified Public Accountants of 125 E. 23rd Street, New York, N.Y., to make monthly examinations of the books and records of the Debtor-in-Possession and prepare the monthly operating statements as required by this Court and to perform the accounting services set forth in the annexed affidavit and the Debtor-in-Possession is authorized to pay said accountants the sum of not exceeding $250 per month in compensation of the performance by said accountants of said services.

CONSENTED TO:
GOLD, BROWNSTEIN & TAFT, ESQS.

           _____
                  Bankruptcy Judge

By: _____
     Attorneys for Creditors' Committee

UNITED STATES DISTRICT COURT
EASTERN DISTRICT OF NEW YORK _____ x

<table>
<tr><td>In the Matter
of

PEERLESS MANUFACTURING CORP.

_____ Debtor.
_____ x</td><td>PETITION</td></tr>
</table>

The petition of PEERLESS MANUFACTURING CORP. respectfully shows to this Honorable Court and alleges:

1. That your petitioner is the Debtor-in-Possession herein.

2. That at, prior to, and subsequent to the filing of the petition for arrangement herein, your petitioner was engaged in the business of manufacturing aluminum picture frames.

3. That prior to the filing of the petition for arrangement herein, your petitioner had employed Stevens, Cary & Williams, Certified Public Accountants, of 125 E. 23rd Street, New York, NY 10016 as its accountant and has continued to employ them on behalf of your petitioner as Debtor-in-Possession.

4. That the Creditors' Committee of the Debtor herein has approved the continuation of said accounting service by the aforesaid accounting firm.

5. That your petitioner will require the services of said accountants to assist it in the preparation and auditing of its books and records monthly and assist petitioner in preparing the necessary monthly statement of operations as required by this Court.

6. That your petitioner has been advised by said accountants as appears from the annexed affidavit of Stephen Stevens that said accountants estimate that their services will require $250.00 in accounting time per month for said services to be rendered, all of which are more particularly set forth in the aforesaid affidavit.

7. That your petitioner believes it to be for the best interests of the Creditors and the Debtor-in-Possession herein that it be authorized to employ the accountants for the aforesaid purpose.

WHEREFORE, your petitioner respectfully prays for the entry of the annexed order for which no previous application has been made.

DATED: Brooklyn, New York
February 24, 1975

PEERLESS MANUFACTURING CORP.

BY:_____
Charles Gold, Treas.

IN THE UNITED STATES DISTRICT COURT
FOR THE EASTERN DISTRICT OF NEW YORK
———————————————————————x

In the Matter	AFFIDAVIT OF THE
	ACCOUNTANT FOR THE
of	DEBTOR-IN-POSSESSION

PEERLESS MANUFACTURING CORP.

                    Debtor.

For Relief under Sec. 322 of the
    National Bankruptcy Act
———————————————————————x

STATE OF NEW YORK   ⎫
COUNTY OF NEW YORK ⎬ SS:
CITY OF NEW YORK   ⎭

STEPHEN STEVENS, being duly sworn,
deposes and says:

THAT he is a Certified Public
Accountant, and a member of the firm of Stevens, Cary & Williams, Certified
Public Accountants, maintaining offices at 125 E. 23rd Street, New York,
New York 10016.

THAT he was duly licensed to practice
the profession of Certified Public Accountancy by the State of New York,
on June 1, 1943.

THAT the members of deponent's firm
have no association with the debtor, its counsel, any attorney, creditor
nor any party to these proceedings, except that the firm of Stevens, Cary &
Williams may have been retained in similar proceedings to which any of the
aforesaid may be a party.

THAT he has been retained on numerous
occasions to investigate and make examinations of the affairs of debtors in
proceedings in the District Court for the Eastern District of New York, and
therefore has a wide familiarity with the matters to be inquired into in
the audits of debtors.

THAT your deponent has made a
preliminary survey of the books and records of the debtor to determine the
services to be rendered herein.

THAT your deponent proposes to
monthly, examine the books and records of the debtor-in-possession.

THAT these examinations will include a
preparation of monthly operating statements as provided for in the
order permitting the debtor to remain in possession.

THAT your deponent will review the preparation of the statements of cash receipts and disbursements required in this proceeding.

THAT your deponent proposes to prepare budgets and operating surveys.

It will be necessary to meet with counsel to the debtor and its officers and stockholders and their counsel and to appear before the Bankruptcy Judge in connection with the proceedings.

Your deponent estimates that there will be required $250.00 of accounting time per month for the services to be rendered therein.

Wherefore your deponent asks for an order of retention for monthly service in the amount of $250.00 payable upon completion of each monthly examinations.

_____

Sworn to before me this
31st day of January, 1975

_____ x
    Notary Public

Application and Order for Retention of Accountants for a Trustee in Bankruptcy

UNITED STATES DISTRICT COURT
SOUTHERN DISTRICT OF NEW YORK

———————————————————— x

In the Matter

of

TOURS TOUJOURS CORPORATION.

Bankrupt.

———————————————————— x

In Bankruptcy

No. 70 D 224

ORDER FOR RETENTION
OF ACCOUNTANT AS
ACCOUNTANT TO THE
TRUSTEE

Upon the annexed application of Thomas Mann, trustee, by his attorney, Gladys Rollins, and the affidavit of Robert J. Johnson, duly sworn to, and no adverse interest appearing, it is

ORDERED that Thomas Mann, as trustee, be and he hereby is authorized to employ Stevens, Cary & Williams, Certified Public Accountants, as accountants in this proceeding to perform the services set forth and described in the annexed application and affidavit at a maximum compensation of $2,500.00, the exact amount thereof to be fixed by the court upon the filing of a proper application therefor.

Dated: New York, New York
    January 1, 1970

_____H. Edward Brinks_____
Bankruptcy Judge

UNITED STATES DISTRICT COURT
SOUTHERN DISTRICT OF NEW YORK
_____x

In the Matter

of

TOURS TOUJOURS CORPORATION.

Bankrupt.
_____x

TO THE HONORABLE H. EDWARD BRINKS, BANKRUPTCY JUDGE:
 The application of Thomas Mann, trustee, by his attorney, Gladys Rollins, respectfully represents:

 1. That I am the trustee herein, duly qualified and acting.

 2. That the bankrupt was engaged in the business of operating a wholesale and retail travel agency and arranging tours at 250 Broadway, New York, N.Y.

 3. The trustee has collected approximately $20,000.00.

 4. Applicant believes that it is necessary in the best interests of the estate to have a complete examination of the books and accounts of the bankrupt and the debtor-in-possession for the following reasons:

 a) All operations, receipts and disbursements of the debtor-in-possession should be scrutinized in order that the assets of the debtor-in-possession at the date of the adjudication can be reconciled with the assets of the debtor at the date the Chapter XI was filed.

 b) Applicant has taken possession of the books of account of the debtor and debtor-in-possession which should be examined to ascertain what the assets and the liabilities of the estate are and in particular, to scrutinize any transfers or payments out of the ordinary course of business.

 c) Applicant is negotiating for the sale of certain property and capital stock in subsidiaries and for the collection of certain payments due under property, all of which require the assistance of an accountant regarding assets and liabilities of subsidiaries and accountings for money previously collected.

 d) Applicant may be required to file tax returns for which the assistance of an accountant is required.

 5. That by reason of the premises aforesaid, applicant desires to retain the services of Stevens, Cary & Williams to make the necessary examination and report. Said accountants are known to applicant to be experienced and knowledgeable in the field of public accounting and in particular, in the area of insolvency. Said accountants have advised applicant that the cost of the

proposed services would be $3,000.00. Applicant verily believes said proposed fee to be reasonable and proper.

WHEREFORE, applicant prays that an order be made authorizing the employment of Stevens, Cary & Williams as accountants at a maximum compensation of $3,000.00, the exact amount thereof to be fixed by the court upon the filing of a proper application therefor, for all of which no previous application has been made.

Dated: New York, New York
　　　　November 3, 1970　　　　　　　　　Gladys Rollins

　　　　　　　　　　　　　　　　　By:＿＿＿＿＿＿＿＿＿＿＿＿＿＿＿
　　　　　　　　　　　　　　　　　　　Bruce Bachers, a partner
　　　　　　　　　　　　　　　　　　　Attorney for Trustee

Examining Accountant's Report to a Creditors' Committee

FINANCIAL STATEMENTS
THE PENGUIN LAUNDRY, INC.
DEBTOR-IN-POSSESSION
January 1, 1972

CONTENTS

Whippet, Marcum & Company
Certified Public Accountants
238 Avenue of the Americas
New York, New York 10012

The Penguin Laundry, Inc.
Debtor-in-Possession
Brooklyn, New York

  The accompanying statement of assets and liabilities of The
Penguin Laundry, Inc., Debtor-in-Possession as of January 1, 1972, the related
statement of operations and accumulated deficit for the year then ended
and the supplemental information presented herein were not audited
by us, and accordingly we do not express an opinion on such statements and
information.

  The statements and information described above were prepared
solely for the purpose of assisting the company and counsel in formulating a
proposal to submit to creditors in connection with the pending Chapter
XI proceeding. Accordingly, the statements have been prepared on a
going-concern basis and the liabilities reflected in the accompanying statement
of assets and liabilities have been specially classified. Moreover, in
addition to the departures from generally accepted accounting principles
described in Notes 4 and 5 to the financial statements, the statement of changes
in financial position, which would ordinarily be required in accordance
with generally accepted accounting principles, has been omitted.

  The accompanying statements and supplemental information
should be considered in conjunction with the schedules filed in the Chapter
XI proceeding as well as the claims filed by creditors in that proceeding.

               Whippet, Marcum & Company

New York, New York
May 23, 1972

THE PENGUIN LAUNDRY, INC.
Debtor-in-Possession
STATEMENT OF ASSETS AND LIABILITIES
January 1, 1972
(unaudited)

ASSETS

Current Assets

Cash			$ 3,970
Accounts receivable (Note 2)			
Unbilled		$ 13,146	
Billed, less allowance for doubtful accounts of $2,723		100,141	113,287
Inventories (Note 3)			
Production supplies		62,499	
Linens in circulation		111,396	173,895
Prepaid expenses			8,840
Total current assets			299,992

Fixed Assets (Pledged) (Note 4)

Land and buildings		1,122,480	
Building equipment		275,551	
Machinery and equipment		251,668	
Furniture and fixtures		6,161	
Leasehold improvements		18,142	
Delivery equipment		6,300	
		1,680,302	
Less accumulated depreciation		686,894	993,408

Other Assets

Investment at amortized value—$22,000 New York City, 3% due 6/1/80 (held as deposit by New York State Industrial Commission)		22,500	
Due from Irving Heath (Note 7)		73,000	
Utility deposits		5,700	
Due from 2525 Prospect Avenue Corp. (Note 5)		16,000	
Deferred mortgage costs, net of amortization of $3,491 (Note 6)		66,328	
Cash—security deposit	$4,000		
Less security deposit payable	(4,000)	—	183,578
			$1,476,978

The accompanying notes are an integral part of this statement.

LIABILITIES

Collateralized Liabilities

11% mortgage payable, Sackman-Galliard Corporation (Note 7)		$ 589,095
Other (Note 8)		41,946
		631,041

Debtor-in-Possession Liabilities (Note 9)

Bank overdraft	$ 13,424	
Accounts payable	5,006	
Taxes payable	16,664	
Wages payable	16,568	
Accrued expenses	5,782	57,444
Debtor priority liabilities		
Taxes payable (subject to audit by taxing authorities)	26,559	
Wages and vacations payable (subject to claims for vacation and termination pay)	3,467	
Due to union—dues withheld from employees	3,618	
Other	4,488	38,132
General liabilities		
Accounts payable	425,250	
Employment contracts payable (Note 10)	12,029	
Due to the Greater New York Savings Bank or The Penguin Laundry, Inc. Employment Retirement Plan (Note 11)	80,000	
5% twenty-five year debentures (Note 12)	257,842	
Debenture bond subscription paid	1,919	
Due to Ralph W. Zinn (Note 13)	100,000	
Due to Julius Berman (Note 14)	25,108	902,148
		1,628,765

Contingencies (Note 18)

Deficit in Stockholders' Equity

Common stock—authorized, 80,000 shares, no par value; issued, 20,000 shares	200,000	
Capital contributed	41,205	
Appraisal surplus	590,304	
Accumulated deficit	(797,100)	
	34,409	
Less 7,161 shares of common stock in treasury—at cost	(186,196)	(151,787)
		$1,476,978

Subject to claims filed in the proceedings.

THE PENGUIN LAUNDRY, INC.
Debtor-in-Possession

STATEMENT OF OPERATIONS AND ACCUMULATED DEFICIT
Year ended January 1, 1972
(unaudited)

Sales		$1,983,097
Prime cost of sales		
Production labor	$512,053	
Production supplies and linens (Note 3)	191,297	703,350
Prime gross profit		1,279,747
Operating overhead		1,289,410
		(9,663)
Consulting fees (Note 17)	55,900	
Employment contract payments (Note 10)	71,869	
General and administrative expenses	320,987	
Interest expense	103,230	551,986
		(561,649)
Other income (includes rental income of $25,965)		28,565
Net loss before extraordinary item		(533,084)
Extraordinary item—excess of par value over cost of 5% twenty-five year debentures redeemed (Note 20)		110,170
NET LOSS		(422,914)
Accumulated deficit—January 3, 1971		(374,186)
Accumulated deficit—January 1, 1972		$ (797,100)

The accompanying notes are an integral part of this statement.

THE PENGUIN LAUNDRY, INC.
Debtor-in-Possession
NOTES TO FINANCIAL STATEMENTS
January 1, 1972
(unaudited)

NOTE 1—HISTORICAL INFORMATION

The company, which was incorporated under the laws of the State of
New York on June 25, 1894, is engaged in the laundry and dry cleaning
business for the retail trade and is providing linen services and
rentals to institutional customers.

Sales activities are conducted primarily in the New York metropolitan
area and customers are serviced via rented delivery vehicles.

Laundry and dry cleaning operations are conducted at the company's
owned premises at 2525 Prospect Avenue, Brooklyn, New York
and the company also owns garage premises at 8201 Woodfield Road,
West Hempstead, New York.

The company's president and chief executive officer is Mr. Ralph W. Zinn,
who assumed that office on November 22, 1971. Prior to that date
Mr. Isidore Heath was the company's president and Mr. Julius Berman,
secretary/treasurer.

On December 13, 1971, the company filed a petition for arrangement
under Chapter XI of the National Bankruptcy Act in the Eastern
District of New York. The matter was referred to the Honorable Joseph V.
Costa, Bankruptcy Judge, who thereafter continued the debtor-in-
possession.

At the date of the filing of the Chapter XI petition, the company's
stockholders were Ralph W. Zinn, Julius Berman and Isidore Heath,
each of whom owned one third of the company's outstanding common
shares (12,839 shares). Mr. Zinn acquired his shares in November,
1971 from Messrs. Heath and Berman, who had acquired the company's total outstanding shares on October 22, 1970, pursuant to the
terms of an escrow and purchase agreement.

Counsel to the company advises that as the result of various defaults
under the escrow and purchase agreement, the ownership of the shares
may be at issue.

NOTE 2—ACCOUNTS RECEIVABLE

Unbilled accounts receivable represent amounts invoiced to customers in
1972 for laundry and dry cleaning for the last week of December
1971.

NOTES TO FINANCIAL STATEMENTS (continued)

NOTE 2 (continued)

Billed accounts receivable consist principally of amounts due from
retail charge customers for weekly home delivery of laundry and dry
cleaning and include approximately $15,000 in amounts carried in
the name of the routemen or drivers.

The allowance for doubtful accounts is considered adequate by management
and is reflected at an amount equal to the company's accounts receivable write-offs for the year.

NOTE 3—INVENTORIES

Production supplies are reflected at cost less periodic adjustments for
consumption.

Linens in circulation are reflected at cost less amortization at the rate
of $1/12$ each month from the date of purchase of the linens. Amortization for
the period from May 1, 1971 (inception of linen rental operations)
to January 1, 1972 totalled $59,498.

NOTE 4—FIXED ASSETS

Fixed assets are reflected at book value which includes cost plus
an appraisal revaluation of $590,304 which was recorded prior to 1960.
Depreciation is computed at varying rates on the straight-line
method and is reflected in the same amount as recorded for the year
1970. No depreciation has been taken on 1971 fixed asset additions,
which approximated $68,000. In addition, as in prior years, no depreciation
has been reflected in the appraisal revaluation, a practice which is at
variance with generally accepted accounting principles.

NOTE 5—DUE FROM 2525 PROSPECT AVENUE CORP.

This represents advances to this corporation whose sole stockholders
are Julius Berman and Irving Heath (see Note 1), in connection with the
purchase in February 1971 of certain dry cleaning equipment for
the use of the company. The total purchase price to 2525 Prospect Avenue
Corp. was $47,000. After payment of the initial $16,000 deposit ad-
vanced by the company, the balance of $31,000 plus financing costs
aggregating $13,175 were to be paid in sixty monthly installments of
$763.25. The company has been paying $1,000 per month to 2525
Prospect Avenue Corp. which the company's records have reflected as
rent for the use of the equipment.

Pursuant to the terms of a purchase money security agreement, Northern
Commercial Corporation holds a lien against the equipment, and

NOTE 5 (continued)

Schedule A-2 in the Chapter XI proceeding reflects a $40,000 liability to that company. This liability is not reflected in the company's records or on the accompanying statement of assets and liabilities, a practice which is at variance with generally accepted accounting principles.

NOTE 6—DEFERRED MORTGAGE COSTS

These represent mortgage fees, closing costs and mortgage brokerage fees in connection with the first mortgage to Sackman-Galliard Corporation, which are being amortized over the fifteen year period of the mortgage.

NOTE 7—11% MORTGAGE, PAYABLE TO SACKMAN-GALLIARD CORPORATION

This mortgage is collateralized by land, buildings, fixtures and equipment, and is payable in monthly installments of $6,280, including interest. The final payment is due on February 1, 1986.

This mortgage was obtained on February 24, 1971. The principal amount was $600,000 and after the repayment of a previously existing mortgage, the net cash proceeds of $354,283.65 were deposited in the company's account at the Bankers Trust Company. However, the company's general ledger entry of that date reflected a cash receipt of $244,708.25 and the difference of $109,575 was charged to construction costs ($97,575) and prepaid expenses ($12,000).

At or around that time, the following five checks, totalling the identical $109,575 were issued and not recorded on the company's books:

Date (all 1971)	Check no.	Payee	Amount
February 25	356	Irving Heath*	$ 10,000
25	353	Isidore Heath	50,000
26	476	Isidore Heath	13,000
25	355	Julius Berman	24,500
25	354	First National Bank of Glen Head	12,075
			$109,575

As at October 31, 1971, subsequent to preliminary inquiry by Whippet, Marcum & Company, the previous charges to construction costs and prepaid expenses were eliminated and the loan accounts of Isidore

*Endorsed Irving Heath, Isidore Heath

NOTES TO FINANCIAL STATEMENTS (continued)

NOTE 7 (continued)

Heath and Julius Berman were charged for $73,000 and $36,575, respectively, by journal entry.

NOTE 8—OTHER COLLATERALIZED LIABILITIES

Other collateralized liabilities consist of the following:

Chattel mortgage payable—American Laundry Machinery Industries	$12,172
5% loan payable—Bankers Trust Company	18,123
Note payable—Manufacturers Hanover Trust Company	2,811
New York City water and sewer charges	8,840
	$41,946

The chattel mortgage is payable at the rate of $500 per month and is collateralized by a gas heater tumbler acquired by the company in May 1971 for $17,172. The 5% loan to Bankers Trust Company is collateralized by a second lien on the gas heater tumbler and is payable at $653.72 per month, including interest. The note to Manufacturers Hanover Trust Company is collateralized by the assignment of a subtenant's lease and was due and payable in December, 1971.

NOTE 9—DEBTOR-IN-POSSESSION LIABILITIES

These are obligations incurred by the debtor corporation subsequent to the filing, on December 13, 1971, of a petition for Reorganization under the National Bankruptcy Act (see Note 1).

NOTE 10—EMPLOYMENT CONTRACTS PAYABLE

At January 1, 1972, pursuant to the terms of employment contracts entered into at the time the company's stock was purchased by Messrs. Berman and Heath (see Note 1), the company was obligated to former stockholders in the amount of $12,029. In addition to this unpaid balance, payments to such stockholders during the year aggregated $59,840.

NOTE 11—DUE TO THE GREATER NEW YORK SAVINGS BANK
OR THE PENGUIN LAUNDRY, INC. EMPLOYMENT
RETIREMENT PLAN

This represents the balance due for loans made during 1971 secured by the pledge of a savings passbook of the Employment Retirement Plan. The company's schedules in the Chapter XI proceeding (see Note 1) indicate that the indebtedness is due to the savings bank. However, the schedule further indicates that the bank alleges that the loan

NOTE 11 (continued)

was made to the Retirement Plan. Accordingly, pending disposition of the matter, the financial statements list both creditors.

NOTE 12—SERIES B, 5% TWENTY-FIVE YEAR DEBENTURE

This represents the unpaid balance of an original issue of $780,000 issued in units of $26.00 or multiples thereof. These debentures were originally sold to employees and paid for by payroll deductions. The filing of the Chapter XI proceeding has accelerated the due date of the debentures, as set forth on the face of the debentures, which are all now due and payable.

NOTE 13—DUE TO RALPH W. ZINN

This represents non-interest-bearing loans made to the company in 1971 by an officer-stockholder (see Note 1).

NOTE 14—DUE TO JULIUS BERMAN

This represents non-interest-bearing loans made to the company in 1970 and 1971 by a stockholder and former officer (see Note 1) reduced by the journal entry discussed in Note 7.

NOTE 15—FEDERAL INCOME TAX STATUS

In 1971, the company elected to be taxed as a Subchapter S corporation, and accordingly will not benefit from net operating loss deductions for the year. In the event that the Subchapter S election is terminated, net operating loss carry-forwards in an amount which has not yet been determined may be available to the company.

NOTE 16—PURCHASES OF LINENS IN OCTOBER
        AND NOVEMBER, 1971

In October and November 1971, the company purchased approximately $104,000 of linens. The total of all linen purchases for 1971 approximated $171,000. The company's counsel has indicated that the creditors' committee approved the return to creditors of all linens shipped to the company subsequent to November 2, 1971. Approximately $27,000 of merchandise was returned to suppliers under this understanding.

NOTE 17—CONSULTING FEES

During the period March 1, 1971 to October 31, 1971, the following approximate weekly amounts of cash were withheld from the company's

NOTES TO FINANCIAL STATEMENTS (continued)

NOTE 17 (continued)

daily receipts and charged to various expenses on the company's books and records:

March 1, 1971 to May 10, 1971	$2,000
May 10, 1971 to June 15, 1971	1,500
June 15, 1971 to October 31, 1971	1,050

As at October 31, 1971, subsequent to preliminary inquiry by Whippet, Marcum & Company, the company recorded the following journal entry which reclassified the various expenses and charged the aggregate amount to consulting fees:

Debit	
Consulting fees	$55,900.09
Credit	
Production supplies	$ 297.00
Repairs	2,156.05
Plant cleaning	430.18
Machinery repairs	1,403.24
Factory expenses	850.50
Welfare	2,837.12
Receiving and shipping	638.96
Collection and delivery	4,246.23
Auto rental	445.72
West Hempstead auto expenses	1,425.72
Sales promotion	10,595.31
Discounts and commissions	6,535.06
Office expenses	8,095.17
Postage	3,268.00
Professional expenses	581.00
Executive office expense	8,299.70
General expense	3,795.13

During the month of November 1971, cash withheld from receipts and charged to various expense accounts approximated $4,000. There was no journal entry reclassifying these items.

NOTE 18—CONTINGENCIES

(a) Schedule A-2 filed by the company in the Chapter XI proceeding (see Note 1) reflects the following liabilities which are not recorded in the company's books or included in the accompanying financial statements:

Chase Manhattan Bank—lease agreement covering equipment leased (with option to purchase) from Tiddy Equipment Leasing	$ 8,950
Northern Commercial Corporation—secured by lien on machine originally sold to 2525 Prospect Avenue Corp. (see Note 5)	40,000

(b) Schedule A-3 to the Chapter XI proceeding reflects the following suit pending against the company in the amount of $350,000:

The company together with Julius Berman and Isidore Heath (see Note 1) commenced an action in New York State Supreme Court, County of Nassau, against Malcolm Koenigsberg and Leonard Cohen in the amount of $150,000 for damages sustained as the result of the defendants' failure to lend $250,000 to the company for working capital. The amended complaint recites that the defendants were each to receive a 12½% interest in the company in exchange for this loan. The defendants have denied liability and have brought countersuit for $350,000 alleging, among other matters, the following:

1. That each owned 12½% of the company's stock.

2. That the individual plaintiffs withheld various sums from the company's cash receipts.

3. That the individual plaintiffs received kickbacks from various of the company's suppliers.

4. That the individual plaintiffs used cars made available to them by the company for their own use and the use of their families.

5. That the individual plaintiffs donated certain assets of the company to 2525 Prospect Avenue Corp.

6. That the company sustained losses in excess of $350,000 for which the defendants hold the plaintiffs responsible.

7. That the company employed Harvey Berman, brother of Julius Berman, and Peter Heath, son of Isidore Heath in a manner which was detrimental to the company's affairs.

8. That various other acts were committed which were improper and were to the company's detriment.

The plaintiffs have orally indicated that they deny the allegations. Although the company has included in Schedule A-3 the sum of $350,000 as a contingent liability, suit pending, counsel has advised that the counterclaim is not against the company and that Schedule A-3 will be amended.

NOTES TO FINANCIAL STATEMENTS (continued)

NOTE 18 (continued)

(c) Schedule B-3 to the Chapter XI proceeding reflects the following pending legal actions wherein the company is involved:

Julius Berman, Isidore Heath and Penguin Laundry, Inc. v. Malcolm Koenigsberg and Leonard Cohen (Subject to counterclaim—see above)	$150,000
Penguin Laundry, Inc. v. Realm Printing Corp. (suit to recover overcharge—a counterclaim of $1,609 has been made)	6,944
Harold Borman and Bertram Hill, Esq. v. Penguin Laundry, Inc. (breach of employment contract—a counterclaim of $50,000 has been interposed against Mr. Borman)	20,000

NOTE 19—CERTAIN TRANSACTIONS

(a) Possible preferential payment to Bankers Trust Company

In August 1971, the company borrowed $50,000 from the Bankers Trust Company. The debt was subsequently repaid by the payment of $20,000 in October 1971 and $30,000 in November 1971.

(B) Officers' salaries

The following disbursements were charged to officers' salaries during the year:

Julius Berman	$6,400
Irving Heath	6,600
Ralph W. Zinn	2,550

(c) Professional fees

The following disbursements were among those included in professional fees:

Julius Berman	$7,700
Irving Heath	5,400
Wives of Mr. Berman, Mr. Ross Messrs. Heath and Koenigsberg	1,400

NOTE 19 (continued)

(d) Payments to Julius Berman in November 1971

The following checks were drawn to the order of Julius Berman in November 1971:

Date	Check no.	Amount	Account charged
November 12, 1971	892	$2,500	Professional services
November 26, 1971	534	1,150	Machinery and equipment expenses
November 26, 1971	433	850	Repairs (building overhead)

(e) Other disbursements which may require further inquiry:

Date	Check no.	Payee	Amount	Charged to
June 24, 1971	1282	Dr. Elliot Feinstein	$ 975.00	Repairs and maintenance
June 4, 1971	1219	Harvey Berman	150.00	Linen supply
April 30, 1971	1007	Harvey Berman	150.00	Linen supply
February 26, 1971	459	Realm Printing Co.	15,274.72	Printing
February 25, 1971	354	First National Bank of Glen Head	12,075.00	Construction costs*

NOTE 20—EXTRAORDINARY ITEM

During the year the company redeemed $140,920 of its 5% twenty-five-year debentures from the holders thereof at a cost of $30,749. The resulting difference between the face value of the redeemed debentures, and the cost of redemption has been reflected in the statement of operations and accumulated deficit as an extraordinary credit.

---

*Transferred by journal entry as a charge to loan payable, Julius Berman as of October 31, 1971 (see Note 7).

SUPPLEMENTAL INFORMATION

THE PENGUIN LAUNDRY, INC.
Debtor-in-Possession
SUPPORTING SCHEDULES
Year ended January 1, 1972
(unaudited)

Operating overhead	
Superintendent labor	$ 62,576
Indirect labor	86,947
Power plant labor	14,231
Power expense	79,512
Building overhead (including depreciation of $24,595)	81,252
Machinery overhead (including depreciation of $17,900)	40,942
Factory expenses	29,359
Factory labor	28,637
Welfare and pension costs	94,965
Payroll taxes	81,170
Workmen's compensation	24,786
Labor—routemen	329,955
Collection and delivery expenses (including depreciation of $342)	304,600
Vacation payroll	30,478
Total operating overhead	$1,289,410
General and administrative expenses	
Officers' salaries	$ 15,550
Sales promotion	27,155
Claims	20,508
Claim department expenses	9,953
Office salaries	82,615
Office expenses (including depreciation of $383)	32,957
Bad debts	3,600
Professional fees	53,976
Executive office payroll and expenses	30,209
Other taxes	712
General expenses	43,752
Total general and administrative expenses	$ 320,987

Exhibit I

Examining Accountant's Report to a Trustee in Bankruptcy

TENTATIVE FINANCIAL STATEMENTS
LOEMAN MACHINERY CO., INC., BANKRUPT
November 8, 1972

CONTENTS

Exhibit I **219**

WITTE SILVER & CO.
Certified Public Accountants

Jay M. Halpert, Esq.
Trustee in Bankruptcy of
Loeman Machinery Co., Inc., Bankrupt

The tentative balance sheet of Loeman Machinery Co., Inc., Bankrupt, as of November 8, 1972, and the related tentative statements of excess of costs, expenses and other charges over revenue and other credits for the periods from June 19, 1970 to November 8, 1972, and the supplemental information presented herein were not audited by us, and accordingly we do not express an opinion on such statements and information.

The statements and supplemental information referred to above were prepared solely for the purpose of assisting you in the liquidation of Loeman Machinery Co., Inc. Accordingly, the accompanying financial statements do not purport to present financial position and results of operations, in conformity with generally accepted accounting principles.

The books and records of the bankrupt were incomplete. The following data and records were not available:

>General ledger for the period June 19, 1971
>>to June 17, 1972
>
>Bank statement and cancelled vouchers for
>>October 1972
>
>Bank reconciliations for the period June 1972
>>to September 1972
>
>Contract files
>
>Rent lease agreement
>
>Corporation income tax returns and franchise
>>tax returns for 1970 and 1971

The bankrupt did not maintain subsidiary ledgers for accounts receivable and accounts payable nor were any detailed analyses found in the debtor's files for notes receivable held for collection, loans payable and exchanges. The tentative schedules of accounts receivable, accounts payable, loans payable, exchanges receivable and exchanges payable were prepared by analyses of the detail of the total cash postings to these accounts and by reference to data, such as sales invoices, unpaid invoices on hand, etc.

Accordingly, all statements and schedules included in this report should be considered as tentative and subject to further adjustment.

Witte Silver & Co.

New York, New York
March 15, 1973

LOEMAN MACHINERY CO., INC., BANKRUPT
TENTATIVE BALANCE SHEET
November 8, 1972
(unaudited)

ASSETS

Current Assets

Cash in bank—tax account				$ 13
Receivable arising from sale of office furniture and fixtures				342
Merchandise inventory (stated at auction proceeds) (Note 2)				12,598
Notes receivable held for collection		$12,107		
Less estimated uncollectibles		11,722		385
Accounts receivable				21,165
Notes receivable—uncollectible (Note 8)				—

Fixed Assets (Note 3)

	Cost	Accumulated depreciation	Net	
Land and building	$35,856	$21,342	$14,514	
Automobile (1968 Oldsmobile)	3,736	1,801	1,935	
	$39,592	$23,143		16,449

Other Assets

Deposits receivable			1,079	
Exchanges receivable			12,356	13,435

				$64,387

The accompanying notes are an integral part of this statement.

Exhibit I **221**

LIABILITIES

*Secured Liabilities Incurred Prior to Debtor-in-
Possession Period*

Mortgage payable to Ida Greenfield (Note 3) (collateralized by land and building)	$ 20,000	
Interest payable on above mortgage	1,800	$ 21,800

Liability Incurred Prior to Debtor-in-Possession Period

Due to Leasing Service Corp. and Walter Heller & Co. (collateralized by inventory, machinery and equipment) (Note 3)	133,039

*Priority and General Liabilities Incurred During
Debtor-in-Possession Period—June 19, 1970 to
November 8, 1972:*

Priority liabilities			
Taxes payable		1,247	
General liabilities			
Due to Merchants Bank of N. Y. (overdraft) (Note 4)	$ 4,240		
Accounts payable	5,637		
Loans payable	2,400		
Exchanges payable	14,173	26,450	27,697

*Priority and General Liabilities Incurred Prior to
Debtor-in-Possession Period*

Priority liabilities			
Taxes payable		665	
General liabilities			
Due to Bankers Trust Company (overdraft)	22,605		
Accounts payable	33,686		
Notes payable to Ford Motor Corp.	317		
Due on defaulted equipment leases ("S & K")	26,500		
Liabilities as guarantor or endorser of "Vitra" and "S & K" indebtedness	233,160		
Due to National Bank of North America	17,405	333,673	334,338

Due to Officers	32,188

Due to Related Company—Brothers Industries Corp. (Note 5)	10,946

Deficit in Stockholders' Equity

Balance—June 18, 1970—as previously reported	(430,455)	
Adjusted to restate liabilities	10,000	
As restated	(420,455)	
Accumulated deficit—June 19, 1970 to November 8, 1972	(75,166)	(495,621)
		$ 64,387

LOEMAN MACHINERY CO., INC., BANKRUPT

TENTATIVE STATEMENTS OF EXCESS OF COSTS, EXPENSES AND OTHER CHARGES OVER REVENUE AND OTHER CREDITS

(unaudited)

	Period June 19, 1970 to June 17, 1971		Period June 18, 1971 to June 17, 1972		Period June 18, 1972 to November 8, 1972	
Revenue and other credits						
Sales		$ 99,808		$129,948		$ 2,176
Adjustment of accounts receivable control account						2,687
Unidentified receipts (Note 6)		795				
		100,603		129,948		4,863
Costs, expenses, other charges and other income						
Cost of goods sold						
Inventory—opening	$ 76,142		$ 57,754		$75,043	
Purchases	32,457		78,245		1,789	
	108,599		135,999		76,832	
Less inventory—end (Note 2)	57,754		75,043		12,598*	
Cost of goods sold		50,845		60,956		64,234
Gross profit (loss)		49,758		68,992		(59,371)
Gross profit percentage		(49.5%)		(53.1%)		—
Operating expenses						
Selling	3,451		10,839		1,064	
General and administrative	56,259	59,710	58,511	69,350	19,687	20,751
		(9,952)		(358)		(80,122)
Other charges						
Loss sustained on Lincoln automobile (wrecked)				(3,246)		
Loss on office furniture and fixtures sold at auction						(434)
Other income						
Leasing, appraisal and commission income		13,011	5,935	2,689		
Excess of costs, expenses and other charges over revenue and other credits		$ 3,059		$ 2,331		$(80,556)
Accumulated deficit for the period from June 19, 1970 to November 8, 1972						$(75,166)

*Stated at net auction proceeds.
The accompanying notes are an integral part of these statements.

Exhibit I **223**

LOEMAN MACHINERY CO., INC., BANKRUPT
NOTES TO TENTATIVE FINANCIAL STATEMENTS
November 8, 1972
(unaudited)

NOTE 1—HISTORICAL COMMENTS

Loeman Machinery Co., Inc. was incorporated in New York State in January 1960. The company, located at 176 Grand Street, New York, New York, was engaged as a dealer in used machinery.

The president was Joseph Loeman, 21 East 73rd Street, Brooklyn, New York. The secretary was Nicholas Loeman, 165-15 86th Street, Howard Beach, New York.

On June 18, 1970 the company petitioned for relief under Chapter XI, Section 321 of the Bankruptcy Act.

The debtor was continued in possession to November 8, 1972 on which date the company was formally adjudicated a bankrupt.

NOTE 2—MERCHANDISE INVENTORY

The net proceeds realized on the auction sales of the inventory on January 11, 1973 consists of the following:

Gross	$14,773
Prorated auctioneer's expenses	2,175
Net proceeds	$12,598

Inventory at November 8, 1972 approximated $74,551 calculated as follows:

Inventory at June 18, 1972		$75,043
Purchases		1,789
		76,832
Less sales (including adjustment of accounts receivable control account of $2,687 which was considered as sales for purpose of inventory computation)	$4,863	
Deduct 53.1% which represents the gross profit percentage per tentative statement of operations for the year ended June 17, 1972	2,582	
Cost of sales		2,281
Computed inventory at November 8, 1972		$74,551

Based on the above, approximately 20% of the computed inventory before applicable auction expenses was realized on the sale.

NOTES TO TENTATIVE FINANCIAL STATEMENTS (continued)

NOTE 2 (continued)

For the period June 18, 1972 to November 8, 1972 the bankrupt's books and records reflect only the following two sales:

July	17, 1972	Transco Envelope Co.	$1,500
August	9, 1972	Ampco Printing Advertisers Offset Co.	
		(cash sale)	618
			$2,118

Inventory listings were not located. No sales journal postings were made after July 17, 1972.

NOTE 3—FIXED ASSETS

The attorney for the trustee has indicated that the land and building located at 148 Baxter Street, New York, New York are being held for future sale. It is subject to a $20,000 mortgage payable to Ida Greenfield of 2250 East 4th Street, Brooklyn, New York, and may be subject to other liens by Leasing Service Corp. and Walter Heller & Co. The sole tenant of the Baxter Street property is Zeisel Machinery Co., Inc. Zeisel Machinery Co., Inc. is also the landlord of Loeman Machinery Co., Inc. at 176 Grand Street, New York, New York. The trustee's attorney has indicated that rents are collected from Zeisel Machinery Co., Inc. at 148 Baxter Street under an arrangement for an adjusted rental for the 176 Grand Street building.

The auto has not been disposed of. The official auctioneers, Underwriters Salvage Co. of N.Y., have indicated that the auto is located at Jerry's Auto Parts, 135-26 Cross Bay Boulevard, Ozone Park, New York.

Exhibit I **225**

NOTE 4—DUE TO MERCHANTS BANK OF NEW YORK (OVERDRAFT)

The bank balances were not reconciled to the books at November 8, 1972 because of the unavailability of the October 1972 bank statement and cancelled vouchers.

NOTE 5—DUE TO RELATED COMPANY—BROTHER INDUSTRIES CORP.

The records of the debtor indicate that Mr. Joseph Loeman owned or controlled Brother Industries Corp.

NOTE 6—UNIDENTIFIED RECEIPTS—$795.00

Represents cash received on December 1, 1970 and credited to the accounts receivable account without specifying the name of the customers.

NOTE 7—OFFICERS' SALARIES

Officers' salaries were continuously drawn for the 16-week period from June 18, 1972 to October 6, 1972 at the rate of $300.00 per week for Mr. Joseph Loeman and at the rate of $250.00 per week for Mr. Nicholas Loeman. Sales for the period from June 18, 1972 to November 8, 1972 amounted to $2,176.00.

NOTE 8—NOTES RECEIVABLE—UNCOLLECTIBLE

Notes receivable—uncollectible are indicated to amount to $1,119,789.

Exhibit I **227**

SUPPLEMENTAL INFORMATION

LOEMAN MACHINERY CO., INC., BANKRUPT
TENTATIVE SCHEDULE OF NOTES RECEIVABLE HELD FOR COLLECTION
November 8, 1972
(unaudited)

	Balance November 6, 1972	Estimated uncollectible at June 18, 1970	Balance estimated collectible November 8, 1972
Abacus Electronics	$ 1,885		$ 1,885
Control Welding	5,950	$ 5,950	
Micron Dynamics	3,132	4,632	(1,500)*
New Jersey Production Engineering	1,140	1,140	
	$12,107	$11,722	$ 385

*$4,632 was balance at June 18, 1970, all of which was estimated uncollectible at that time. $1,500 was collected thereafter.

LOEMAN MACHINERY CO., INC., BANKRUPT

TENTATIVE SCHEDULE OF ACCOUNTS RECEIVABLE

November 8, 1972
(unaudited)

Name	*Address*
Conumatic Corp.	2099 Jericho Turnpike, New Hyde Park, New York
Ball Machine Co., Inc.	West Street, Barre, Massachusetts 01005
T. Bonanno & Co.	19 Welse Road, Essex Falls, New Jersey
Servo Components, Inc.	10 Hudson Terrace, Dobbs Ferry, New York
Connecticut Laser Co.	28 Maple Row, Bethel, Connecticut
Ace Welding Corp.	116 8th Street, Brooklyn, New York
Fairfield Graphics, Inc.	1275 Bloomfield Avenue, Fairfield, New Jersey
Clarified Air, Inc.	50 Riverside Drive, New York, New York
Best Supply	1 Maple Street, East Rutherford, New Jersey
MicroWave Industries, Inc.	116 8th Street, Brooklyn, New York
Shapes Unlimited, Ltd.	15 River Drive, Garfield, New Jersey
Radial Tool Co.	199 Centre Street, New York, New York
Merrimac Machine Co.	230 N. Windsor Avenue, Narberth, Pennsylvania
Rhondo Machine Industries, Inc.	31-25 45th Street, Long Island City, New York
Rhondo Manufacturing, Inc.	31-25 45th Street, Long Island City, New York
Stratford Machinery Corp.	Stratford, Connecticut

Exhibit I **229**

Amount	Per bankrupt's schedules	
$ 94.50		
1,850.00	$ 1,850.00	
2,240.00		
1,800.00		
	2,400.00	
815.00		
1,347.26	2,700.00	("Discounted at Merchants Bank")
2,000.00		
	2,000.00	("Discounted at Merchants Bank")
100.00		
1,500.00		
30.00		
2,750.00		
2,000.00		
3,888.07	4,000.00	
	2,000.00	("Discounted at Merchants Bank")
750.00		
$21,164.83	$14,950.00	

LOEMAN MACHINERY CO., INC., BANKRUPT
TENTATIVE SCHEDULE OF NOTES RECEIVABLE—
UNCOLLECTIBLE
November 8, 1972
(unaudited)

Vitra Instrument & Electronics Corp. (loans)		$ 347,328
Accur-Tronics, Inc. (sale of Vitra)	$208,764	
Accur-Tronics, Inc. (loans)	54,322	263,086
S & K Machine & Tool Corp. (loans)		52,526
Precision Ultrasonics Corp. (loans)		85,952
Bonadonna Instrument Co. (loans)		70,000
All Mill Supply Corp. (loans)		28,502
Rooster Plastics, Inc. (loans)		172,600
Intertech Industries, Inc., Bankrupt (loans)		98,534
Armand Marcucilli		1,261
		$1,119,789

Exhibit I **231**

LOEMAN MACHINERY CO., INC., BANKRUPT
TENTATIVE SCHEDULE OF DEPOSITS RECEIVABLE
November 8, 1972
(unaudited)

Name	Address	Amount
Consolidated Edison Co. of New York	4 Irving Place, New York New York	$ 75
Eastern Air Lines, Inc.	P.O. Box 252, Church Street Station, New York, New York	425
New York Telephone Co.	P.O. Box 387, Church Street Station, New York, New York	400
Waldorf Auto Leasing, Inc.	1712 East 9th Street, Brooklyn, New York	179
		$1,079

Subject to creditors' claims.

LOEMAN MACHINERY CO., INC., BANKRUPT
TENTATIVE SCHEDULE OF EXCHANGES RECEIVABLE
November 8, 1972
(unaudited)

Advance Machinery Exchange Joint Venture	$ 661
Carlson Industries	100
Henry F. Meola	942
Michael E. Meola	614
Alfred Merolla	8,889
Louis Savotok	150
Alexander Thohuries	1,000
	$12,356

Exhibit I **233**

LOEMAN MACHINERY CO., INC., BANKRUPT

TENTATIVE SCHEDULE OF TAXES PAYABLE

For period of Debtor-in-Possession
June 19, 1970 to November 8, 1972
(unaudited)

District Director of Internal Revenue (withholding taxes and F.I.C.A. taxes)		$ 513
New York State Income Tax Bureau (withholding taxes)		95
New York State Unemployment Insurance Fund		36
New York State Sales Tax Bureau		234
New York State Corporation Tax Bureau (franchise taxes)		225
New York City Department of Finance		
Withholding taxes	$94	
Corporation income tax	50	144
		$1,247

LOEMAN MACHINERY CO., INC., BANKRUPT
TENTATIVE SCHEDULE OF ACCOUNTS PAYABLE
For period of Debtor-in-Possession
June 19, 1970 to November 8, 1972
(unaudited)

Name	Address	Amount	Per bankrupt's schedules
Alba Carting Co.	540 Hungry Harbor Road, No. Woodmere, New York	$ 100.00	$ 100.0
American Oil Co.	165 North Canal Street, Chicago, Illinois	25.62	25.6
American Paper Towel Corp.	303 West 42nd Street, New York, New York	20.55	20.5
Angelo Restaurant	146 Mulberry Street, New York, New York	180.65	180.6
Apeco	2100 West Dempster Street, Evanston, Illinois	34.36	34.3
Arrow Office & Window Cleaning Co.	231 Centre Street, New York, New York	111.36	111.3
Con Edison Co.	4 Irving Place, New York, New York	400.00	400.0
The Drawing Board	256 Regal Row, Dallas, Texas		17.9
Federal Machinery Corp.	134 Grand Street, New York, New York	400.00	
Garguilo's Restaurant	215 Centre Street, New York, New York	41.70	41.7
Grand Machinery Exchange, Inc.	245 Centre Street, New York, New York	300.00	900.0
Hamburg Machinery Co.	189 Centre Street, New York, New York		8,750.0
Headquarters Tavern	174 Grand Street, New York, New York	129.31	129.31
New York Telephone Co.	P.O. Box 387, Church Street Station, New York, New York	500.00	500.0
176 Grand St. Corp.	208 Centre Street, New York, New York	1,950.00	1,950.0
Robert Rosenberger	43 Bronx River Road, New York, New York	200.00	200.0
Shoham Tool Co.	215 Centre Street, New York, New York		1,200.0
Texaco Oil Co.	P.O. Box 2000, Bellaire, Texas	97.28	97.28
Travelers Insurance Co.	80 John Street, New York, New York	168.25	
Eugene A. Zerdin Insurance	105 Remsen Street, Brooklyn, New York	978.00	978.0
Zeisel Machinery Co.	208 Centre Street, New York, New York		765.0
		$5,637.08	$16,401.73

Exhibit I **235**

LOEMAN MACHINERY CO., INC., BANKRUPT

TENTATIVE SCHEDULE OF LOANS PAYABLE

For period of Debtor-in-Possession
June 19, 1970 to November 8, 1972
(unaudited)

55 Building Corp.	$2,000
Henry I. Zeisel	400
	$2,400

LOEMAN MACHINERY CO., INC., BANKRUPT
TENTATIVE SCHEDULE OF EXCHANGES PAYABLE
For period of Debtor-in-Possession
June 19, 1970 to November 8, 1972
(unaudited)

Advance Machinery Exchange	$ 3,172
Carney Machinery Company (joint venture)	539
Centre Machinery	1,033
Connecticut Microwave	348
Gallo Pet Supply	2,000
Charles H. Gimple	718
Louis Ribble	200
Salvatore Sorisi	1,200
"Smith"	2,975

Unidentified cash receipts credited
  by Bankrupt to exchanges payable:

1972			
Jan.	9	$ 25.28	
	11	273.09	
	14	96.80	
	15	300.00	
Aug.	15	18.56	
	28	9.18	
	8	276.30	
		278.67	
		280.97	
		300.12	
Sept.	19	178.25	
	19	(50.00)	1,988
			$14,173

Exhibit I **237**

LOEMAN MACHINERY CO., INC., BANKRUPT

TENTATIVE SCHEDULE OF TAXES PAYABLE

For period prior to Debtor-in-Possession
November 8, 1972
(unaudited)

New York State Unemployment Insurance Fund	$ 50
New York State Sales Tax Bureau	202
New York State Corporation Tax Bureau (franchise taxes)	25
New York City Department of Finance (New York City real estate taxes)	388
	$665

LOEMAN MACHINERY CO., INC., BANKRUPT

TENTATIVE SCHEDULE OF ACCOUNTS PAYABLE

For period prior to Debtor-in-Possession
November 8, 1972
(unaudited)

Name	Address	Amount
Arrow Office & Window Cleaning Co.	231 Centre Street, New York, New York	$ 113.44
Armstrong-Blum Manufacturing Co.	5700 W. Bloomingdale Avenue, Chicago, Illinois	150.89
Alba Carting Co.	540 Hungry Harbor Road, N. Woodmere, New York	45.00
United Air Lines, Inc.	277 Park Avenue, New York, New York	328.55
American Airlines, Inc.	633 Third Avenue, New York, New York	44.10
Brown & Bigelow—Dept. 31	216120 Quality Park, St. Paul, Minnesota	46.16
A. C. Colby Machinery Co., Inc.	226 E. Jericho Turnpike, Mineola, New York	18.63
Center Detective Bureau	5 Centre Market Place, New York, New York	22.00
Eastern Air Lines, Inc.	P.O. Box 252, Church Street Station, New York, New York	266.59
Farber Corp. Machinery Movers, Inc.	132 Washington Avenue, Brooklyn, New York	100.00
New York City Fire Department	110 Church Street, New York, New York	10.00
Industrial Machinery News	16171 Meyers Road, Detroit, Michigan	517.00
J. B. Sales Co., Inc.	314 Main Street, Ft. Lee, New Jersey	180.00
John E. Knetzer, Jr.	90-14 161st Street, Jamaica, New York	2,000.00
Lightning Cleaner Corp.	2940 Ocean Parkway, Brooklyn, New York	19.50
Montes Venetian Room	451 Carroll Street, Brooklyn, New York	46.00
Martin Manufacturing Co.	707 S. Market Street, Wilmington, Delaware	65.00
Mobil Oil Corp.	150 E. 42nd Street, New York, New York	35.81
New York Telephone Co.	P.O. Box 387, Church Street Station, New York, New York	93.97
Morty Nathan	70-19 174th Street, Flushing, New York	50.00
Patron Transmission Co., Inc.	129 Grand Street, New York, New York	16.08
Max Shur, Inc.	165 Grand Street, New York, New York	18.42
Standard Oil Co.	Louisville, Kentucky	163.25
Sol Tool Co., Inc.	164 Lafayette Street, New York, New York	256.05
Star Sheet Metal Machinery, Inc.	216 Lafayette Street, New York, New York	1,000.00
Used Equipment Directory, Inc.	70 Sip Avenue, Jersey City, New Jersey	247.80
Villa Pensa	198 Grand Street, New York, New York	424.35
Waldorf Auto Leasing, Inc.	1712 E. 9th Street, Brooklyn, New York	357.00
Zeisel Machinery Co., Inc.	148 Baxter Street, New York, New York	1,050.79
Jude Tooling Corp.	102 Wavel Avenue, Syracuse, New York	13,000.00
Apex Screw Machine Products	2550 West 13th Street, Brooklyn, New York	13,000.00
		$33,686.38

Exhibit I **239**

LOEMAN MACHINERY CO., INC., BANKRUPT

TENTATIVE SCHEDULE OF LIABILITIES DUE ON DEFAULTED EQUIPMENT LEASES—"S & K"

For period prior to Debtor-in-Possession
November 8, 1972
(unaudited)

James Talcott, Inc.	$20,000
General Electric Credit Corp.	6,500
	$26,500

LOEMAN MACHINERY CO., INC., BANKRUPT

TENTATIVE SCHEDULE OF LIABILITIES AS GUARANTOR OR ENDORSER OF "VITRA" AND "S & K" INDEBTEDNESS

For period prior to Debtor-in-Possession
(November 8, 1972
(unaudited)

Joseph Bonanno	$ 27,607
Commercial Capital Corp.	63,395
Zeisel Machinery Co.	65,989
Hamburg Machinery Co.	64,169
L & F Co.	12,000
	$233,160

Exhibit I **241**

LOEMAN MACHINERY CO., INC., BANKRUPT
TENTATIVE SCHEDULE OF LIABILITY DUE TO NATIONAL BANK OF NORTH AMERICA
For period prior to Debtor-in-Possession
November 8, 1972
(unaudited)

Balance—September 1, 1970*		$54,605
Less		
Estimated notes held for collection	$10,000	
825 shares Western Union stock as collateral		
(at market)	27,200	37,200
		$17,405

*Represents $27,000 loans on securities plus returned notes from S & K Tool & Machine Co.

LOEMAN MACHINERY CO., INC., BANKRUPT
TENTATIVE SCHEDULE OF LOANS DUE TO OFFICERS
November 8, 1972
(unaudited)

Joseph Loeman	$29,037
Nicholas Loeman	3,151
	$32,188

LOEMAN MACHINERY CO., INC., BANKRUPT
TENTATIVE SCHEDULES OF SELLING AND GENERAL AND ADMINISTRATIVE EXPENSES
(unaudited)

	Period June 19, 1970 to June 17, 1971	Period June 18, 1971 to June 17, 1972	Period June 18, 1972 to November 8, 1972
Selling expenses			
Commissions	$ 325	$ 4,825	
Advertising	112	10	
Automobile and delivery	1,865	3,017	609
Travel and entertaining	1,149	2,987	455
	$ 3,451	$10,839	$ 1,064
General and administrative expenses			
Officer's salary—Joseph Loeman	$15,600	$15,900	$ 4,800
—Nicholas Loeman	13,000	13,000	4,000
Salaries—other	11,685	11,985	2,635
Insurance	3,865	4,414	1,339
Telephone	2,693	3,670	848
Rent	1,800	1,845	1,950
Accounting and professional fees	1,500	1,320	400
Electricity	946	1,198	627
Bank charges and interest	475	1,134	1,999
Office expense	751	589	181
Cleaning and maintenance	399	525	111
Payroll taxes	2,287	1,984	776
New York State franchise tax		125	
New York City corporation income tax		25	
New York City real estate tax	856	420	
New York City vault tax	15	111	
New York City occupancy tax	34	34	15
Licenses and permits		85	
Unidentified charges	353		
General expense		147	6
	$56,259	$58,511	$19,687

Order Authorizing Payment of Unpaid Wages

UNITED STATES DISTRICT COURT
SOUTHERN DISTRICT OF NEW YORK
_____ x

In the Matter	In Proceedings for

of

an Arrangement
_____

No. 72 B750

SWITCH CORPORATION OF AMERICA.

Debtor.
_____ x

ORDER AUTHORIZING
PAYMENT OF UNPAID
WAGES
_____

At New York, New York, in the said District on the 3rd day of August, 1972.

Upon the annexed application of SWITCH CORPORATION OF AMERICA, the above named debtor-in-possession, no adverse interest being represented, and due deliberation having been had thereon, and sufficient reason appearing therefor, it is

NOW, on motion of KRAUSE, HIRSCH & GROSS, attorneys for the debtor and debtor-in-possession

ORDERED, that SWITCH CORPORATION OF AMERICA, debtor-in-possession, be and it hereby is authorized and empowered to pay unpaid wages up to $600 per employee due in the normal course of business (but not including overdue wages) at the time of the filing of the petition to its employees, which are entitled to priority, pursuant to the provisions of Section 64(a) of the Bankruptcy Act.

_____
Bankruptcy Judge

UNITED STATES DISTRICT COURT
SOUTHERN DISTRICT OF NEW YORK
————————————————————————x

In the Matter	In Proceedings for an Arrangement
of	
	No. 72 B750
SWITCH CORPORATION OF AMERICA.	
Debtor. ————————————————x	APPLICATION

TO HONORABLE EDWARD J. RYAN, BANKRUPTCY JUDGE:

The application of SWITCH CORPORATION OF AMERICA, debtor and debtor-in-possession, respectfully sets forth and alleges:

1. Applicant filed a petition to effect an arrangement with its creditors pursuant to the provisions of Chapter XI, Section 322 of the Bankruptcy Act, on August 2, 1972.

2. On said date, this Court made and entered an order authorizing the debtor to operate its business and manage its property as debtor-in-possession, which it is presently doing.

3. Applicant is engaged in the business of manufacturing switches for household products, farm machinery, electronic equipment, and other industrial products, and maintains 12 divisional plants and operations throughout the United States.

4. In connection with its manufacturing facilities, applicant employs approximately 3,800 employees who are paid at varying times throughout the month, depending upon the particular division by which they are employed.

5. By reason of the fact that applicant has filed its petition herein, certain of the payrolls due to employees encompass wages earned prior to August 2, 1972, the date upon which the petition was filed.

6. It is essential that applicant's employees continue their employment with applicant in order that applicant may fulfill numerous government as well as private industry contracts which it is presently performing, and for its other operations to continue without interruption.

7. Applicant is extremely concerned that if the payroll due its employees is not met as and when it falls due, that irreparable harm to its continued business operations and its relationship with its customers will be caused.

8. Applicant wishes to point out that with the depressed employment market, its employees are dependent solely upon income derived from applicant for their sustenance.

9. Applicant submits to the Court that under any circumstances, said employees' claims are for wages and would be entitled to a priority in

payment pursuant to the provisions of Section 64(a) of the Bankruptcy Act, and further, that substantially all of said wage claims are less than $600 in amount, and all have been earned within three months of the filing of the petition.

10. Applicant further submits that in the interest of maintaining the debtor-in-possession as a viable entity, that it should be permitted to pay its employees the payrolls as and when they fall due which encumber any period prior to August 2, 1972. As a result thereof, applicant will be able to maintain its working facilities intact, and be able to continue the operation of its business in a normal, ordinary fashion.

11. The authorization sought herein will be in the best interest of the estate and creditors.

WHEREFORE, applicant prays for the granting of the annexed order for which no previous application has been made to this or any other court.

Dated: New York, New York   KRAUSE, HIRSCH & GROSS
       August 3, 1972   Attorneys for Applicant

By_____
           Salvatore A. Adorno
               A Partner

Exhibit K:

Stipulation for Payment of Federal Taxes

UNITED STATES DISTRICT COURT
EASTERN DISTRICT OF NEW YORK
————————————————————————x

In the Matter of the Application

           of

    EQUIPOISE, INC.

————————————————————Debtor.————x

Docket No. 71-B-885

STIPULATION FOR PAYMENT
OF FEDERAL TAXES

WHEREAS, the debtor filed a petition proposing a plan of arrangement under Chapter XI of the Act of Congress relating to bankruptcy on or about August 20, 1971; and

WHEREAS, the District Director of Internal Revenue, Brooklyn, New York, filed an amended proof of claim on or about August 15, 1973, in the amount of $57,032.04;

NOW, THEREFORE, the attorney for the debtor and the United States Attorney for the Eastern District of New York, as attorney for the United States of America, stipulate that the claim, plus statutory additions, shall be allowed in full and paid according to the following terms:

1. The amount due and owing ($57,032.04) shall be paid to the District Director of Internal Revenue, Brooklyn, New York, Attention: Special Procedures Staff, as follows:

   Upon confirmation of the Plan of Arrangement, $10,000.00 shall be due and paid immediately.

   The balance of the liabilities ($47,032.04) shall be paid in twenty-four (24) equal consecutive monthly payments beginning thirty (30) days after confirmation of the Plan of Arrangement.

2. With the last monthly payment due and payable twenty-four (24) months after confirmation of the Plan of Arrangement, there shall be paid any remaining balance which may be due and owing.

Statutory additions will be billed by the appropriate District Director after the final installment payment has been made. This amount shall be payable upon demand or upon terms prescribed by the District Director.

2a. The debtor agrees to remit to the District Director an amount equal to any payment made to the unsecured non-governmental creditors, under the terms of the plan of arrangement, which at any time exceeds the aggregate of the payments made to the District Director pursuant to Paragraph 1 of this stipulation. Payments to the District Director will not exceed the sum of all federal taxes and statutory additions due and owing.

  b. Payments to the District Director under this provision will be made at the same times that payments are made to the unsecured creditors. Any amounts received by the District Director as a result of this provision will be applied to the installment payments due pursuant to Paragraph 1 of this stipulation in inverse order, that is, to the last installment first.

3. Time is of the essence as to deferred payments. If there is a default in making the deferred payments of federal taxes plus statutory additions, or if all federal taxes accruing during the pendency of the proceeding are not paid in full on the due dates as prescribed by law, or if there is any other violation of this stipulation, the United States of America or the appropriate District Director shall have the right to declare the remaining installments due and payable. The balance may be collected by levy or by any other proceeding authorized by law for the collection of federal taxes.

4. All statutes of limitation on the assessment and collection of federal taxes plus statutory additions for the claimed years and periods are suspended from the date of filing the petition for an arrangement to the date of the entry of the order confirming a plan of arrangement, and for two years thereafter.

5. If additional federal taxes and statutory additions which have not been claimed prior to confirmation of a plan of arrangement are determined to be due from the debtor, they will be paid in full by the debtor immediately after notice. However, the appropriate District Director may permit the additional taxes and statutory additions to be paid in installments.

6. The debtor shall have the right to make the deferred payments plus accrued interest before the due date.

7. While any amount is owing under the stipulation, the debtor will segregate and hold separate and apart from all other funds all moneys deducted and withheld from amounts owed or paid to

employees or collected from others for taxes under any law of the United States and deposit the amounts so withheld or collected in a separate tax account. These amounts shall be deposited, and used and disbursed only for the particular purposes for which they are set aside or as set forth below:

All federal taxes required to be deducted and withheld from amounts owed or paid to employees and all social security taxes required to be contributed by the debtor shall be remitted by the debtor, together with a federal tax deposit form, to a bank which is an authorized federal depositary for taxes, not later than the end of the second business day next succeeding the day upon which taxes were required to be deducted or withheld. All Federal Unemployment Tax Act taxes listed on Form 940 and all federal excise taxes listed on Quarterly Federal Excise Tax Return Form 720 which the debtor is required to collect or for which liability is incurred shall be deposited in the tax account by the end of the calendar week next succeeding the week during which the amounts are required to be collected or liability for them is incurred. All tax funds on deposit at the end of the second calendar week shall be remitted at once by the debtor, together with the federal tax deposit form, to a bank which is an authorized federal depositary for taxes. At the end of the calendar week, after making any remittances to a depositary for federal taxes, the debtor shall furnish the appropriate District Director with evidence of the remittances on forms and under conditions prescribed by the District Director.

8. All federal taxes incurred during the pendency of this proceeding will be paid on the date of confirmation of the Plan of Arrangement. All federal taxes incurred while any amount is owing under this stipulation shall be paid in full on the due date.

9. While federal taxes plus statutory additions remain unpaid, the debtor shall not create any security interest respecting the assets of the debtor without first obtaining the written consent of the appropriate District Director, nor shall the debtor sell or otherwise dispose of assets other than in the ordinary course of business without first obtaining the District Director's written consent, except that a security interest securing a $50,000 debt to Carl Marx & Co., Inc. or its designee and a security interest securing a $25,000 debt to Mr. Harold Harran will be allowed provided these security interests are executed and properly recorded within 15 days after confirmation. The District Director will not file notices of federal tax lien until after 15 days from date of confirmation. These security interests will attach to all accounts receivable and contract rights of the debtors, its equipment, its goods and inventory together with the proceeds of the above assets.

10. In its petition for an order confirming the present or any amended Plan of Arrangement in this proceeding the debtor shall not seek

an order in any manner restraining the United States of America from collecting the federal taxes and statutory additions determined or which may be determined to be due from the debtor.

11. If the debtor is entitled to a net operating loss deduction during the period that the federal taxes provided for herein, plus statutory additions, remain unpaid, then an amount equal to the tax savings to the debtor resulting from such deduction shall, on the date due for filing the appropriate returns, be paid to the District Director for application to the liabilities, provided for herein, without regard to the payments otherwise due. However, the payment to the United States of the tax savings attributable to any year affected by the operating loss shall not exceed the net taxable income for such specific year (without regard to the operating loss deduction) less the installment payments provided for herein applicable to that year.

12. Any refunds or credits, to which the debtor may become entitled at any time before the federal taxes, plus statutory additions, have been fully satisfied, may be credited administratively against the federal taxes and statutory additions. If any refund check is received by the debtor prior to the full satisfaction of the federal taxes plus statutory additions, the check shall be endorsed and delivered at once to the appropriate District Director.

13. The debtor will notify the court that any disbursements to which it may be entitled, from funds which were submitted to the Bankruptcy Court for the purpose of paying unsecured creditors, will instead be remitted to the appropriate District Director. Any amounts so received will be applied to the installment payments due under the terms of this stipulation in inverse order, that is, to the last installment first.

14. While the federal taxes plus statutory additions remain unpaid, no stock options shall be issued and no assets shall be paid or otherwise transferred as loans, gifts, salaries, fees, or in any other form, which the appropriate District Director in his discretion considers unreasonable or unnecessary.

15. While the federal taxes plus statutory additions remain unpaid, the debtor shall not declare or pay any dividends upon its stock, declare stock dividends or make any other distribution of its stock, or purchase, redeem, or otherwise acquire shares of its stock, without the prior written consent of the appropriate District Director.

16. Any amount paid or credited on account of federal taxes plus statutory additions shall be applied in the manner determined by the appropriate District Director.

17. The following are definitions of terms used in this stipulation:

    a. "Debtor" includes any partnership or corporation organized or used for effectuating the plan of arrangement and any natural person, and shall be singular or plural, as the case may be.

    b. "District Director of Internal Revenue" or "District Director" includes successors in office.

    c. "Statutory additions" includes penalties and interest provided by the Internal Revenue Code.

18. The provisions of this stipulation shall apply in lieu of the deposit required under the provisions of Section 337(2) of the Bankruptcy Act. However, if the debtor has materially mis-represented any fact, or if the order of confirmation or any other order entered in this proceeding does not comply with the terms of this stipulation, then this stipulation shall be of no force and effect.

19. The provisions of this stipulation shall be made a part of the plan of arrangement and shall be incorporated by reference in the order confirming the plan.

20. This stipulation is contingent upon the entry of an order of confirmation of a plan of arrangement which shall incorporate this stipulation on or before _____ October 31, _____ 1974.

21. The United States reserves the right to withdraw its consent to this stipulation prior to the confirmation of a plan of arrangement.

Dated _____ August 20, _____ 1974

                          Krause, Hirsch & Gross
                          Attorney for the Debtor

                By _____
                          A Partner

                UNITED STATES ATTORNEY
                EASTERN DISTRICT OF NEW YORK
                Attorney for the United States

                By _____
                        Assistant United States
                          Attorney

This stipulation is approved.

<u>EQUIPOISE, INC.</u>
Debtor

_____

President of the Debtor

MARVIN E. HAGEN
Regional Counsel
Internal Revenue Service
North-Atlantic Region (New York)

By _____

Donald Schwartz
Staff Assistant to the
Regional Counsel

Exhibit L

Characteristic Debtor Testimony at a Hearing on Confirmation

Precisotron Corporation of America

TESTIMONY TO BE ADDUCED WITH RESPECT TO BEST INTEREST

Q. Are you an officer of the Debtor corporation?

A. Yes.

Q. What office do you hold in the corporation?

A. I am President and Chief Executive Officer.

Q. How long have you been President and Chief Executive Officer of the Debtor?

A. Since September 1970.

Q. And before that, what positions did you hold with the Debtor and for what periods of time did you hold them?

A. I started with the Formatic Division in 1961 and became a Group Vice President of the Debtor in May of 1970.

Q. How long have the other officers of the Debtor been with the Debtor?

A. Edward T. Mahoney, a Director, Vice President, Counsel and Secretary, has been employed by the Debtor since 1953.

Frank Petry, Jr., Executive Vice President, has been with the Debtor since December 1970.

Albert M. Ryan, a Director, and Vice President of Marketing, has been with the Debtor since November 1973.

Arthur Hartfield has been Vice President of Manufacturing since May 1973.

Q. Do you contemplate any change in the management of the Debtor?

A. No.

Q. Are you familiar with the Plan of Arrangement as amended which was filed with the Court and accepted by the creditors?

A. Yes, I am.

Q. Can you please state a synopsis of the Plan for the Court?

A. The Plan, as filed with the Court and approved by the creditors, provides for the payment of all administration expenses in cash upon confirmation or upon such terms as may be agreed upon between the Debtor and the respective administration creditors.

Approximately $3,200,000 has been budgeted for the payment of administration expenses. This consists of approximately $1,500,000 for the payment of accounts payable and approximately $1,700,000 for the payment of all other administration expenses.

Priority claims will be paid in full, in cash, upon confirmation or upon such other terms as may be agreed upon between the Debtor and the respective priority creditors. Priority claims are estimated at approximately $1,800,000 and consist principally of federal income tax assessments and deficiency interest.

Each general creditor will receive upon confirmation his pro rata share of $15,000,000, provided that the aggregate of allowed claims does not exceed $51,500,000 or, in the alternative, 28½% of his allowed claim, whichever is greater, unless the Debtor has applied to the Official Creditors' Committee for its approval of a payment in a lesser amount. In addition, general claimants will receive the proceeds, if any, from the winding up proceedings of the Debtor's International Division presently pending in the High Court of Justice of the United Kingdom.

In addition, for each $100.00 of claim allowed, each general creditor shall receive one share of Common Stock of the company and one newly created share of non-voting stock, each with a par value of 10¢ per share, which shares shall be identical in all respects except for the difference in voting rights. Non-voting shares will be convertible into Common Stock on the 5th anniversary of the issuance thereof or such earlier date as may be determined by the Board of Directors of the company. No fractional shares will be issued and each general creditor will receive the lowest whole number of shares to which he is entitled.

The shares to be issued to general creditors will have registration rights providing in effect for demand registration rights encompassing a single registration statement through the end of 1983 and so called "piggy-back" registration rights and a second demand registration right if the company's new lenders do not exercise their registration right with respect to the shares underlying the warrants to be issued to them.

All Executory Contracts with respect to warrants or stock options shall be terminated except for presently outstanding stock options with respect to 63,500 shares heretofore granted and the new Stock Purchase Agreements with respect to 650,000 shares to be purchased by 18 employees of the Debtor and option agreements which may be entered into pursuant to the Debtor's 1974 Stock Option Plan.

Prior to confirmation, the liquidator of the International Division appointed by the Court shall have determined that all general creditors of the company outside of the United Kingdom may prove their claims in

Exhibit L **255**

said liquidation proceedings and receive a distribution on the basis of their claims. If such determination is not made, claims of creditors domiciled or residing in the United Kingdom, with certain exceptions, will be deemed disputed claims in the Chapter XI Proceeding and appropriate provisions will be made therein.

(I should like to advise the Court that next week we are going to London to implement these arrangements.)

The shareholders of the Debtor must, prior to confirmation:

(1) Approve the Plan and its implementation.

(2) Approve the Amendment to the Restated Certificate of Incorporation which provides for a reduction of the par value from $1.00 to 10¢ per share and the authorization of 600,000 shares of non-voting Common Stock.

(3) Approve the Stock Purchase Agreement and the 1974 Stock Option Plan.

With respect to these conditions, proxy material for a meeting of share-holders has been cleared by the Securities and Exchange Commission and has been mailed to all shareholders of record of the Debtor. The meeting will be held November 21, 1974. On the basis of proxies received to date, it is reasonable to assume that the foregoing proposals will be approved by the shareholders.

The Court will retain jurisdiction over the Marine Midland Bank with respect to distribution received by them from the liquidation of the International Division or these Chapter XI Proceedings. Such funds shall be distributed ratably to all general creditors in addition to the monies previously mentioned.

Q.   Were there any conditions to the Plan, and if so, please advise the Court whether the conditions have been fulfilled and if not, what provision is being made for the fulfillment of those not yet completed?

A.   None other than those previously described and the fact that the litigation with Albert Christie and his claim in these proceedings must be either settled or fully adjudicated. The essential terms of a settlement have been worked out with Mr. Christie through his representatives and are currently being reduced to writing. The terms of the settlement will not affect the viability of the Debtor in its ongoing operations; will not affect the distributions to be made pursuant to the Plan and have been approved by the Chemical Bank whose loan will fund the Plan and the ongoing operations of the Debtor.

Q.   What is the business of the company?

A.   (Herein a summary of the company's operations by division.)

For the benefit of the Court we have prepared consolidating and consolidated pro forma balance sheets as at August 31, 1974 which reflect the status of each division of the Debtor and its subsidiary and give effect to the results of a liquidation of the Debtor. From these we have prepared a summary of the estimated amount of the distribution which would be available for general unsecured creditors.

These are designated Exhibit 1—Consolidating Pro Forma Balance Sheet.
Exhibit 2—Consolidated Pro Forma Balance Sheet.
and Exhibit 3—Summary of Realizable Value upon liquidation and estimated funds available for distribution to general unsecured creditors.

(Note: Have eight (8) copies available.)

I wish to add that the Debtor's Formatic Division is in the middle of a major contract with the Department of Defense of the United States Government. The dollar amount of liability to the U.S. Government upon liquidation would be substantial and undeterminable. Our best estimate is that such liability would be more than double the amount reflected in the foregoing pro forma statements.

Q. Are the assets of the company subject to the claims of a secured creditor? If so, state the nature of the security interest and the amount of the claim.

A. Substantially all of the creditors were unsecured. The only secured interests which were outstanding were mortgages, and these have been paid.

Q. With respect to general unsecured claims, have you reviewed the filed and scheduled claims?

A. Yes.

Q. What is the aggregate amount of general unsecured claims as of today?

A. Approximately $56,000,000.

Q. Based on your review of the claims filed, have you filed any objections?

A. Yes.

Q. In aggregate dollar amount, how many claims have been objected to?

A. Approximately $5,000,000, the principal one of which is a claim of $4,500,000 filed by the liquidator of a German subsidiary.

Q. On the basis of the data contained in Exhibits 1, 2 and 3 and assuming that the company were adjudicated a bankrupt and its assets liquidated under the National Bankruptcy Act, would there be monies available from such liquidation for the payment of general unsecured creditors after payment of the administration expenses, priority claims and secured claims?

A. Yes, but substantially less than is available under the Plan. The realizable dollar amount available to general unsecured creditors upon liquidation

Exhibit L **257**

of the company under the National Bankruptcy Act is approximately $8,150,000 which would result in a distribution of less than 16.5% on scheduled general unsecured claims.

Q.   If the Plan is confirmed, what would shareholders' equity be following such confirmation and the fulfillment of the conditions referred to above?

A.   Based on the pro forma consolidated balance sheet as at June 30, 1974, approximately $20,000,000 or, after all dilution approximately $2.77 per share.

Q.   Is the Common Stock of Precisotron trading? If so, where?

A.   The Common Stock is trading in the over-the-counter market but it is reported only in the "pink sheets" distributed among brokers.

Q.   Could you give the prices at which it has been traded over the past year?

A.   It has traded from a low bid of 25¢ per share to a high bid of $1.00 per share and a low asked of 50¢ per share and a high asked of $1.375 per share.

Q.   Do you have knowledge of the recent bid and asked prices?

A.   On __Nov. 5__ 1974 I am informed that the bid price was __⅝__ and the asked price was __⅞__.

Q.   Does the stock currently have a net worth?

A.   No. There is a deficit net worth, but upon the implementation of the Plan of Arrangement, the pro forma book value per common share will be approximately $2.77 per share.

Q.   What is the fair value of the stock to be issued pursuant to the Plan?

A.   A member firm of the New York Stock Exchange was engaged by the company to determine the fair value of the shares to be issued under the Plan, and said firm has determined the fair value to be 30¢ per share.

Q.   Do you have the report of that brokerage firm supporting such determination?

A.   Yes, I have.

(Have 8 copies available to be offered in evidence.)

Q.   In your opinion on the basis of the testimony you have given and the evidence presented to this Court in the course of this proceeding, is this Plan in the best interest of creditors?

A.   Yes.

FEASIBILITY

Q.   In your previous testimony, you summarized the amount of administration expenses filed, priority claims filed and potential priority claims, all of which aggregate $5,000,000. What provision is made for the payment of the aforesaid claims?

A.   We have reserved $5,000,000, available in cash, for the payment of all priority claims and all administration expenses.

Q.   Where is the company obtaining the $15,000,000 for the principal cash payment to be made to general unsecured creditors?

A.   From a group of banks and bank affiliated secured lenders headed by the Chemical Bank. This consortium of banks are committed to lend $17,000,-000 of which $2,000,000 is earmarked for working capital and $15,000,000 for funding the Plan. The agreement between the Debtor and the banks is being finalized and will be submitted to the Court prior to confirmation. (The agreement between the Debtor and the banks, substantially in the form in which we anticipate it will be executed, including exhibits, has been approved by the Board of Directors of the Debtor and by the banks. We offer the form of the loan agreement and those exhibits presently available in evidence.) The loans will be secured by all eligible accounts receivable of the company, all of the fixed assets of the company and all of the inventory of the company's Formatic Division. The loan will bear interest at a rate of 4½% over the prime rate in effect at Chemical Bank. The respective lenders will receive their ratable portion of not more than 569,000 warrants to purchase a like number of common shares of the company at an exercise price of 37½¢ per share and exercisable for a period of 5 years. The common shares underlying the warrants are entitled to one demand registration right and so-called piggy back registration rights and contain normal antidilution provisions.

Q.   Will the company be able to carry and repay the debt incurred?

A.   Yes.

Exhibit M

Application for Allowance of the Accountant for the Debtor-in-Possession

UNITED STATES DISTRICT COURT
EASTERN DISTRICT OF NEW YORK

In the Matter	APPLICATION FOR ALLOWANCE OF THE
of	ACCOUNTANT FOR THE
PEERLESS PAINT & VARNISH CO., INC.	DEBTOR-IN-POSSESSION
Debtor.	

To the Honorable Judges of the United States District Court for the
Eastern District of New York

The petition of ROBERT A. WIENER respectfully shows and alleges:

That he is a Certified Public Accountant, maintaining offices at
1185 Avenue of the Americas, New York, New York.

That he is a member of the firm of ROBERT A. WIENER & CO. who
were accountants to the debtor-in-possession in accordance with an order
dated May 14, 1970 providing for maximum compensation of $4,000 for certain
accounting services.

That in addition thereto your petitioner's firm was retained to render
monthly accounting services at $500 a month.

That there is nothing due to your petitioner's firm in connection with
the monthly accounting services. Application is being made herein only for
the services rendered in connection with the order of retention setting the
maximum compensation at $4,000.

That in connection with the above, your petitioner prepared a report of
the affairs of the debtor-in-possession as of April 21, 1970 which included the
following:

Exhibit A   Balance Sheet as at April
21, 1970

Schedule A-1   Taxes Payable

Exhibit B	Comparative Statement of Operations for the Periods: Year Ended 2/28/68 Year Ended 2/28/69 Year Ended 2/28/70 March 1, 1969 to April 21, 1970
Schedule B-1	Manufacturing Overhead
Schedule B-2	Selling and Promotion Expenses
Schedule B-3	Other Income and Expenses
Schedule B-4	Shipping and Delivery Expenses
Exhibit C	Analysis of Cash Receipts and Disbursements for the period January 1, 1970 to April 21, 1970
Exhibit D	Comparison of Sales, Purchases, Labor and Payments to Trade Creditors for the period March 1, 1969 to April 21, 1970
Exhibit D	Summary of Transactions with Large Trade Creditors for the Period January 1, 1970 to April 21, 1970

A copy of the aforesaid report is attached hereto and made a part of this application.

The following services were rendered in connection with the report dated April 21, 1970.

A trial balance was prepared as of February 28, 1970 of the general ledger of the debtor.

Thereafter the transactions for the period from March 1, 1970 to April 21, 1970 were journalized for the following transactions:

Cash Receipts
Cash Disbursements
Collection of Accounts Receivable
Sales
Collection of Notes Payable
Purchases
Payments to Creditors
Cash Receipts from A.I.C. Financial Co.
Cash Transmitted to A.I.C.
Financial Co.
Taxes Payable
Taxes Paid
Loans Received from S. Bong and
repayments

Subsequent schedules for the transactions were recorded summarizing
the transactions so that they could be posted to the trial balance for
all of the above transactions where applicable.

In addition thereto, the following adjusting journal entries at April 20,
1970 were prepared:

To record unentered invoices.

To reverse outstanding checks at the First Israel Bank.

To correct posting of accounts to the First Israel Bank and Manufacturers
Hanover Trust Co.

To adjust cash at the First Israel Bank.

To record unrecorded cash disbursements at the Chemical payroll
account.

To record payment to the union pension and welfare funds from Manufacturers Hanover Trust Co.

To adjust the cash in bank at Manufacturers Hanover.

To adjust the accounts receivable control account.

To record an additional allowance for bad debts.

To provide a reserve for sales.

To accrue interest due to A.I.C. Financial.

To adjust the books of account to the statement received from A.I.C. Financial.

To adjust for notes collected according to a report from A.I.C. Financial.

To accrue payroll and real estate taxes.

To write off the balance in the petty cash account.

To adjust the officers' life insurance cash value.

To accrue the payroll for the week ended April 22, 1970.

To accrue vacation pay.

To record interest on the S.B.A. loan.

To record the liability for the pension and profit sharing plan.

To record additional unrecorded invoices.

To adjust the accounts payable general ledger to the detailed list.

To record the estimated depreciation.

To provide for the estimated inventory at April 20, 1970.

The aforesaid adjusting entries were posted to the trial balance. The trial balance and adjustments and transactions were extended into the balance sheet and profit and loss columns and was then used in the financial statements set forth above in your petitioner's report.

The following services were rendered in connection with the report and the review of the records of the debtor:

Reconciliation of cash in bank—Chemical Bank.

Reconciliation of cash in bank—Chemical Bank—payroll account.

Reconciliation of account with A.I.C. Financial Corp.

Preparation of a schedule of interim transactions—cash receipts.

Preparation of a schedule of interim transactions—cash disbursements.

Preparation of a schedule of interim transactions—sales.

Preparation of a schedule of interim transactions—purchases.

Preparation of a schedule of interim transactions—payroll.

Preparation of a schedule providing for computation of inventory.

Preparation of a memorandum relating to accounts receivable.

Preparation of an analysis of doubtful accounts.

Preparation of an analysis of officers' life insurance.

Preparation of an analysis of the liability for vacation pay.

Preparation of an analysis of accounts payable adjustments.

Preparation of an analysis and adjustments of a detailed schedule of accounts payable consisting of 9 pages.

Preparation of an analysis of real estate taxes payable.

Preparation of an analysis of taxes payable.

Preparation of an analysis of loan—S. Bong subordinated to the S.B.A. loan.

Analysis of the loan with Leonard Bong.

Analysis of the Equitable Life Insurance account, collateral loan— officers' life insurance policy.

Analysis of the Prudential Insurance Company's loan.

Preparation of a memorandum relating to the S.B.A. loan.

Preparation of a memorandum relating to Titanium Pigment Division, National Lead Co.

Preparation of an analysis of the account with Allis Chalmers.

Preparation of an analysis of the loan with S. Bong.

Preparation of an analysis of the petty cash account.

Preparation of an analysis of the travel and entertainment account.

Preparation of an analysis of large trade creditors' account.

Preparation of an analysis of cash disbursements for January, February, March and April, 1970.

Preparation of a schedule of unpaid invoices.

Preparation of a schedule of unusual checks.

Your petitioner thereafter met with the debtor and his counsel and with creditors regarding the matters which arose from the examination of the books and records.

The services herein rendered consisted of 50 days of accounting time at an average rate of $100 per day.

Wherefore, your petitioner requests payment of $4,000 in accordance with the invoice annexed.

_____

State of New York ⎫
City of New York ⎬ SS:
County of New York ⎭

ROBERT A. WIENER, being duly
sworn, deposes and says:

That he has read the foregoing
petition and knows the contents thereof.

That the same is true to his own
knowledge.

_____

Sworn to before me this
25th day of July
1973.

_____

JUSTINE M. RODE
NOTARY PUBLIC,
State of New York
No. 03-8611450
Qual. in Bronx County
Cert. filed in
New York County
Commission Expires
March 30, 1974

UNITED STATES DISTRICT COURT
EASTERN DISTRICT OF NEW YORK

In the Matter

of

PEERLESS PAINT & VARNISH CO., INC.

Debtor.

STATE OF NEW YORK
CITY OF NEW YORK
COUNTY OF NEW YORK

ROBERT A. WIENER, being duly sworn, deposes and says:

That he is the Certified Public Accountant in the above-entitled matter and a member of the firm of ROBERT A. WIENER & CO., Certified Public Accountants, the applicants for the allowance for services rendered as accountants to the Debtor-in-Possession, to be paid out of the assets of the proceeding.

That he did not enter into any agreement, written or oral, express or implied, with any other party in interest, or any attorney of any other party in interest in the proceeding for the purpose of fixing the amount of the fee or other compensation to be paid to any party in interest or any attorney of any party in interest in these proceedings for the services rendered in connection therewith, and that no division of compensation is being made by the applicant.

Sworn to before me this
25th day of July
1973.

JUSTINE M. RODE
NOTARY PUBLIC,
State of New York
No. 03-8611450
Qual. in Bronx County
Cert. filed in
New York County
Commission Expires
March 30, 1974

ROBERT A. WIENER & CO.

Certified Public Accountants

1185 Avenue of the Americas
New York, New York 10036

July 25, 1973

Peerless Paint & Varnish Co., Inc.

Fifty days of Accounting Time @ $100 per day $5,000.00

Maximum in Accordance with Order of Retention $4,000.00

Exhibit N

Application for Allowance for Accountants for Trustee in Bankruptcy

UNITED STATES DISTRICT COURT
EASTERN DISTRICT OF NEW YORK

In the Matter	APPLICATION FOR ALLOWANCE OF THE ACCOUNTANT FOR THE TRUSTEE IN BANKRUPTCY
of	
SHATTERSBURG GLASS CORPORATION	
Bankrupt.	No. 68 B 1234

To the Honorable Judges of the United States District Court for the Eastern District of New York

The petition of Stephen Stevens respectfully shows and alleges:

That he is a Certified Public Accountant, maintaining offices at 125 E. 23rd Street, New York, New York.

That he is a member of the firm of Stevens, Cary & Williams who were retained in accordance with an Order dated January 1, 1968 to render certain accounting services as accountant to the debtor-in-possession.

That pursuant to this Order your petitioner's firm rendered such accounting services, the details of which are set forth in an Application for Allowance for $1,500.00 which was filed in this proceeding in November, 1972.

That the services exhausted the aforementioned Order of Retention.

That in addition thereto your petitioner's firm was retained as accountant to the debtor-in-possession at a monthly fee of $300.00 per month until and including August   , 19--.

That thereafter, your petitioner's firm rendered accounting services on behalf of the Trustee in Bankruptcy through an Order signed by the Honorable Boris Brainerd, Bankruptcy Judge, on _____(date)_____.

That the services rendered by your petitioner's firm, Stevens, Cary & Williams pursuant to the Order were as follows:

1. Prepared the schedule of unpaid accounts receivable at 10/31/70 consisting of eleven pages.

2. Prepared the 1970 final Employer's Quarterly Federal Tax Return for the debtor-in-possession and prepared the 1970 W-2 forms which were forwarded to the employees.

3. Responded to numerous inquiries for employment data from the New York State Department of Labor— Division of Employment.

4. Examined, listed in detail and analyzed all tax claims listed on the claims docket of the bankruptcy court to determine which ones were the latest valid claims.

5. Corresponded with and conferred with Trustee's counsel numerous times on matters relating to tax claims from Federal and State taxing authorities.

6. Corresponded numerous times with Federal and State taxing authorities to ascertain the propriety of their claims.

7. Prepared the final return for the New York State withholding taxes.

Your petitioner's firm reviewed the following administration claims:

1. Internal Revenue Service for unemployment insurance in the amount of $608.14

2. New York State Income Tax Bureau, Department of Taxation and Finance, withholding taxes in the amount of $1,045.68

3. New York State Unemployment Insurance, Division of Employment, unemployment insurance in the amount of $62.03

4. New York State Sales Tax Bureau, Department of Taxation, Bureau of Law, sales taxes in the amount of $360.00

Your petitioner reviewed the following debtor claims:

1. Internal Revenue Service:

a) Withholding and FICA Taxes

3rd quarter 1969	$ 9,792.08
4th quarter 1969	11,308.87
1st quarter 1970	7,907.65

b) Federal Unemployment Insurance

1969	$822.52
1970	$509.57

c) Excise taxes, 1st quarter 1970, $86.62

2. New York State Income Tax Bureau, Department of Taxation and Finance, Bureau of Law, Withholding taxes—12/1/69 to 12/31/69—$514.00

3. New York State Unemployment Insurance, Division of Employment, unemployment insurance in the amount of $628.35

4. New York State Sales Tax Bureau, Department of Taxation, Bureau of Law, sales taxes in the amount of $185.40

Schedulized our findings for the above with appropriate remarks and submitted them to the Trustee's attorney.

Your petitioner was asked to review 19 claims which had been filed with the office of the Bankruptcy Judge by the Judge's office and by counsel to the Trustee. These claims included a portion of administration expense as well as a portion which related to the period prior to the filing of the petition. It was necessary to examine the claims and the supporting information which relates thereto and to reclassify the claims into general and administration claims. Your petitioner thereafter furnished the aforesaid schedule to counsel to the Trustee who in turn forwarded it to the office of the Judge.

The services rendered herein consisted of 20 days of accounting time at an average rate of $100 per day or a total therefore of $2,000.

WHEREFORE your petitioner requests payment of $1,500 the maximum allowable under the Order of Retention.

Stevens, Cary & Williams
Certified Public Accountants
125 East 23d Street
New York City

Shattersburg Glass Corp.
307 Monroe Boulevard
Carstairs, New York

Twenty (20) days of accounting time @ $100 per day $2,000.00

Maximum in Accordance with Order of Retention $1,500.00

STATE OF NEW YORK
CITY OF NEW YORK } SS:
COUNTY OF NEW YORK

_____ *(Name)* _____, being duly sworn,
deposes and says:

That he has read the foregoing
petition and knows the contents thereof.

That the same is true to his own
knowledge.

_____

Sworn to before me this
            day of   197 .

_____

UNITED STATES DISTRICT COURT
EASTERN DISTRICT OF NEW YORK

In the Matter

of

SHATTERSBURG GLASS CORPORATION,

Bankrupt.

AFFIDAVIT OF
ACCOUNTANT IN
CONNECTION WITH
APPLICATION FOR THE
ALLOWANCE FOR THE
ACCOUNTANT FOR THE
TRUSTEE

State of New York
City of New York 〉 SS:
County of New York

Stephen Stevens being duly sworn,
deposes and says:

That he is the Certified Public
Accountant in the above-entitled matter, the applicant for the allowance for
services rendered as accountant to the trustee, to be paid out of the assets
of the bankruptcy proceeding.

That he did not enter into any
agreement, written or oral, express or implied, with any other party in interest,
or any attorney of any other party in interest, in this proceeding for the purpose
of fixing the amount of the fee or other compensation to be paid to any party in
interest or any attorney of any party in interest in these proceedings for the
services rendered in connection therewith, and that no division of
compensation is being made by the applicant.

_____

Sworn to before me this
        day of

Exhibit O

Specification of Objections to a Bankrupt's Discharge

UNITED STATES DISTRICT COURT
SOUTHERN DISTRICT OF NEW YORK
————————————————————————x

In the Matter of

MANFRED B. SETT.

Bankrupt.
————————————————————————x

SPECIFICATIONS OF
OBJECTIONS

TO THE HONORABLE RUPERT L. ARMAND, BANKRUPTCY JUDGE

James Stern of 580 Fifth Avenue, New York, N.Y. in the Southern District of New York, trustee of the Estate of the above-named bankrupt, having examined into the acts and conduct of the said bankrupt and being satisfied that probable grounds exist for the denial of the discharge of said bankrupt, does hereby oppose the granting to the bankrupt herein of discharge from his debt and for the grounds of such opposition does file the following specifications:

1. For the reason that he has failed to keep or preserve books of account or records from which his financial condition and business transactions might be ascertained in that he has failed to record all of his transactions made during the course of his business and in the 18 months preceding the filing of the petition against him herein.

2. That on and after May 29, 1969, subsequent to the first day of the 12 months immediately preceding the filing of the petition, the bankrupt transferred certain of his property to wit: diamonds to Doffstader, Stein & Co., William L. Lewis Inc. and others for an inadequate consideration with intent to hinder, delay or defraud his creditors.

3. That the bankrupt during the course of these proceedings, although requested to do so, failed to explain satisfactorily, losses of assets between November 12, 1968 and May 29, 1970 and failed to explain satisfactorily a deficiency of assets in the amount of approximately $600,000.00 at the time of the filing of the petition in bankruptcy to meet his liability.

4. That on or about the 12th day of November, 1968 the bankrupt, while engaged in business as a sole proprietor, obtained for said business money or credit or a renewal thereof from Prudential National Bank and Trust

Co. of New York by making or causing to be made a materially false statement in writing, respecting his financial condition to wit: that he stated he owned real estate and that he had personal assets of $190,000 and personal liabilities not in excess of $7,000 and additionally stated that he had diamond business assets consisting of accounts receivable and inventory valued at at least $60,000 with business liabilities not in excess of $20,000.00.

5. That on September 7, 1967 the bankrupt, while engaged in business as a sole proprietor, obtained for said business money or credit or a renewal thereof from Prudential National Bank and Trust Co. of New York by making or causing to be made a materially false statement in writing, respecting his financial condition to wit: that he had a net worth of $180,000 consisting of cash, stock, bonds and real estate and liabilities of only $3,500 in addition to diamond business assets consisting of accounts receivable and inventory valued at at least $40,000 with liabilities thereon not in excess of $10,000.00.

WHEREFORE, objection is made to the granting of such application for discharge.

_____
                             Trustee

Jasper R. Toms
Attorney for Trustee

Exhibit P

Final Report of Bankruptcy Judge

REPORT OF BANKRUPTCY JUDGE ON ASSET AND NOMINAL ASSET CASES TERMINATED IN STRAIGHT BANKRUPTCY

FILED UNDER: Straight Bankruptcy ☐ or Relief Chapter No._____
Date converted to Straight Bankruptcy (if applicable) _____
Date case reopened (if applicable) _____

CONSOLIDATION:

List Case Numbers of all cases consolidated with this case:_____
_____ Date of Consolidation_____
Has any part of the claims against bankrupt, or distribution shown on this JS-19 been included in another JS-19?
☐ Yes   ☐ No   If "Yes", explain on reverse.

DISTRICT	OFFICE			DISCHARGE	BANKRUPTCY JUDGE CODE	DATE CLOSED
		1	1 ASSET	1 GRANTED		
			5 NOMINAL	2 DENIED		
				3 WAIVED		

DOCKET NUMBER	IN RE:	DATE FILED
	1 (Last Name, First, M. I.)	

OBLIGATIONS OF BANKRUPT

PRIORITY	SECURED	UNSECURED	TOTAL	ROUND ALL AMOUNTS TO NEAREST DOLLAR
2 $	+ $	+ $	= $	

RECEIVER'S COMMISSIONS	RECEIVER'S EXPENSES	TRUSTEE'S COMMISSIONS	REFEREE'S SALARY AND EXPENSE FUND	SPECIAL CHARGES
3 $	+ $	* + $	+ $	+ $ +

REPORTING FEES	ACCOUNTANT'S FEES	AUCTIONEER'S FEES	APPRAISER'S FEES	ATTORNEY FEES FOR CREDITORS
4 $	+ $	+ $	+ $	+ $ +

ATTORNEY FEES FOR TRUSTEE	ATTORNEY FEES FOR RECEIVER	ATTORNEY FEES FOR BANKRUPT	OTHER ATTORNEY FEES	RENTAL EXPENSES
5 $	+ $	+ $	+ $	+ $ +

TRUSTEE'S OTHER EXPENSES	TOTAL COSTS & EXPENSES OF LIQUIDATION	PRIORITY CLAIMS PAID		
		WAGES	TAXES	OTHER
6 $ *	= $	+ $	+ $	+ $ +

SECURED PAYMENTS	UNSECURED PAYMENTS	OTHER DISTRIBUTIONS	NET PROCEEDS REALIZED	
7 $	+ $	+ $ *	= $	

NET PROCEEDS REALIZED	AMOUNT PAID BANKRUPT IN LIEU OF EXEMPTION	TOTAL STRAIGHT BANKRUPTCY OPERATING EXPENSES	OTHER DISBURSEMENTS	TOTAL DISTRIBUTION
$	+ $	+ $	+ $ *	= $

BY RECEIVER   BY TRUSTEE

Bankruptcy Judge

J.S. 19 (Rev. 7-75)   *Itemize on reverse side

RETURN FORM TO: Administrative Office of the United States Courts, D.I.S.— Operations Branch —— Supreme Court Building, Washington, D.C. 20544

276

Application and Order Permitting Trustee to Abandon and Destroy Books, Papers, and Records of the Bankrupt

UNITED STATES DISTRICT COURT
EASTERN DISTRICT OF NEW YORK
——————————————————x

In the Matter
of

BETTER BEVERAGE COMPANY.

Bankrupt.
——————————————————x

In Bankruptcy
No. 56 A 987

ORDER PERMITTING TRUSTEE
TO ABANDON AND DESTROY
BOOKS, PAPERS AND RECORDS
OF BANKRUPT.

At Jamaica, New York, in said District, on the 23rd day of May, 1973.

Upon the annexed application of JOHN WALKER, Trustee in Bankruptcy herein, by his attorneys, dated May 22nd, 1973, and it appearing that it is in order for the Trustee to abandon and destroy the books and records of the bankrupt herein, it is ordered that JOHN WALKER as Trustee, be and is hereby authorized to abandon and destroy the books, papers and records of the bankrupt.

—————————————————
Anthony Peersens
Bankruptcy Judge

UNITED STATES DISTRICT COURT
EASTERN DISTRICT OF NEW YORK
————————————————————————x

In the Matter

of

BETTER BEVERAGE COMPANY.

Bankrupt.
————————————————————————x

In Bankruptcy
No. 56 A 987

APPLICATION FOR ORDER PER-
MITTING TRUSTEE TO ABANDON
AND DESTROY BOOKS, PAPERS
AND RECORDS OF BANKRUPT.

TO THE HONORABLE ANTHONY PEERSENS, BANKRUPTCY JUDGE:

This is an application to abandon and destroy the books, papers and records of the above-named bankrupt.

Applicant respectfully alleges:

1. That he is the Trustee herein, duly elected and qualified as such.

2. That on or about May 8, 1973, the Trustee's Supplemental Final Report and Account was filed with the Court.

3. That he has been advised by the accountant retained by him on behalf of the bankrupt that there is no further need for the books, papers and records of the bankrupt.

4. That the office of the Honorable Anthony Peersens has advised counsel for the Trustee that the Trustee's Final Report and Account has been accepted by the Court and that it is proper for the instant application to be made.

WHEREFORE applicant prays for an order authorizing the Trustee to abandon and/or destroy the books, papers and records of the bankrupt.

Dated: New York, New York
May 22nd, 1973.

_____
JOHN WALKER

Trustee in Bankruptcy

BY _____
Attorney

INDEX

INDEX

A

U